Tilde *skills*

Design and Develop Complex Text Documents

plus Challenges & Assessment Tasks

plus Manage Business Document Design Development

Microsoft Word 2013

Tilde Publishing and Distribution

Tilde *skills* Design and Develop Complex Text Documents
Microsoft Word 2013
1st edition, 3rd printing

Authors
Tilde Publishing and Distribution

ISBN: 978-0-7346-0852-9
ISBN: 978-0-7346-2079-8

Copyright

Text copyright © 2014 by Tilde Publishing and Distribution.
Illustration, layout and design copyright © 2014 by Tilde Publishing and Distribution.

Under Australia's *Copyright Act* 1968 (the Act), except for any fair dealing for the purposes of study, research, criticism or review, no part of this book may be reproduced, stored in a retrieval system, or transmitted in any form or by any means without prior written permission from Tilde Publishing and Distribution. All inquiries should be directed in the first instance to the publisher at the address below.

Copying for education purposes

The Australian *Copyright Act* 1968 (the Act) allows a maximum of one chapter or 10% of this book, whichever is the greater, to be copied by an educational institution for its educational purposes provided that that educational institution (or the body that administers it) has given a remuneration notice to Copyright Agency Limited (CAL) under the Act.

Details of the CAL licence for educational institutions are available from the agency's website <www.copyright.com.au>.

Disclaimer

All reasonable efforts have been made to ensure the quality and accuracy of this publication. Tilde Publishing assumes no responsibility for any errors or omissions and no warranties are made with regard to this publication. Neither Tilde Publishing nor any authorised distributors shall be held responsible for any direct, incidental or consequential damages resulting from the use of this publication.

Published in Australia by:
Tilde Publishing and Distribution
PO Box 72
Prahran VIC 3181, Australia
Tel: 1300 880 935
www.tilde.com.au

Contents

Preface ix

Topic 1 – Document layout review 1
    Document layout 1
    Changing document views 1
    Document views 2
    Adding page breaks, blank pages and cover pages 2
    Changing columns for part of a document (Section breaks) 4
    Deleting a section break 5
    Changing document margins 5
    Changing page size 6
    Selecting a paper source 6
    Setting tab stops 7
    Setting leader characters 9

Topic 2 – Working with tables 10
    Creating and modifying a table 10
    Selecting within a table 11
    Moving within a table – keyboard methods 11
    Table styles, borders and shading 11
    Changing column width and row height 12
    Moving and copying rows/columns 13
    Aligning table text 13
    Merging and splitting cells 14
    Converting text to tables 14
    Sorting information 16
    Modifying uneven rows or columns 17
    Deleting rows, columns or cells 17
    Terms & concepts review 17

Topic 3 – Creating templates and designing forms 20
    Creating a custom template 20
    Editing a template 21
    Creating a template for Fill-in fields 22
    Printing field codes 23
    Designing forms 27
    Planning the content 27
    Laying out your design 28
    Creating your form (with content controls) 29
    Modifying your form 33
    Terms & concepts review 33

Topic 4 – Inserting shapes & WordArt 37
    Inserting and modifying basic shapes 37
    Fundamentals in shapes 37
    Fundamentals in adding colour and effects 38
    Selecting and working with multiple objects 39
    Creating a text box 40
    Inserting WordArt 40

Topic 5 – Complex mail merge 44
    Mail merge for form (standard) letters 44
    Creating a data source 45
    Commencing the merge 47
    Completing your merge 49
    Creating labels 50
    Creating custom labels 51
    Merging only some of your data 53

Removing your mail merge selection criteria 55
Using a Fill-in field in a merge 56
Using an If field in a merge 60
Terms & concepts review 64

Topic 6 – Working with long documents 65
Text presentation 65
Document design 66
Picture placement 66
Consistency when using styles 67
Applying a quick style 67
Updating a quick style 68
Working with heading styles and outlining 69
Managing your documents with Outline view 71
Numbering your headings automatically 74
Creating a table of contents 77
Updating your table of contents 78
Adding a header & footer 80
Advanced headers & footers 82
Different headers & footers for document sections 83

Topic 7 – Expanding and enhancing documents 87
Creating an index 87
Inserting footnotes and endnotes 91
Applying page borders and watermarks 94
Building long documents by importing data 95
Inserting a text file 96
Inserting a picture file 96
Importing data from other sources 97
Linking to an Excel workbook 98

Topic 8 – Inserting charts and SmartArt 101
Inserting a chart object 101
Creating an organisation chart using SmartArt 106

Topic 9 – Adding comments, tracking changes & comparing content 112
Adding comments to your document 112
Tracking document changes 114
Comparing and merging content 116

Topic 10 – Calculations in Word 120
Inserting automatic totals 120
Inserting custom calculations 122
Explaining table cell references 122
Explaining bookmarks and formulas 122
Interpreting number formats 123
Building your calculation 123
Creating your own formula 124

Topic 11 – Customising and automating tasks 128
Customising the Quick Access Toolbar 128
Customising shortcut keys (direct key combinations) 129
Assigning a Quick Part item to a shortcut key 132
Assigning Quick Parts to the Quick Access toolbar 134
Recording a macro 134
Running a macro 136
Assigning a macro to a shortcut key 137
Assigning a macro to the Quick Access Toolbar 138
Modifying a command button image 139
Creating a customised template 141

Topic 12 – Creating a master document 144
Inserting subdocuments 144

Workplace scenarios 147
Skills Challenges & Assessment tasks 155
Creating a working area 155

Assessment tasks **172**
Skills Challenges & Assessment tasks **177**
    Creating a working area 177
Assessment tasks **186**
Appendix I **193**
    Shortcut keys: Direct key combinations 193
    Shortcut keys: Word 2013 access keys 195
Appendix II **197**
    Saving to PDF 197
    Using Help 197
Index **199**

Preface

Introduction

This publication can be used as a tutorial for self-paced learning or for instructor-led teaching. Its purpose is to enable students to become competent in the design and development of business documents using the complex technical features of Microsoft Word 2013. If kept conveniently near your computer workstation it can also be used as your primary reference, reminding you of the most efficient ways to approach word processing tasks.

Business Services Training Package

The contents of this publication can contribute to achieving the following unit of competency in the Business Services Training Package: *BSBITU401A Design and develop complex text documents* and *BSBADM506B Manage business document design & development.*

Pre-requisites

The following pre-requisites or equivalent knowledge apply:

Tilde skills Produce Simple Word Processed Documents, and
Tilde skills Design and Produce Text Documents

Learning outcomes - Business Services Training Package
Unit BSBITU401A Design and develop complex text documents

1. **Prepare to produce word processed documents**

    1.1. Use safe work practices to ensure ergonomic, work organisation, energy and resource conservation requirements are addressed

    1.2. Identify document purpose, audience and presentation requirements, and clarify with relevant personnel as required

    1.3. Identify organisational requirements for text-based business documents to ensure consistency of style and image

    1.4. Evaluate complex technical functions of the software for their usefulness in fulfilling the requirements of the task

    1.5. Match document requirements with software functions to provide efficient production of documents

2. **Design complex documents**

    2.1. Design document structure and layout to suit purpose, audience and information requirements of the task

    2.2. Design document to enhance readability and appearance, and to meet organisational and task requirements for style and layout

    2.3. Use complex software functions to enable efficient manipulation of information and other material, and ensure consistency of design and layout

2.4. Use manuals, user documentation and online help to overcome problems with document design and production

3. **Add complex tables and other data**

    3.1. Insert a standard table into document, changing cells to meet information requirements

    3.2. Format rows and columns as required

    3.3. Insert images and other data, formatting as required

4. **Produce documents**

    4.1. Use complex operations in the development of documents, to achieve required results

    4.2. Preview, adjust and print documents in accordance with organisational and task requirements

    4.3. Name and store documents in accordance with organisational requirements and exit the application without information loss/damage

    4.4. Prepare documents within designated time lines and organisational requirements for speed and accuracy

Learning outcomes - Business Services Training Package
Unit BSBADM506B Manage business document design & development

1. **Establish documentation standards**

    1.1. Identify organisational requirements for information entry, storage, output, and quality of document design and production

    1.2. Evaluate organisation's present and future information technology capability in terms of its effect on document

    1.3. Identify types of documents used and required by the Organisation

    1.4. Establish documentation standards and design tasks for organisational documents in accordance with information, budget and technology requirements

2. **Manage template design and development**

    2.1. Ensure standard formats and templates suit the purpose, audience and information requirements of each document

    2.2. Ensure document templates enhance readability and appearance, and meet organisational requirements for style and layout

    2.3. Test templates, obtain organisational and user feedback, and make amendments as necessary to ensure maximum efficiency and quality of presentation

3. **Develop standard text for documents**

    3.1. Evaluate complex technical functions of software for their usefulness in automating aspects of standard document production

    3.2. Match requirements of each document with software functions to allow efficient production of documents

    3.3. Text macros to ensure they meet the requirements of each document in accordance with documentation standards

4. **Develop and implement strategies to ensure the use of standard documentation**

    4.1. Prepare explanatory notes of the use of standard templates and macros using content, format and language style to suit existing and future users

    4.2. Develop and implement training on the use of standard templates and macros and adjust the content level of detail to suit user needs

    4.3. Produce, circulate, name and store master files and print copies of templates and macros in accordance with organisational requirements

5. **Develop and implement strategies for maintenance and continuous improvement of standard documentation**

    5.1. Monitor use of standard documentation templates and macros, and evaluate the quality of documents produced against documentation standards

    5.2. Review documentation standards against the changing needs of the organisation, and plan and implement improvements in accordance with organisational procedures

How this publication is organised

This publication contains **12** topics. Each topic contains: concept overviews; detailed **How to** explanations; and abundant **Hands-on** exercises.

Consolidation tasks are used at intervals to bring skills together, and the course finishes with a number of **Workplace scenarios, Skills challenges** and **Assessment tasks** which firmly place knowledge in a workplace setting and can act as assessment tools.

Information contained in the **Appendices** can be brought into the course at any time.

Tilde conventions

The following conventions are used throughout Tilde publications.

Convention explained	Example
Each topic begins with an overview of relevant theory (a narrative). In narratives, important terms are shown in **bold**.	'Using **styles** you can ensure a consistent and professional ...'
Narratives are often followed by examples or useful additional information (an aside).	*For example ...* *As an aside ...*
A set of **How to** steps follows a narrative. These steps detail the procedure required to perform a task. These can be read by a student, presented by a trainer, or referred to when using the manual as a reference.	**How to: Apply a quick style** 1. ... 2. ... 3. ...
A command button is shown beside the relevant **How to** step, and often as a reminder in **Hands-on exercises**.	
In **How to** steps, names of command buttons are highlighted in **bold**. Steps also include the name of the ribbon where the button is located, and the group.	'Display the Home ribbon, point to any option in the **Quick Styles Gallery** (Styles group).'

Keyboard shortcuts can often save you time and effort. These are illustrated with the required keys from the keyboard.	New document `Ctrl` `N`
An exercise to be undertaken by a student is called a **Hands-on exercise**. Each exercise step is described in detail and is used to practise and reinforce the skill being learned.	**Hands-on exercise X**
In exercises, file names are shown in *italics*. Key actions are also highlighted in bold.	'**Open** the document *Health centre*.'
Additional useful **Hints & tips** are used to help students apply their skills more successfully, overcome problems and extend their knowledge.	
Terms & concepts review questions are used to review key terms and concepts covered in a topic.	
To review or consolidate student skills a **Consolidation task** is used. This task can be undertaken individually by students, or as a team review in the classroom.	**Consolidation task X**
To help students apply their new skills in realistic scenarios a work-based task called a **Workplace scenario** is used.	

How to use this publication in a self-paced manner

Read through the **How to** step(s), and then work through the following **Hands-on** exercise.

Accompanying exercise files are required to work through the exercises. These can be downloaded from the Tilde website <www.tilde.com.au>, or obtained from the publisher. It is recommended that they are pre-loaded into a suitable folder on a hard/network drive, or used directly from a (USB) flash drive.

Downloaded with the accompanying files is a document used for reference within the course. Please print out the following file prior to course commencement: *OH&S guide*.

How to use this publication in an instructor-led classroom

Present to students the material in the **How to** steps; then, have them work through the **Hands-on** exercises.

Accompanying exercise files are required to work through the exercises. These can be downloaded from the Tilde website <www.tilde.com.au>. It is recommended that they be pre-loaded into a suitable folder on a hard/network drive, or used directly from a (USB) flash drive. Exercise files can be freely copied onto student PCs, instructor PCs, or network drives when used for education purposes with a Tilde™ publication.

Spelling

The Macquarie dictionary is used except for the names of features from the application, e.g. Center Align, where the original (American) spelling is used.

Instructor email list

To be notified regularly of new educational developments from Tilde Publishing, go to the Tilde Publishing website www.tilde.com.au.

The Tilde *skills* series

This publication is just one in the Tilde *skills* series that addresses the educational needs of adults in the workplace. It is suitable for anyone wishing to learn using Tilde's enjoyable methodology.

Another Tilde imprint for the business services training package is Tilde *business*. These books integrate the latest educational material with the outcomes of the national curriculum. Each Tilde *business* publication is education, accessible, and affordable.

For more information on Tilde *skills* or Tilde *business*, please visit our website www.tilde.com.au.

Before you start

To ensure you get the best results from this course please check that you are using the standard settings from a fresh installation of Microsoft Office 2013 (for example, remove Developer ribbon and nothing in the Quick Access toolbar except save, undo and redo)

Downloaded with the student exercise files is an *OH&S guide* PDF. Please print this file and keep handy for future reference.

A note about operating systems

This course was written using Microsoft Office 2013 running on Windows 8. If your personal computer or network is running a different operating system, e.g. Windows 7, you may notice some differences. These differences will be minor and are unlikely to affect the course content and exercises. The differences will most likely be noticed in relation to Taskbar operation and navigation within Save As and Open dialogue boxes.

New to Office 2013

Office 2013 suite of programs incorporates many new features in terms of its interface and the functionality it provides. You can configure many of these software features by selecting Options from within Backstage view and locating the appropriate section. More information can be found by searching on the specific aspect within Help.

Depending on the setup of your network or personal computer, as a user of Office 2013, you may have the option to 'sign in' using a Hotmail account when you use the software. Once signed in, you can use the SkyDrive to save and access files. SkyDrive is a Cloud-based storage feature that enables you to store and access files from multiple devices.

Topic 1 – Document layout review

The following topic is a review of some basic document layouts. There are no exercises in this topic as these skills were taught in earlier courses so if you require more exercise please see *Tilde Publishing and Distributions Simple Word Processed Documents* or *Design and Produce Text Documents*.

Document layout

Word offers a variety of document views. Each view has particular benefits at different stages of document creation and editing. Changing the view of a document does not affect its printed appearance.

The five main document views are Print layout, Full Screen Reading, Web Layout, Outline and Draft.

Changing document views

In this topic you look at the variety of views available, then begin looking at document layout tasks.

How to: Change your view

1. Click on the required **View icon** (far right of Status bar)
   ~or~
   Display the View ribbon and click on the required button
   (Views group).

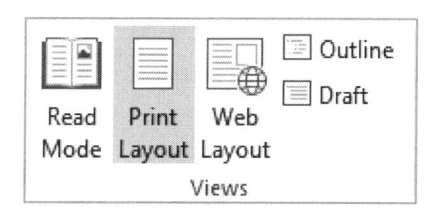

Document views

	Print Layout	Shows a document as it will appear when printed, e.g. graphics in true position, headers and footers.
	Read Mode	This view presents your documents in 'book' format with two pages displayed at a time. Pages are rearranged to read well, so may not be what is printed. A number of useful tools for reviewing are also displayed. Press `Esc` to exit.
	Web Layout	This is a specialised view for creating web pages and other documents that you expect to be seen on screen rather than on paper. It wraps text to fit the window and places graphics on screen the same way they would appear in a browser.
	Outline	This view is designed for working with long documents that use heading styles. It allows you to view selected headings and to quickly re-organise text. For more information on styles see *Tilde Publishing and Distribution's Design and Produce Text Documents*. To exit click on the **Close Outline View** button.
	Draft	This view is the fastest for entering plain text. However, you cannot see text in the margin areas (e.g. headers and/or footers), or some graphics in their true (printed) location (dependant on text wrapping option selected). Useful for very large documents where speed is an issue, and for working with section breaks. For more information on section breaks see *Tilde Publishing and Distribution's Design and Produce Text Documents*.

Hints & tips

In Print Layout view you can hide the white space at the top and bottom of your page (header and footer area). Point to the space between two pages and the **Hide White Space** *icon is displayed (two arrows pointing inwards).*

Double-click and the white space disappears leaving a thick blank line to define pages. To return to full **Print Layout** *view, double-click on the thick black line.*

Adding page breaks, blank pages and cover pages

When you fill a page Word inserts an **automatic** page break and starts a new page. As you edit, Word is constantly recalculating and repositioning the automatic page breaks.

Serif typefaces

Serif, or "roman", typefaces are named for the features at the ends of their strokes. Times Roman and Garamond are common examples of serif typefaces. Serif fonts are probably the most used class in printed materials, including most books, newspapers and magazines.

"Roman" and "oblique" are also terms used to differentiate between upright and italic variations of a typeface.

An automatic page break in Draft view

You can add your own page breaks. Page breaks that you add are called **manual** page breaks. You can delete manual page breaks but automatic page breaks are controlled by Word.

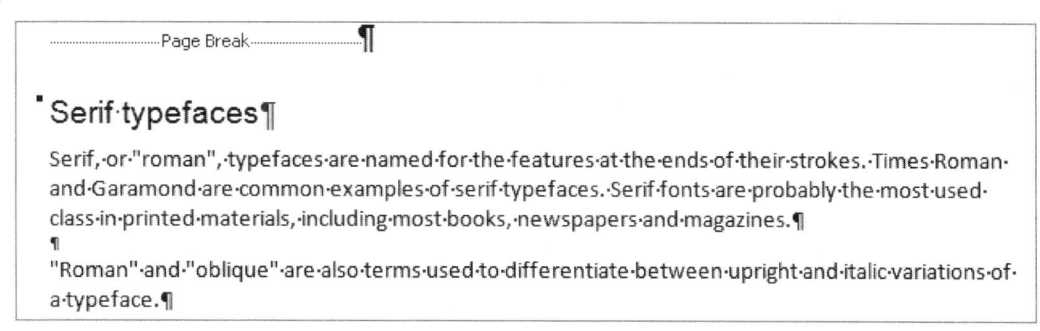

A manual page break in Draft view (Show/Hide button on).
Note that with the insertion of a manual page break the automatic page break has disappeared as it is no longer needed.

In Draft view page breaks are shown as a line across the page as shown in the examples above. In Print Layout view a new page is displayed.

You can also insert an entire blank page into a document and a pre-designed cover page.

How to: Insert a manual page break

1. Click your insertion point where the break is required (usually at the beginning or end of a line of text).
2. Display the Insert ribbon, then click on the **Page Break** button (Pages group).
3. Information after the insertion point now starts a new page.

Page Break   Ctrl Enter

How to: Remove a manual page break/blank page

1. Switch on the **Show/Hide** button (Home ribbon, Paragraph group).
2. Click the insertion point on the page break location (at the start of the line).
3. Press Delete

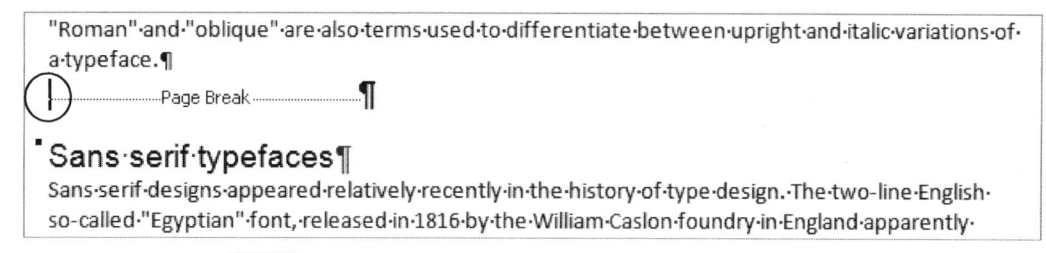

How to: Insert a cover page

1. Display the Insert ribbon, then click on the **Cover Page** button (Pages group).
2. Click on a pre-designed cover from the gallery of options presented.

3. Replace any sample text with your own text.

How to: Remove a cover page

1. Display the Insert ribbon, click on the **Cover Page** button (Pages group), then click on the **Remove Current Cover Page** option.

As an aside ... If you insert another cover page it replaces any existing cover page.

Changing columns for part of a document (Section breaks)

In a longer document you may have areas that require a different header and/or footer or different page orientations.

For example ... A different header and/or footer for the executive summary before the body of the report. A landscape orientation for a large chart.

In a document containing no section breaks, all document formatting (e.g. number of columns, margins, page orientation, headers and footers, etc.) flows through the entire document. By inserting section breaks, you create 'compartments' that can contain different document formatting, e.g. you can have a two-column layout in one section, followed by a three-column layout in the next section.

A section break displays as a double-dotted line when the **Show/Hide¶** button is activated.

There are four different types of section break: **Next page**, **Continuous**, **Even page** and **Odd page**.

A **Continuous** section break starts the new section on the same page. This is most commonly used for multiple column layouts.

The **Next page, Even page** and **Odd page** section breaks force the next section onto the next page. **Next page** is most commonly used where the following page has a different page layout, e.g. landscape orientation. **Even page** and **Odd page** section breaks are most commonly used for books, where new chapters must start on a particular odd or even page.

When creating sections it is a good idea to display section numbers on the Status bar.

How to: Display section numbers on the Status bar

1. Right-click on the Status bar. The Customize Status bar list is presented.
2. Click on **Section** in the list presented. The section number is added to the start of the Status bar.
3. Click anywhere in the document to close the list.

How to: Insert a section break

1. Position your insertion point where you want the new section to begin.
2. Display the Page Layout ribbon, then click on the **Breaks** button (Page Setup group).
3. Under Section Breaks in the list presented, click on a section break option.

Deleting a section break

Sections breaks can be removed - just like page breaks - if they are no longer required. However, it is useful to be aware of how section formatting is stored before attempting to delete a section break.

A section break stores the formatting for the section **above** the break. If you remove a section break, the section takes on the formatting of the section **below** it.

> *For example ...* Your document is formatted into two sections; the first containing a two-column layout, the second a three-column layout. If you delete the section break separating the two sections, your document will be left in a three-column layout.

How to: How to: Delete a section break

1. Display your non-printing characters (Home ribbon, Paragraph group).
2. Click on the section break (double dotted line).
3. Press Delete

Changing document margins

Margins are the borders on all four sides of a page which surround your document's text. Your document's text is surrounded by the margins. Margins are not always empty. They can contain text, graphics, page numbers, etc.

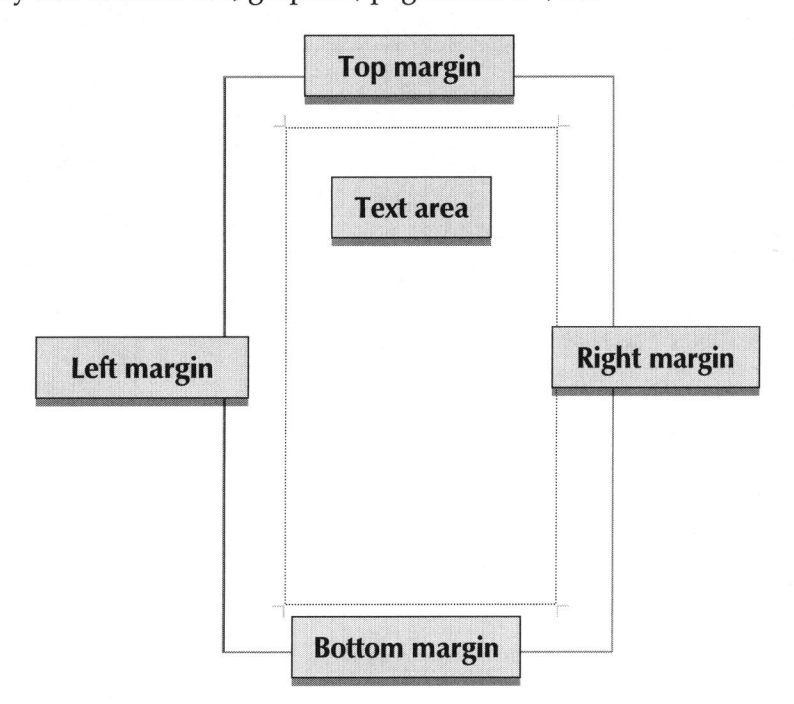

```
          Top margin
         
          Text area
Left margin        Right margin
         
         Bottom margin
```

How to: Change document margins (predefined options)

1. Display the Page Layout ribbon, then click on the **Margins** button (Page Setup group). Select a predefined option from the list presented. Margins are applied to the whole document.

How to: Change document margins (custom)

1. Display the Page Layout ribbon, click on the **Margins** button, then click on **Custom Margins** (Page Setup group). The Page Setup dialogue box is presented.

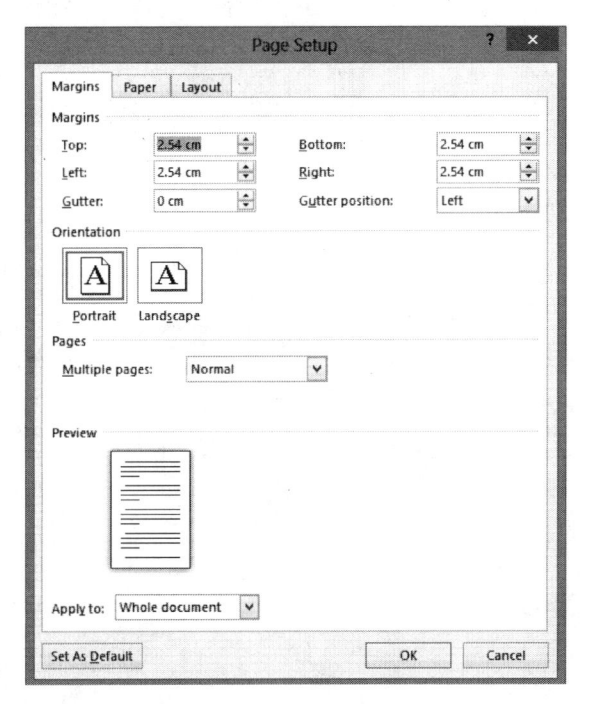

2. Ensure the Margins tab is selected, then adjust the margin settings (**Top**, **Bottom**, **Left**, **Right**) as required.

3. Under **Apply to** select **Whole Document** or **This point forward** or **Selected text**.

4. Click on **OK**.

> *As an aside* ... *To change the margins for all new documents that you create, set your requirements in the dialogue box then click on* **Set As Default**. *Respond* **Yes** *to the question that follows.*

> *As an aside* ...*Using the* **This point forward** *option for margins introduces a section break into your document which starts a new page with the new margin measurements, e.g. a continuation sheet for a letter. Use it instead of a page break when different margins are required.*

Changing page size

The standard Australian page size is A4 (210 x 297mm).

How to: Change standard page size

1. Display the Page Layout ribbon, then click on the **Size** button (Page Setup group). Select an option from the list presented.

> *As an aside* ... *To change the page size default select* **More Paper Sizes** *from the list presented. Set your Paper size, then click on* **Set As Default**. *Respond* **Yes** *to the question that follows.*

Selecting a paper source

If your printer has a selection of paper sources, e.g. two paper trays, you can choose where various pages of your document are printed from.

> *For example* ... *You may select the first page of your letter to print from the top tray (which holds your letterhead paper), and the remaining pages from the second tray (which holds your continuation paper).*

Topic 1 – Document layout review

How to: Choose a paper source

1. Display the Page Layout ribbon, click on the **Size** button, then click on **More Paper Sizes** (Page Setup group). The Page Setup dialogue box is presented. Ensure the Paper tab is active.

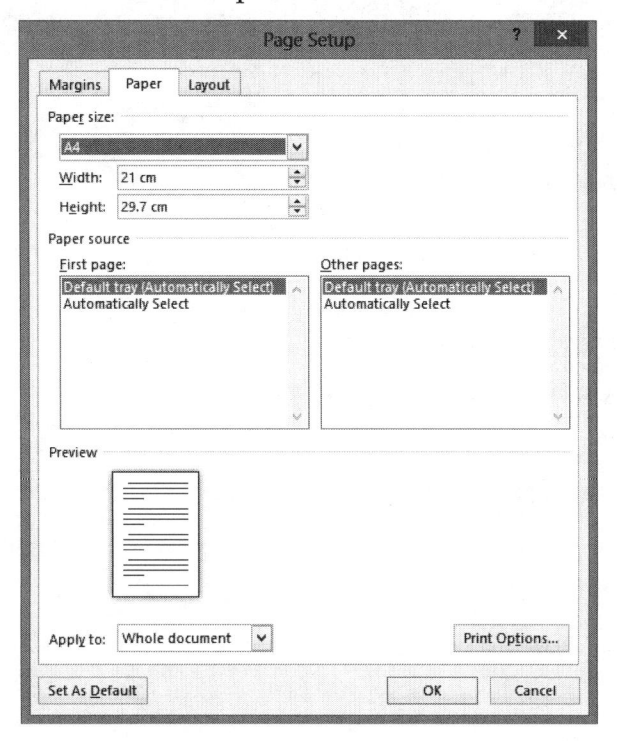

2. Click on the option required for the **First page**.
3. Click on the option required for the **Other pages**.
4. Click on **OK**.

As an aside ... Options available in this dialogue box depend on the capabilities of the printer you are connected to. To change options for all new documents that you create, set your requirements then click on Set As Default. Respond Yes to the question that follows.

Setting tab stops

Tab stops are another useful document layout technique. By setting tab stops you can align text on a page in vertical columns. Setting tab stops is useful for short, simple columns of text (larger, more complex layouts should be aligned using the Tables feature.

There are four main types of tab stop *alignment* as illustrated below: **Left**, **Center**, **Right** and **Decimal**.

Board Members and Fees Owing

Mark Jones	President	1/3/2001	20.00
Philippa Beechworth	Vice President	20/4/2009	65.00
Nigel Chapman	Secretary	16/12/1999	65.00
Rebecca Smithson	Board Member	1/5/2012	20.00
Henry Wong	Board Member	19/3/2011	15.00

A short list of information aligned using tabs: left, centre, right and decimal.

Default tab stops are already available in your document. These can be seen as dark grey markers on the grey bar running beneath your horizontal ruler (positioned approximately every centimetre). (If your ruler is not visible see **How to display your ruler**.)

You can set your own tab stops, and the default tab stops are cleared.

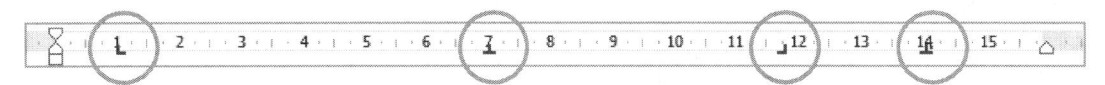

To move to or align to a tab stop, you press `Tab` to produce a tab character.

How to: Display your ruler

1. Display the View ribbon, then click on the **Ruler** option (Show group). (Both are on/off features.)

How to: Set tab stops using the ruler

1. Position the insertion point in the required paragraph ~or~ Select the required paragraphs.
2. Click on the **Tab** button on the far left of the horizontal ruler until the required tab is displayed.

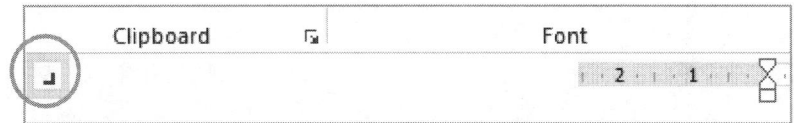

Tab stops

	Left Tab	Text aligns to the left of the tabbed column.
	Center Tab	Text aligns to the centre of the tabbed column.
	Right Tab	Text aligns to the right of the tabbed column.
	Decimal Tab	Text aligns to the decimal point in the tabbed column.

3. Click on the horizontal ruler at the measurement where the tab stop is required.
4. Repeat as necessary.

How to: Move a tab stop

1. Select the required paragraphs. (The tab settings are contained in each paragraph mark ¶.)
2. Drag the tab to a new position on the horizontal ruler.

As an aside ... To clear a tab stop, select the required paragraphs and drag the tab marker off the ruler into the document area and release.

Setting leader characters

Leader characters 'lead up' to tab stops. They can be used in a variety of ways including questionnaires and forms.

For example ...

Flight	From
QF4589	Sydney
AN5940	Sydney
AN5678	Sydney
AN533	Ballina

~or~

Where will you be going on your summer vacation this year?..

Where did you go last year?..

Leader characters can be dots, lines or dashes.

For example ...

Where will you be going on your summer vacation this year? _____

Where did you go last year? _____

Leader characters can also be used across the entire page.

....

(Tear off at the dotted line.)

To create leader characters you use the Tabs dialogue box.

How to: Set leader characters

1. Set your basic tabs using the ruler.
   ~or~

   Position the insertion point in the required paragraph *~or~*
   Select the required paragraphs.

2. Display the Home ribbon, locate the **Paragraph** group, then click on the dialogue box launcher.
   The Paragraph dialogue box is displayed. Click on **Tabs**.
   The Tabs dialogue box is presented displaying any existing tab settings.

3. Click on the required **Tab stop position**.

4. Click on the **Leader** option of your choice.

5. Click on **Set**.

6. Repeat steps 5-7 as necessary.

7. Click on **OK**.

As an aside ... You can also double-click on any existing tab stop on the ruler to display the Tabs dialogue box.

Topic 2 – Working with tables

Creating and modifying a table

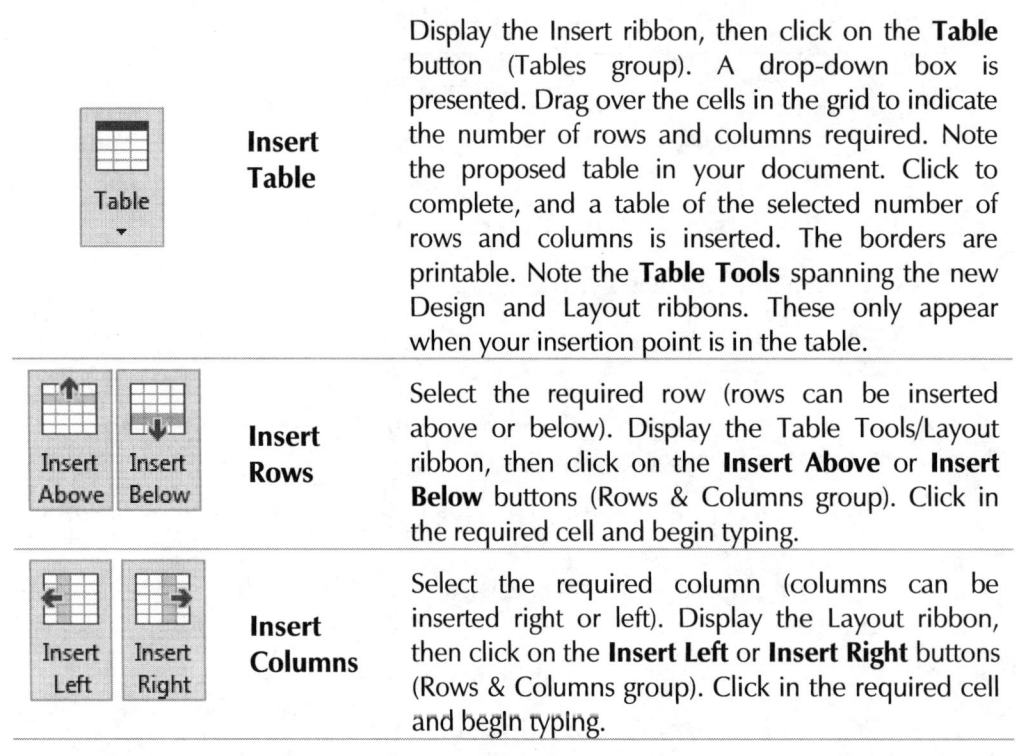

	Insert Table	Display the Insert ribbon, then click on the **Table** button (Tables group). A drop-down box is presented. Drag over the cells in the grid to indicate the number of rows and columns required. Note the proposed table in your document. Click to complete, and a table of the selected number of rows and columns is inserted. The borders are printable. Note the **Table Tools** spanning the new Design and Layout ribbons. These only appear when your insertion point is in the table.
	Insert Rows	Select the required row (rows can be inserted above or below). Display the Table Tools/Layout ribbon, then click on the **Insert Above** or **Insert Below** buttons (Rows & Columns group). Click in the required cell and begin typing.
	Insert Columns	Select the required column (columns can be inserted right or left). Display the Layout ribbon, then click on the **Insert Left** or **Insert Right** buttons (Rows & Columns group). Click in the required cell and begin typing.

As an aside ... When you highlight a row or column, Word will add a plus button between the row or column. Click on the plus button and a new row or column is added after.

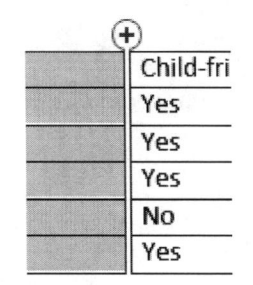

Selecting within a table

Table	Rest the mouse pointer on the table until the **table move handle** ⊞ appears in the top-left corner of the table, then click on the handle. (Ensure you are in **Print Layout** view.)	
Row	Position the mouse pointer outside the table, beside a row. The mouse pointer becomes a white arrow. Click once to select the whole row.	
Column	Position the mouse pointer at the top of a column until a black down-arrow is displayed, then click once to select the whole column.	
Cell	Position the mouse pointer in the cell to the left of the text. The mouse pointer becomes a black arrow. This space left of the text is the **cell selection bar**. Click in the cell selection bar.	

As an aside ... To select multiple cells, rows or columns, select the required item then drag to extend the selection. To select non-adjacent cells, rows or columns, select the first required item, hold down [Ctrl] and continue to select all other required items.

Moving within a table – keyboard methods

How to: Move within a table - keyboard methods

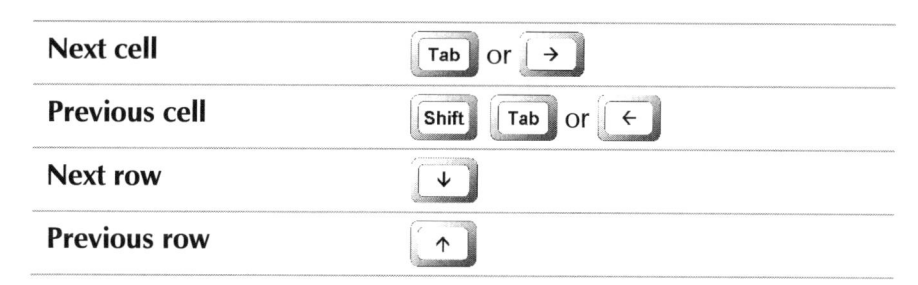

Next cell	[Tab] or [→]
Previous cell	[Shift] [Tab] or [←]
Next row	[↓]
Previous row	[↑]

Table styles, borders and shading

How to: Apply table styles

1. Click in the table.

2. Display the Table Tools/Design ribbon, point to any option in the **Tables Styles** group to see the design effect previewed on your table. Click on the **More** arrow to display the full gallery of styles.

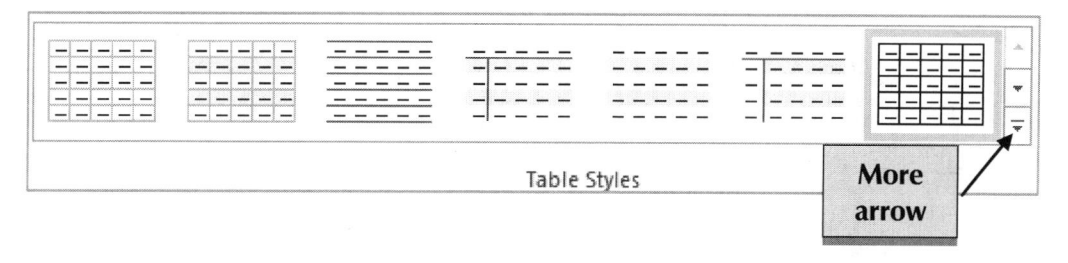

Table Styles

More arrow

3. Click on the required style to apply. The first option on the ribbon is plain.

How to: Adjust table borders

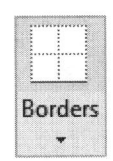

1. Select the required cell, row or column.
2. Display the Table Tools/Design ribbon, click on the **Borders** down-arrow (Table Styles group). A list of options is presented.
3. Click on the required border option.

How to: Adjust table shading

1. Select the required cell, row or column.
2. Display the Table Tools/Design ribbon, click on the **Shading** button (Table Styles group). A gallery of colours is presented organised by themes. Point to a colour selection to see the design effect previewed on your table.
3. Click on a colour of your choice.

Changing column width and row height

How to: Change a column width

1. Position the mouse pointer on the right gridline of the column you want to adjust. The mouse pointer becomes a double-headed arrow. 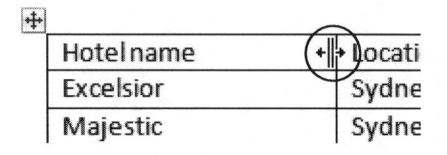
2. Drag the gridline left or right to a new position.

   ~or~

1. Click in the required column, or select the required columns.
2. Display the Table Tools/Layout ribbon, then adjust the measurements on the **Table Column Width** option (Cell Size group).

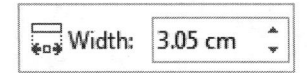

As an aside ... *You can automatically adjust the width of a column to fit its contents by double-clicking on a gridline. The column is automatically resized. This feature is called AutoFit.*

How to: Change a row height

1. Position the mouse pointer on the gridline of the row you want to adjust. The mouse pointer becomes a double-headed arrow.
2. Drag the gridline to a new position.

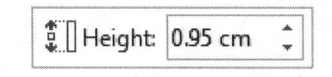

   ~or~

1. Click in the required row, or select the required rows.
2. Display the Table Tools/Layout ribbon, then adjust the measurements on the **Table Row Height** option (Cell Size group).

As an aside ... Hold **Alt** *as you drag a gridline to display measurements on the ruler.*

Moving and copying rows/columns

How to: Move or Copy a row

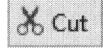

1. Select the row to be moved or copied.
2. Click on the **Cut** or **Copy** buttons (Home ribbon, Clipboard group).
3. Select the destination row.
   (The new row is pasted *above* the selected row.)
4. Click on the top-half of the **Paste** button (Home ribbon, Clipboard group).

Cut Ctrl + X   Paste Ctrl + V

To try to remember the Cut key 'X', think about a pair of scissors—as shown on the Cut button—blades crossing.

How to: Move or copy a column

1. Select the column to be moved or copied.
2. Click on the **Cut** or **Copy** buttons (Home ribbon, Clipboard group).
3. Select the destination column. (The new column is inserted *to the left*.)
4. Click on the **Paste** button (Home ribbon, Clipboard group).

Aligning table text

How to: Align text in cells

1. Select the required cell(s).
2. Display the Table Tools/Layout ribbon, then click on the required alignment button, e.g. **Align Center** (Alignment group).

Examples of alignment buttons

	Align Top Center	Aligns text to top and centre of a cell.
	Align Center	Aligns text to the middle and centre of a cell.
	Align Bottom Center	Aligns text to the bottom and centre of a cell.

How to: Change text direction

1. Select the required cell(s).
2. Display the Table Tools/Layout ribbon, then click on the **Text Direction** button (Alignment group).
3. Click on the button again to continue rotating.

As an aside ... Once text has been rotated, you will notice that the text alignment buttons also rotate.

Merging and splitting cells

How to: Merge cells

1. Select the cells to be merged.
2. Display the Table Tools/Layout ribbon, then click on the **Merge Cells** button (Merge group).

How to: Split cells

1. Select the cell(s) to be split.
2. Display the Table Tool/Layout ribbon, then click on the **Split Cells** button (Merge group). The Split Cells dialogue box is presented.

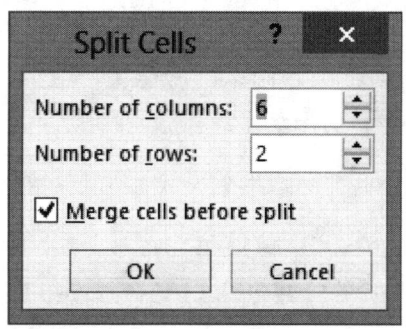

3. Click on the up/down-arrows to select the required **Number of columns**.
4. Click on the up/down-arrows to select the required **Number of rows**.
5. Click on **OK**.

Converting text to tables

When typing lists or figures you may decide that it would be better to align the text in a table instead of straight text. You can convert text into a table instead of retyping your text.

Example with show/hide visible to show tab marks

The work was completed in the quoted time	1	2	3	4
The work was completed in the budget quoted	1	2	3	4

Example of text converted into a table

How to: Convert text into a table

1. Highlight the required text.
2. Display the Insert ribbon and click on the **Table** button (Tables group), then select **Convert Text to Table...**
   The Convert Text to Table dialogue box is presented.

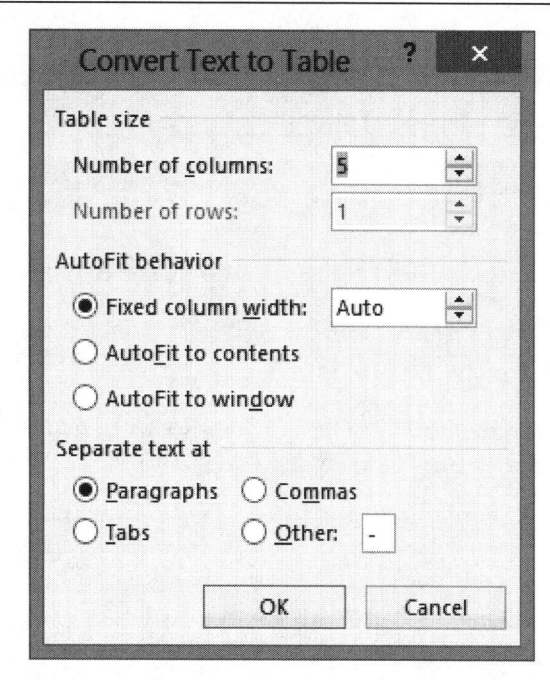

Convert Text to Table dialog

Table size
- Number of columns: 5
- Number of rows: 1

AutoFit behavior
- ● Fixed column width: Auto
- ○ AutoFit to contents
- ○ AutoFit to window

Separate text at
- ● Paragraphs ○ Commas
- ○ Tabs ○ Other: -

[OK] [Cancel]

3. Select the number of columns to be inserted.

4. Select how the initial text has been typed (in the example above, the initial text was typed with tabs in between so I would select Tabs under Separate text at).

5. Click on OK.

6. The text has now been inserted into a table.

Hands-on exercise 1

In this exercise you practice inserting a table by converting text into a table then formatting.

- Start with a blank document.

- Press **Enter** twice.

- Type the following list with tabs in between the numbers.
  To ensure you have inserted tabs in between the numbers, turn the show/high on.

The work was completed in the time quoted	1	2	3	4	5
The work was completed in the budget quoted	1	2	3	4	5
Our staff were polite	1	2	3	4	5
I was pleased with the completed work	1	2	3	4	5

- Select all of the text, then display the Insert ribbon.

- Click on the **Table** button, then select **Convert Text to Table...**
  The Convert Text to Table dialogue box is presented.

- Ensure **Tabs** is selected under **Separate text at.** Leave all other options.

- Click on **OK**.

- Change the height and width of the table to represent the table below.

The work was completed in the time quoted	1	2	3	4	5
The work was completed in the budget quoted	1	2	3	4	5
Our staff were polite	1	2	3	4	5
I was pleased with the completed work	1	2	3	4	5

- Change the alignment of the numbers to **Align Center**.
- Change the text to **Align Center Left**.
- Insert a row at the top of the table.
- Highlight the two cells above the numbers 3 and 4 and click on the **Merge Cells** button (Merge group).
- In the cell above number 1 type: Not applicable
- In the cell above number 2 type: Good
- In the cells above 3 and 4 type: Average
- In the cells above 5 type: Bad
- Select the top row.
- Click on the **Text Direction** button (Alignment group) twice.
- Reduce the font size of the top row to 10 pt and bold.
- Add a shading of your choice to the top row.
- **Save** your document as *Evaluation form*.
- **Close** your document.

Sorting information

When working with tables it is very useful to know the **Sort** feature. This can save you lots of time if text needs to be rearranged.

For example ... You have created a telephone list to which you are often adding new employees, and you need to maintain the list in alphabetical order.

How to: Sort information

1. Click on a table, or select the paragraphs to be sorted.
2. Display the Table Tools/Layout ribbon, then click on the **Sort** button (Data group). The Sort dialogue box is presented. The options in the dialogue box change depending on the text selected.
3. Select the required options.
4. Click on **OK**.

Modifying uneven rows or columns

If you have drawn uneven rows or columns, you can quickly re-distribute them to even them out.

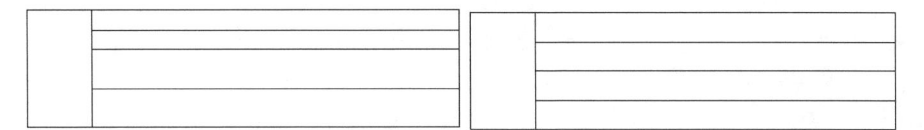

Rows drawn unevenly can be quickly re-distributed

How to: Distribute rows and columns

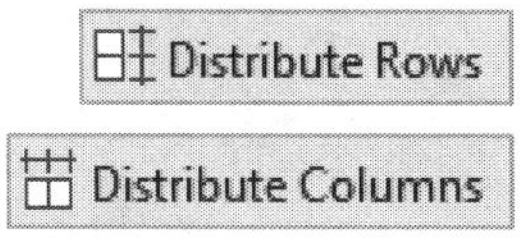

1. Select the required rows or columns.
2. Display the Layout ribbon, then click on the **Distribute Rows** or **Distribute Columns** button (Cell Size group).

Deleting rows, columns or cells

How to: Delete a column, row or cell

1. Select the required column/row or cell.
2. Display the Table Tools/Layout ribbon, then click on the **Delete** button (Rows & Columns group).
3. Select the option you need deleted.

   Note: When you delete a cell, the Delete Cells dialogue box is presented to ask how will the space from the deleted cell will be filled. Make you selection and click on OK.

How to: Delete text only

1. Select the column, row, or cell, and press Delete.

Terms & concepts review

- What are the steps in inserting a table?

  _____
  _____
  _____

- Can you insert text and convert it into a table? If yes, how?

  _____
  _____
  _____

> **Consolidation task 1**

In this exercise you review your basic table skills.

You are employed by a local plumber for administrative duties. Your manager has asked you to create the following table for the plumbers to write estimates when they are out of the office.

- Create the following table in Word. Your manager has given a hand-drawn version from notes taken from the last meeting (see next page).
- Format appropriately.
- If there is space on the page, increase the height of the rows and add more rows.
- Choose appropriate fonts.
- Save as: *Estimate form vs1*.
- Check your spelling.
- Print and review your form.
- Close your document.

Hints

- Use tab stops for the address (See Topic 1)
- Use leader character for date, ph, address and name of customer.
- Create as 3 different tables and press Delete to join them together at the end.

Additional text to be inserted as Terms & Conditions

> Terms & Conditions:
>
> The estimate is for completing the job as described above. It is based on our evaluation and does not include material price increase or additional costs which may be required due to unforeseen circumstances/problems or weather constraints after the work has commenced.

ESTIMATE ← bold

Valid for 30 days

Tom's Plumbing
153 George St
Hawthorn VIC 3122
Ph: 0432 632 026
Ph: 1300 823 026

Date: _____
Ph: _____
Address: _____

Name of customer: _____

~~~~~ DESCRIPTION ~~~~~ ← light blue shading

| ~~~~ LABOUR ~~~~ | HRS | Amount $ |

TOTAL

| QTY | ~~ MATERIALS ~~ | Amount $ |

TOTAL

*terms & conditions. See other sheet for information to type in here

Total labour	$
Total materials	$
Tax, GST etc	$
TOTAL	$

Signature:

Topic 3 – Creating templates and designing forms

Creating a custom template

Word supplies a variety of templates to help you get started. However, advanced users of Word will want to create their own. A template starts with a blank document but you save it a different way to a normal document.

How to: Save your template

1. Click on the **Save** button (Quick Access Toolbar).
2. Click on **Computer**, then the **Browse** button.
3. Type a **File name**.
4. Click on the drop-down box, then select **Word Template**.

   The Custom Office Templates folder is displayed (note the path of this folder in the address bar).

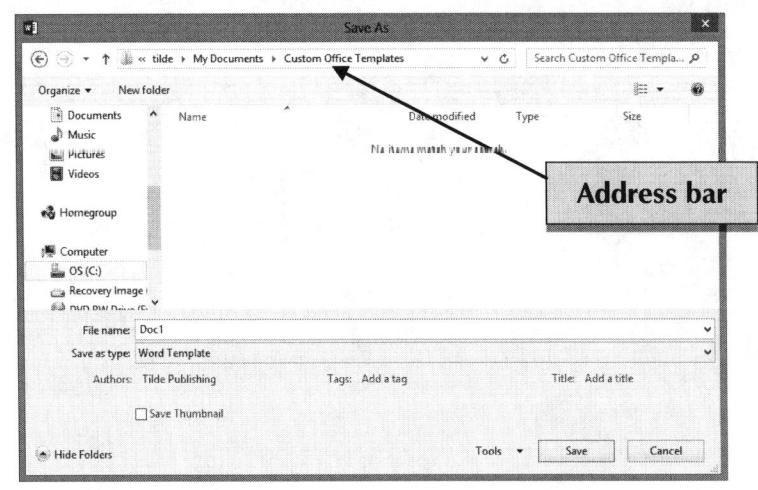

5. Click on **Save**.

Editing a template

To open a template for editing you follow the usual procedure for opening a document. The main difference is selecting your templates folder as your file location.

How to: Open a template for editing

1. Display **Backstage** view.
2. Click on the **Open** button.
3. Click on **Computer**, then click on **Browse**.
4. Navigate to your folder: **Custom Office Templates**
5. Double-click on your template to open it.
   Check for the correct name in the Title bar

Hands-on exercise 2

In this exercise you create a standard document with standard text, then save it as a template. After this has been created, you add Fill-in fields.

- Print out the following document for reference:
  Org style guide – memo standard.

- In a **new** blank document, create a memorandum based on the *Org style guide – memo standard*

Memorandum

To	
Department	
From	
Department	
Email	
Date	
Subject	

Next, you save your layout as a template.

- Using your memo document, click on the **Save** button (Quick Access Toolbar).
- Click on **Computer**, then the **Browse** button.
- Type a **File name** of *Dept memo*.
- Click on the **Save as type** down-arrow, then click on **Word Template**.
- Note the path displayed in the **Address Bar**.
  This is where your templates are stored.
- Write the path:

  _____

- Click on **Save**.

Creating a template for Fill-in fields

As an experienced user of Word, by now you will have encountered various fields within Word, (e.g. date fields, page number fields, merge fields, etc.). Another field of particular interest is the **Fill-in** field.

The **Fill-in** field is used to prompt for information. A Fill-in field generates a dialogue box. The dialogue box can be used to request information to be placed into a document in place of the Fill-in fields.

Shown below is first an example of a Fill-in field, then the dialogue box it generates.

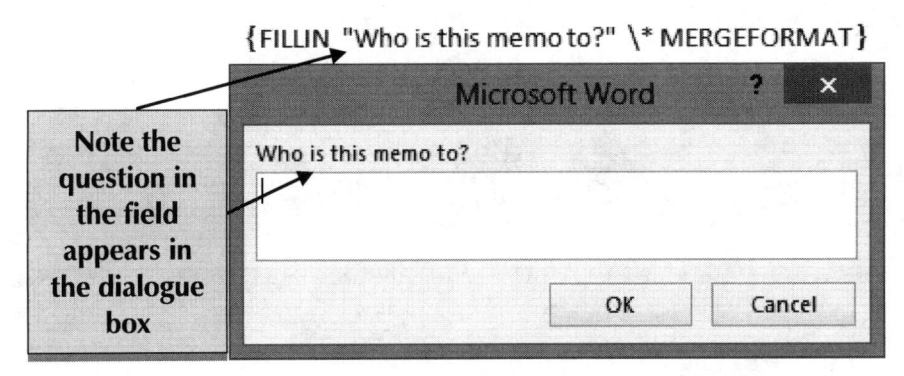

{ FILLIN "Who is this memo to?" * MERGEFORMAT }

Note the question in the field appears in the dialogue box

Dialogue box created by the Fill-in field

A Fill-in field needs to be **updated** to produce a dialogue box. If Fill-in fields are placed in a **template** the update happens automatically as the new document is produced from the template.

To create a standard layout for your Fill-in fields, a **template** is ideal.

How to: Insert the Word field: Fill-in

1. Position your insertion point where you want the dialogue box to prompt for information, e.g. To, From.

2. Display the Insert ribbon, click on **Quick Parts** (Text group), then click on **Field**. The Field dialogue box is presented.

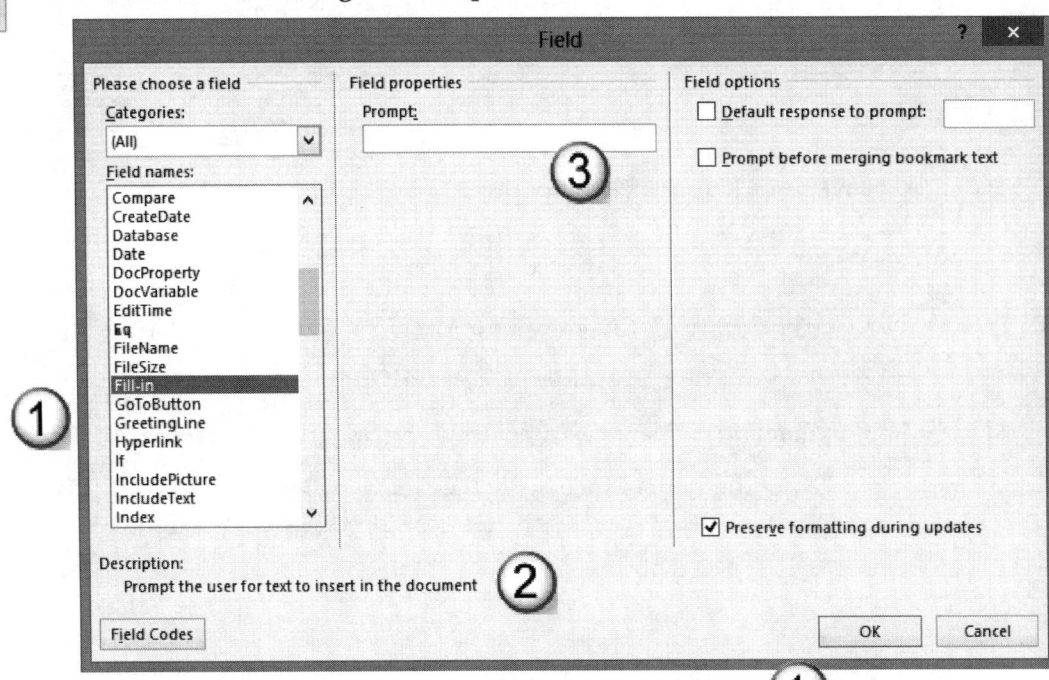

3. Scroll down the **Field names** list and click on **Fill-in**. Note the **Description**.

Topic 3 – Creating templates and designing forms

4. Click in the **Prompt** field properties and type your text, e.g. Who is this memo to?

5. Click on **OK**.
   The created dialogue box is presented. Click on **OK**.

6. Reposition the insertion point and repeat the above steps for all the required prompts.

Printing field codes

After creating a document with fill-in's you may wish to print a copy of the field codes so you can keep the original codes in case the file is accidently deleted.

1. Display **Backstage** view, then click on **Options**.
   The Word Options dialogue box is presented.

2. Click on **Advanced,** then scroll down to the **Print** heading.

3. Click on the check-box: **Print field codes instead of their values**. Then click on **OK**

4. Display your document in **Print Preview** to see the field codes displayed. Remember to remove the check-box once you have printed your document.

Hands-on exercise 3

In this exercise you insert Fill-in fields into the template you created in the last exercise.

- Ensure *Dept memo* (template) is displayed.

- Click your insertion point beside the **To** cell, i.e.

- Display the Insert ribbon, click on the **Quick Parts** button (Text group), then select **Field...** The Field dialogue box is presented.

- Scroll down the **Field names** list and click on **Fill-in**.

- Click in the **Prompt** field and type the following: *Who is memo to?*

- Click on **OK**.
   The created dialogue box is presented. Click on **OK.**

- Press [Alt] [F9] to see the inserted field codes.

- Click into the field codes and edit the text to read: *Who is this memo to?*

Copyright © 2014 Tilde Publishing & Distribution   23

- Click your insertion point beside the **From** cell.
- Click on the **Quick Parts** button, then click on **Field**.
- Scroll down the **Field names** list and click on **Fill-in**.
- Click in the **Prompt** field and type the following: *Who is this memo from?*
- Click in the field **Default response to prompt** and type Your Name.
- Click on **OK**.
  The created dialogue box is presented.
- Copy the field code from the cell beside To: ({FILLIN "Who is this memo to?" *MERGEFORMAT}).
- Paste the field code into the cell beside the first Department.
- Turn show/hide on to see the formatting.
- Carefully edit the field to read: {FILLIN "Which department is the memo going to?" *MERGEFORMAT}
- Turn off show/hide.
- Complete the rest of the fields (Department, Email, Subject) either by copying the field code or inserting via the Quick Parts button.

Next you insert the Date field.

- Click on the **Quick Parts** button (Insert ribbon), then on **Field.**
- Scroll down to **Date** in the **Field names** list.
- Click on the first date in the date formats list (note the format: d/MM/yyyy) then click on **OK**.
- Press [Alt] [F9] to hide the field codes.
- Write down the way the date has been displayed:
- Right click on the date, then select **Edit Field...**
  The Field dialogue box reopens.
- Change the date to the third option: d MMMM yyyy
- Click on OK.
- Write down the way the date has been displayed:
  Notice the difference in the way the date has changed its formatting.
- **Save** your changes.

Next, you print your template with field codes showing (this is always a good idea to keep in a procedure book).

- Display **Backstage** view, then click on **Options.**
  The Word Options dialogue box is presented.
- Click on **Advanced,** then scroll down to the **Print** heading.
- Click on the 5th check-box: **Print field codes instead of their values**.
  Then click on **OK**
- Display your document in **Print Preview** to see the field codes displayed.
- Print your document.

- Go back into the **Backstage** view and un-check: **Print field codes instead of their values**.
- Click on **OK**.
- **Close** your template.

Finally, you create a new *document* based on this template.

- Open Word or, if Word is open, display **Backstage** view then click on New.
- Under the search bar, click on **Personal.**

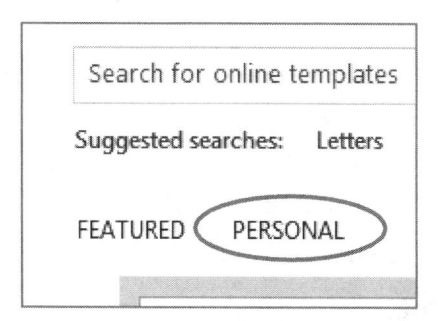

- Click on the *Dept memo* template, then click on **OK**.
- A new *document* is presented based on your memo template and the first dialogue box is presented asking the question "Who is this memo to?".
- Type a name, and then click on **OK**.
  The next dialogue box is presented.
- What is the next dialogue box asking?

___

- Type a response, and then click on **OK**.
  The next dialogue box is presented.
- Respond to all prompts.
- Are all the dialogue box prompts correct?
- If the dialogue box prompts are incorrect, open the template, edit, save and retest.
- Review in **Print Preview**.
- **Save** your completed document as *Dept memo test* (with your other exercise files, not under templates). Note the date of the memo is today's date.
- **Close** your document.

As an aside ... Remember, when creating a new document, a filename field shows the default document name, e.g. Document1 until the document is previewed or printed (when fields are automatically updated).

Hints & tips

If you are displaying file extensions on your computer (when file names are listed) you will notice that Word templates in 2013 have a file extension of .dotx (XML file format).

Syntax of the fill-in field. Fields are surrounded by curly brackets, then comes the field name, then in the case of the fill-in field the prompt surrounded by double quote marks. The default text is preceded by a \d, then the default text (again with double quote marks). The \d is *called a switch. Fields creating using the Field dialogue box automatically include the switch *MERGEFORMAT. This ensures that any formatting applied is retained when an update occurs.*

Consolidation task 2

In this task you produce an automated fax template.

- Print out the following document for reference:
  Org style guide – fax standard.

- In a **new** blank document, create the following fax. Follow your style guide for the fax layout. Check you have setup the following as requested:
    - Margins and page size.
    - Font and font size.
    - Line spacing.
    - Space before/after paragraphs.
    - Row height, column width.
    - Alignment of text in table.

Facsimile

To	
Fax number	
From	
Fax number	
Email	
Date	
Subject	
No. of pages (inc. cover sheet)	

- **Save** your document as a **template** called *Dept fax*.
- Leave the template open.
- Insert Fill-in fields to prompt for the information you require in your template.
- Ensure your insertion point is positioned before you insert a field. (If a field is incorrectly positioned, select the entire field, then press `Delete`.)
- Review your template in **Print Preview**.
- **Print** a copy of your template with field codes showing.
- **Save** your changes.
- **Close** your template.

- Create a **new** document from your template.
- Complete the required details in the dialogue boxes displayed.
- **Save** your document as *Dept fax test*.
- **Close** your document.

Designing forms

A **form** is a document requesting an individual to enter information. Forms usually have a structured and ordered layout.

> *For example ...* Documents that could be effective as forms include: company invoices, weekly timesheets, and registration forms.

You can create a form in Word by starting with a **template** and adding **content controls**, including text boxes, date pickers and drop-down lists. Users can then fill out the form on their computer (in Word).

Before you start creating your form, it is important to take a few moments to plan how you are going to use it. Putting together a draft design can help you finalise your form's content and plan the position of required elements on the form. Ultimately, this approach will save you time, as poorly designed forms often require extensive re-working.

Planning the content

When initially planning the design of your form you need to identify all the information you want to include, and an approximate order or position. This includes both the information you are requesting as well as any information you need to give.

For this purpose, listing the information is a good starting point, as well as indicating any order or position you may think appropriate.

> *For example ...* You have been asked to create a registration form for your company's upcoming road show.

Information to be included...	Nature of information	Order / Position
Name	To be entered	Group 1
Address	To be entered – lengthy field	Group 1
State	To be entered	Group 1
Postcode	To be entered	Group 1
Phone, Fax, Email	To be entered	Group 1
Company logo	Display	Header
Form title	Display	Header
Company contact details	Display	Footer
If want to receive notice of promotions	To be entered – Yes/No response	Group 3
If want to receive quarterly newsletters	To be entered – Yes/No response	Group 3
Provide information on company careers	To be entered – Yes/No response	Group 2
Provide information on company products	To be entered – Yes/No response	Group 2

Provide information on current promotions	To be entered – Yes/No response	Group 2

Laying out your design

Once you have identified the content for your form, you can sketch a basic layout.

Your format must list the information required and allow room for the responses. Some information may need considerable space for the response, e.g. a person's full name, while other information may be shorter, e.g. a postcode. This means that some information may be combined onto one line, e.g. suburb, state and postcode, whereas name and street address are usually given full lines for a response.

> *For example ...* For the form identified in the previous example, a useful sketch of the content would be.

[Sketch of a Registration Form with LOGO box, fields for Name, Address, Suburb/State/P Code, Phone/Fax, Email, checkboxes for "Please provide me with information on: career prospects with your company, current product range, current promotions", checkboxes for "Please include me on the following mailouts: monthly promotions, quarterly newsletter", followed by "Thank you for your interest" and a "Company address details" box]

From this sketch your final form can be developed.

Registration Form

Name: _____
Address: _____
_____

Suburb: _____ State: _____ Postcode: _____
Phone: ( ) _____ Fax: ( ) _____
Email: _____

Please provide me with information on:
- ☐ career prospects with your company
- ☐ current product range
- ☐ current promotions

Please include me in the following mailouts:
- ☐ monthly promotions
- ☐ quarterly newsletter

Thank you for your interest!

Market Research Incorporated
1 Smith Street
Jonestown NSW 2345

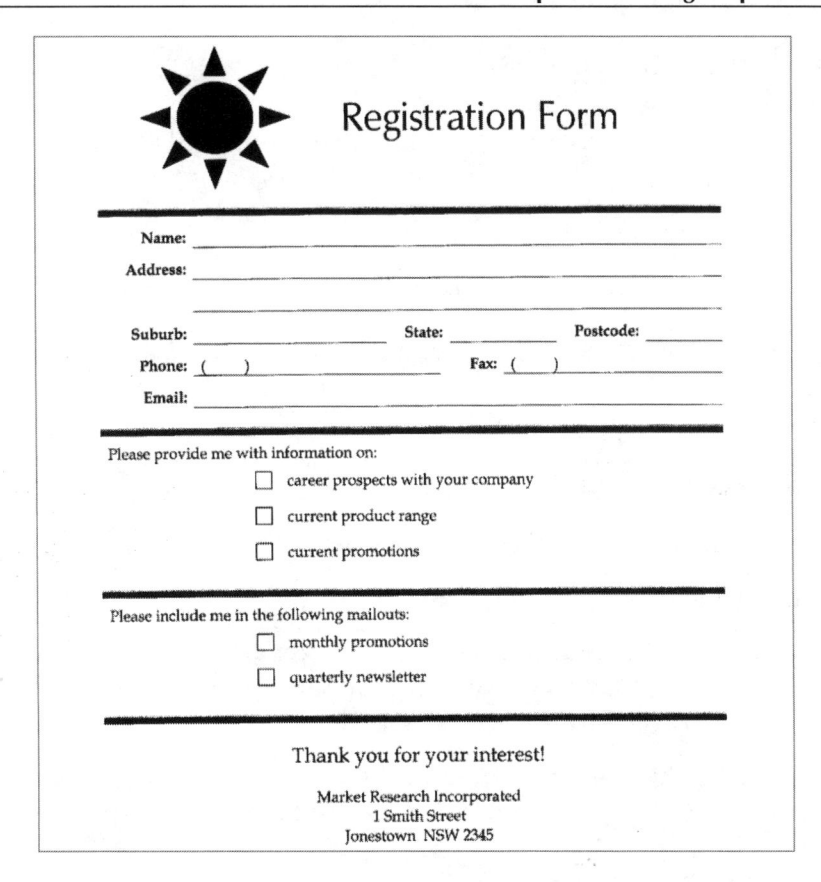

Creating your form (with content controls)

To create a form, insert **content controls** where data input is required. The **properties** of these controls can be adjusted to tailor data input. Before users are allowed to fill out the form, the form is **protected** so that the form itself cannot be modified.

How to: Display the Developer ribbon

1. Display **Backstage** view, then click on **Options**.
   The Word Options pane is presented.

2. Click on **Customize Ribbon** in the left panel.

3. Under **Main Tabs** select the **Developer** checkbox.

4. Click on **OK**.

5. Display the Developer ribbon.

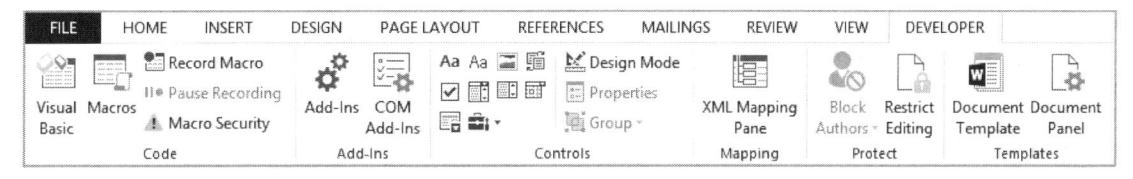

How to: Create a form

1. Display the Developer ribbon.

2. Create a new document or open an existing document containing the layout for the form.

3. Layout/edit your text using tables as appropriate.

4. **Save** as a template.

5. In your template, position your insertion point and insert **content controls** as required (Controls group).

Basic content controls

Aa	**Rich Text**	Use where a formatted text response is required.
Aa	**Text**	Use where a plain text response is required.
	Drop-Down List	Use where a list of alternatives needs to be available from which the user can select, e.g. male, female.
	Date Picker	Use where date entry is required.

6. **Save** your changes.

How to: Adjust control properties

1. Insert the required **content control**.

2. With the control selected, click on the **Properties** button (Controls group).
   The Content Control Properties dialogue box is presented, which differs depending on the control selected.

3. Adjust the properties as required.

4. Click on **OK**.

How to: Protect your form

1. Create your template and insert the required content controls.

2. Click on the **Restrict Editing** button (Protect group).
   The Restrict Formatting and Editing task pane is presented.

3. Click on **Allow only this type of editing in the document**.

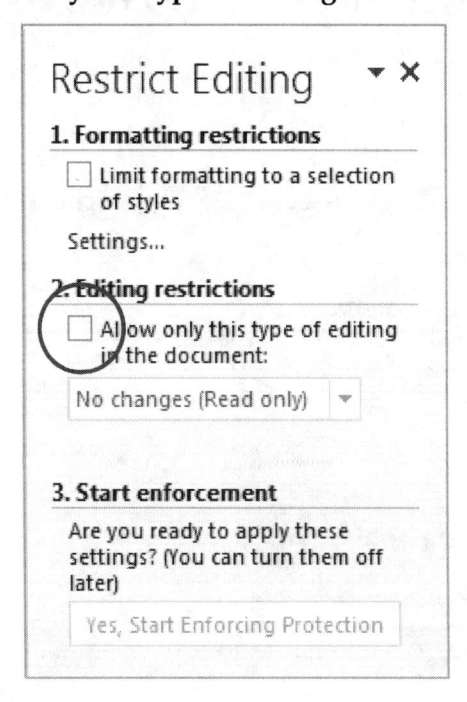

4. Click on the down-arrow for the list of restrictions underneath.
   Click on **Filling in forms.**

5. Click on the **Yes, Start Enforcing Protection** button.
   The Start Enforcing Protection dialogue box is presented.

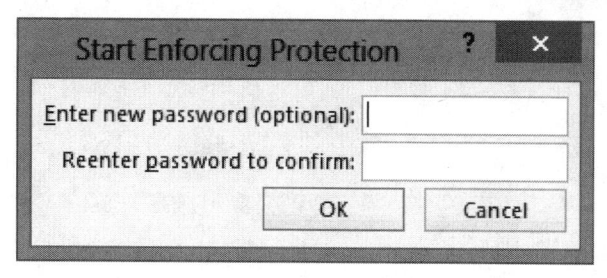

Adding a password is optional but highly recommended when personal data such as addresses is being collected.

6. Add a password, then reenter the password. Click on **OK**.

7. **Close** the task pane.

Hands-on exercise 4

In this exercise you practice creating a form. Your supplied exercises include a template called *Registration form* which is used in this task. This template should have been copied into your Templates folder (see **Preface, Before You Start**).

- **Open** the supplied template *Registration Form*.
  A layout has been created for you using tables.

- Display the Developer ribbon.

- Click your insertion point beside the **Name** cell.

- Click on the **Plain Text Content Control** button (Controls group). Hover your mouse over the control buttons in the ribbon to see its name.

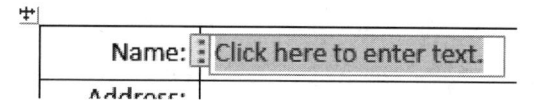

- Click your insertion point beside the **Address** cell.

- Click on the **Plain Text Content Control** button.

- With the control still selected, click on the **Properties** button (Controls group). The Content Control Properties dialogue box is presented.

- Click on **Allow carriage returns (multiple paragraphs)**.

- Click on **OK**.

- Click your insertion point beside the **Suburb** cell.

- Click on the **Plain Text Content Control** button.

- Click your insertion point beside the **State** cell.

- Click on the **Drop-Down List Content Control** button.

- With the control still selected, click on the **Properties** button (Controls group). The Content Control Properties dialogue box is presented.

- Under **Drop-Down List Properties,** click on **Add...** The Add Choice dialogue box is presented

- Type NSW, then click on **OK**.

- Click on **Add**.

- Type QLD, then click on **OK**.
- Click on **Add**.
- Add abbreviations for all the other states, then click on **OK**.
- Back in the form, click on the down-arrow beside the control marker and note the States added.
- With the state control still selected, display the Properties dialogue box again.
- Under **Drop-Down List Properties**, select on *Choose an item*, then click on the **Modify** button.
- Edit to read in both Display Name and Value: Choose a state
- Click on OK then on OK.
- Click on the down-arrow beside the control and select **Choose a state**.
- Add **Text** fields beside **Postcode**, **Phone**, **Fax** and **Email**.
- Click bedside **Career prospects with your company**.
- Click on the **Drop-Down List Content Control** button.
- With the control still selected, click on the **Properties** button (Controls group).
- Add choices for **Yes** and **No**.
- Repeat for all the remaining questions. (You can copy and paste the markers.)

Finally, you add protection to your form.

- Click on the **Restrict Editing** button (Protect group).
  The Restrict Formatting and Editing task pane is presented.
- Click on **Allow only this type of editing in the document**.
- Click on the down-arrow for the list of restrictions underneath.
  Click on **Filling in forms.**
- Under **Start enforcement**, click on the **Yes, Start Enforcing Protection** button. The Start Enforcing Protection dialogue box is presented.
- Add your name as a password then reenter it. Click on **OK**.
- **Close** the task pane.
- **Save** your template and **close**.
- Create a **new** document based on your *Registration form* template.
- Fill out the details. Note how you cannot access areas outside the controls.
- **Save** your form as *Registration form 1*.
- **Close** your form.

Modifying your form

At times you will need to amend the contents of your form.

How to: Modify a form

1. Re-open your 'form' template.
2. Click on the **Restrict Editing** button (Protect group).
   The Restrict Formatting and Editing task pane is presented.
3. Click on **Stop Protection** (you will need to insert a password if originally entered).
4. Amend your form as necessary
5. Re-apply the document protection.
6. **Close** the task pane.
7. **Save** your template.

Hands-on exercise 5

In this exercise you practise modifying a template.

- Re-open your *Registration form* template.
- Click on the **Restrict Editing** button (Protect group).
  The Restrict Formatting and Editing task pane is presented.
- Click on **Stop Protection** (you will need to insert your password).
- Add font colour to the document footer.
- Re-apply the document protection (your name as a password).
- **Close** the task pane.
- **Save** your template and close.

Terms & concepts review

- What is the name of the Word **field** used to prompt with dialogue boxes?

  _____

- Why are **fill-in fields** used in a template?

  _____

  _____

- If the field codes are not visible on your document, what keys do you press to display them?

  _____

  _____

- List some everyday documents where you think **fill-in fields** would be useful.

  _____

  _____

  _____

- Where do you find the following buttons and what do they do?

	Ribbon? Group?	What does this button do?
Aa		
Restrict Editing		
Quick Parts		

Topic 3 – Creating templates and designing forms

Consolidation task 3

You have been asked to create the following order form with content controls to be used complete online.

- Create the following order form with tables (see next page for possible table solution).
- Insert controls to the form (a few hints provided). Insert protection.
- Appropriately format the order form with shading/alignment/font.
- Save your template as *Order form v1*.
- Test your order form.
- Print and close when completed.

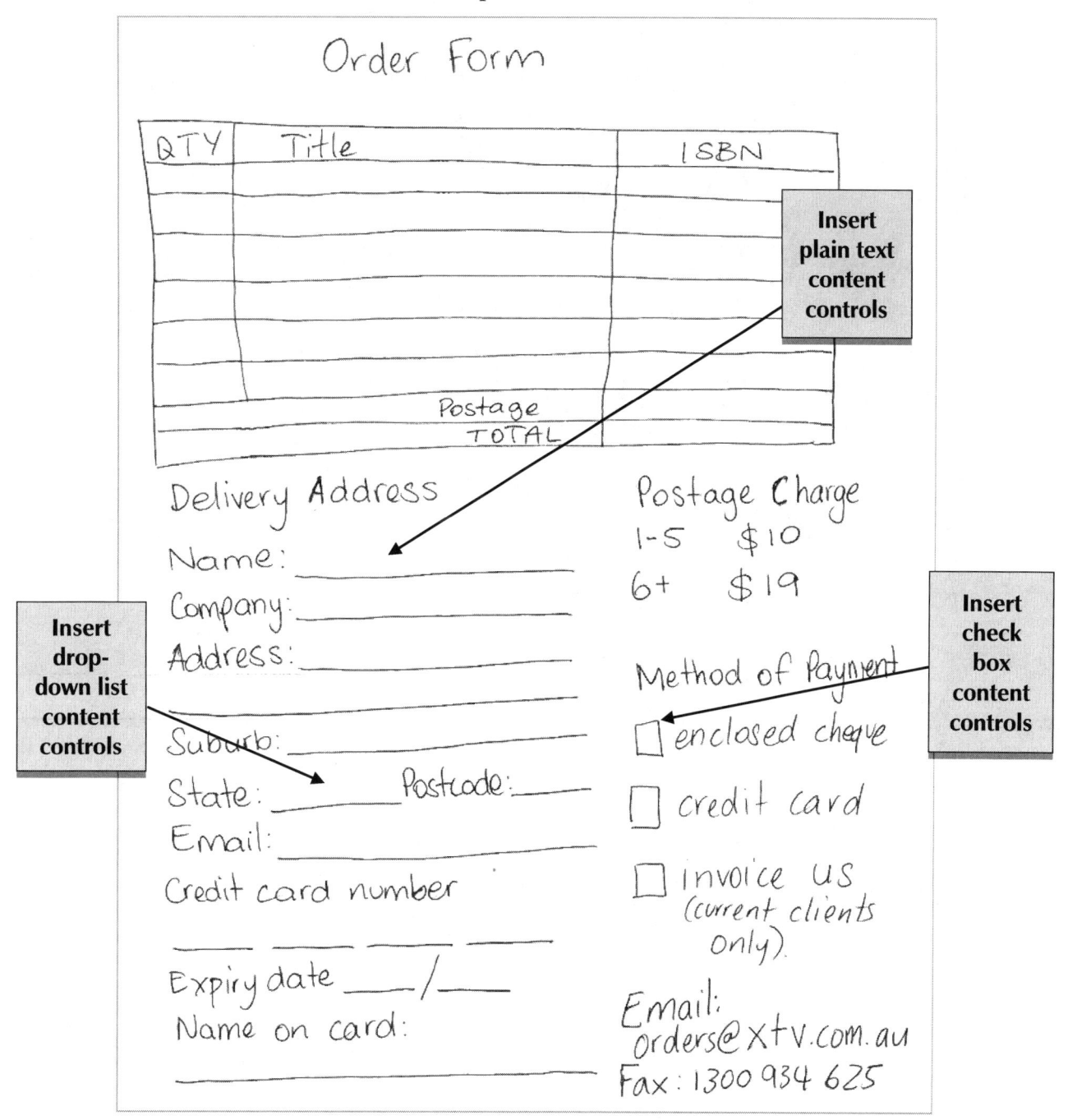

Order Form

QTY	Title	ISBN
		Postage
		TOTAL

Insert plain text content controls

Insert drop-down list content controls

Insert check box content controls

Delivery Address
Name: _____
Company: _____
Address: _____
Suburb: _____
State: _____ Postcode: _____
Email: _____
Credit card number
_ _ _ _ / _ _ _ _ / _ _ _ _ / _ _ _ _
Expiry date ___ / ___
Name on card: _____

Postage Charge
1-5 $10
6+ $19

Method of Payment
☐ enclosed cheque
☐ credit card
☐ invoice us (current clients only)

Email: orders@xtv.com.au
Fax: 1300 934 625

Order form

QTY	Title	ISBN
	Postage	
	Total	

Delivery address			Postage Charge	
Name			1-5	$10
Company			6+	$19
Address				
Suburb			**Method of Payment**	
State			Enclosed cheque	
Email			Credit card	
			Invoice us (current clients only)	
Credit card number				
	|		|	|
Expiry date		/		
Name on card:			Email orders@xtv.com.au Fax: 1300 934 625	

Example of form with table borders showing

Order form

QTY	Title	ISBN
	Postage	
	Total	

Delivery address   Postage Charge

Name _____   1-5 $10
Company _____   6+ $19
Address _____
        _____

Suburb _____   **Method of Payment**
State _____   ☐ Enclosed cheque
Email _____   ☐ Credit card
                                ☐ Invoice us
                                  (current clients only)
Credit card number
_____ | _____ | _____ | _____

Expiry date _____ / _____
Name on card: _____   Email
                                   orders@xtv.com.au
                                   Fax: 1300 934 625

Example of form with selective borders showing

Topic 4 – Inserting shapes & WordArt

Word provides an extensive range of preconfigured shapes that you can insert into your documents. You can choose from a range of basic shapes, or more complex designs using SmartArt (taught later in the book).

Inserting and modifying basic shapes

These include squares, circles, lines and arrows, flowchart symbols and callouts.

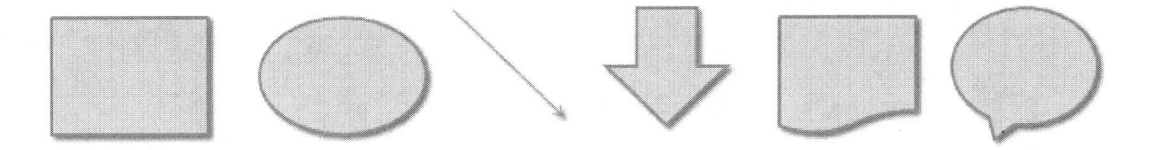

Fundamentals in shapes

Inserting shapes		o Insert ribbon (Illustrations group) o Click on the shape and drag mouse to create shape o Release mouse to finish shape
Resizing shapes		o Click on the shape to display the sizing handles and drag to new size
Moving a shape		o Click on the shape to display the four way arrow and drag to a new position.
Copying a shape		o Click on the shape and press Ctrl and drag.
Rotating a shape		o Select and drag the green rotate handle.

Fundamentals in adding colour and effects

For the following fundamental skills, first click on the shape and display the Format ribbon.

Changing shape fill Shape Fill ▼	o	Click on the **Shape Fill** down-arrow (Shape Styles group) then click on the required colour.
Changing shape outline Shape Outline ▼	o	Click on the **Shape Outline** down-arrow (Shape Styles group) then click on the required colour.
Changing a shape effect Shape Effects ▼	o	Click on the **Shape Effect** down-arrow (Shape Styles group) and point to the required category, then sub-category. Click to select.
Changing a shape style	o	Click on the **More** button in the **Shape Styles** gallery (Shape Styles Group), click to select.
Add text to a shape	o	Right-click on a shape, then click on **Add Text**.

Hints & tips

What if I want to draw a square or a circle?

Press [Shift] as you draw with a Rectangle shape to draw a square.

Press [Shift] as you draw with the Oval shape to draw a circle.

What if I cannot keep my lines straight as I draw?

Press [Shift] as you draw a line to keep it straight.

What if I see an additional yellow sizing handle on an object?

Some of the shapes have an additional yellow adjust handle(s). Point to the handle and drag to change the depth or angle.

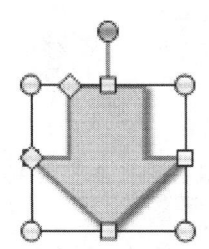

How to: Insert a callout

1. Display the Insert ribbon then click on the **Shapes** button (Illustrations group).

2. Under **Callouts**, click on the callout of choice.
   Your mouse pointer becomes a cross.

3. Hold your mouse down while dragging across the screen to create your callout. Release your mouse when the shape is what you require.

4. You will notice your insertion point is inside the shape. Type the required text.

5. If you need to change the direction of the point, click on the yellow diamond and move your mouse.

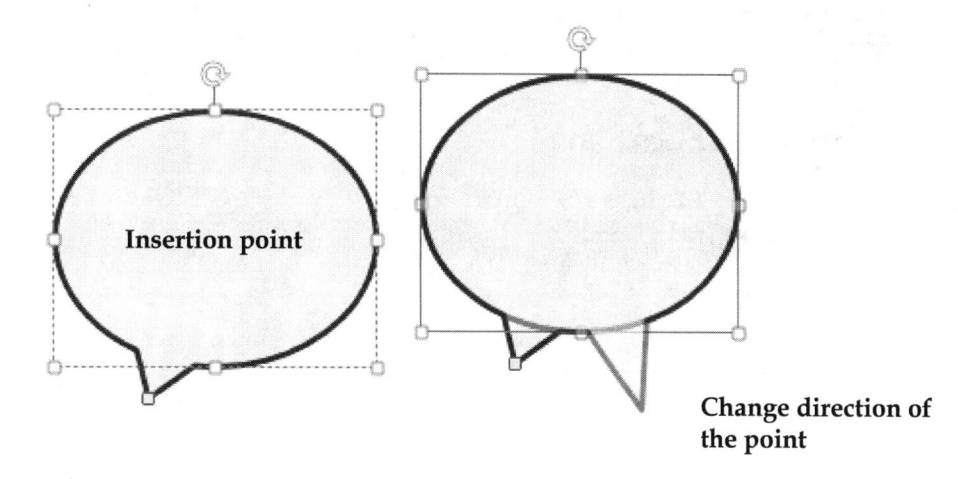

Insertion point

Change direction of the point

Selecting and working with multiple objects

You can work with several objects at the same time, e.g. to save time when applying colour or effects. You can also select several objects together in order to align or group them.

How to: Select multiple object

1. Click on the first object, then press **Shift** and click on subsequent objects.

How to: Align multiple objects

1. Select the required objects. 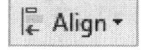
2. Display the Format ribbon, then click on the **Align** button (Arrange group), then click on the required alignment, e.g. Align Top.

How to: Group objects

1. Select the required objects. 
2. Display the Format ribbon, then click on the **Group** button (Arrange group), then click on **Group**.

*As an aside … To ungroup, click on the **Ungroup** option, then click away from the group before you select an individual shape.*

Hints & tips

*To change the order of objects before grouping in the previous exercise, click on an object then click on the **Bring Forward**, **Send Backward** buttons (Arrange group).*

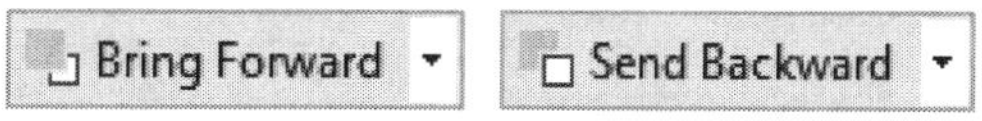

*Note also in the Arrange group the **Rotate** button, to rotate for flip objects.*

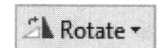

Creating a text box

You can create text boxes to organise information, draw attention to important text, or attractively display headings. Word provides a simple text box or a number of pre-set alternatives.

How to: Insert an empty text box

1. Display the Insert ribbon, then click on the **Text Box** button (Text group). Select Draw Text Box.

2. The text box is inserted into your document.

3. The text box appears surrounded with sizing handles and new Text Box Tools are available on the Format ribbon.

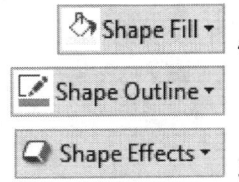

4. To enter text into your text box, simply begin typing. Format your text as required. You can also use the **Shape Fill/ Outline/Effects** buttons (Format ribbon) to format your text box.

5. Drag on a sizing handle to re-size the box. To move the text box, simply point to *the border* and drag it to a new location.

Inserting WordArt

WordArt can be used to create interesting text effects that enhance your documents. Text can be shaped into a variety of styles to create unusual alignments and 3-D effects.

For example ...

Company news

How to: Insert WordArt

1. Display the **Insert** ribbon, then click on the **WordArt** button (Text group). The WordArt Gallery is presented.

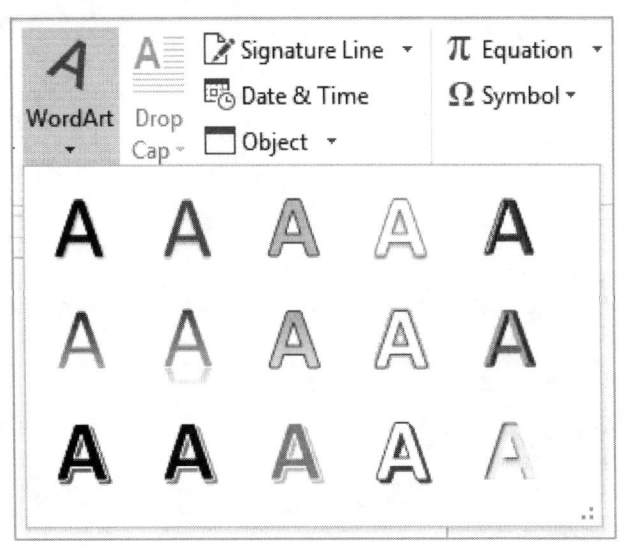

2. Click on the **WordArt style** required.

3. Type your text.

4. Display the Drawing Tools/Format ribbon for more options (WordArt Styles group).

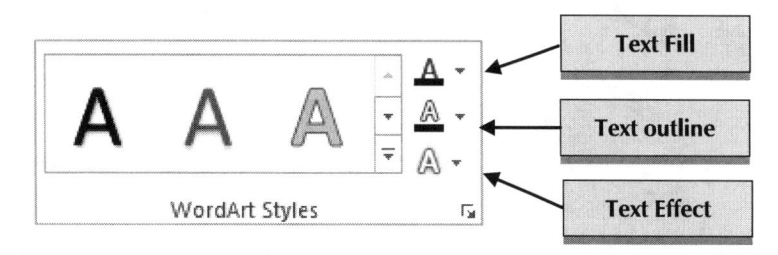

5. Click on the **Text Effects** button to change the alignment of the text (Transform) or to add reflection or shadow.

6. Change the outline colour by clicking on the **Text Outline** button.

7. Change the Text fill colour by clicking on the **Text Fill** button.

8. Double-click on the WordArt object to edit.

Hands-on exercise 6

In this exercise you practice inserting WordArt.

- Open to edit your template *Order form v1*.
- Remove protection.
- Select the heading: **Order Form**.
- Display the Insert ribbon, then click on the **WordArt** button.
- Select **Gradient Fill - Gray** (see graphic).
- Click on the **Wrap Text** button (Format ribbon, Arrange group).
- Select **In Line with Text**.
- Ensure the order form still fits on one page.
- Display in **Print Preview**.
- Select your **WordArt**.
- Click on the **Text Effects** button (WordArt Styles), then select **Transform.**
- Select **Deflate**.
- Change the text fill and text outline to colours of your choice.
- Put the **Protection** back onto the order form.
- **Save** and **close** your template.

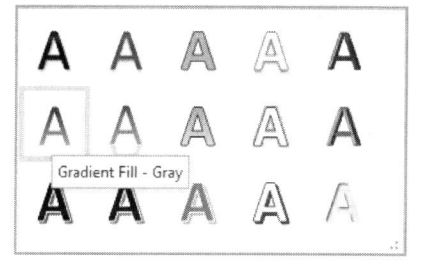

- Test your template.
- **Close** the test without saving.

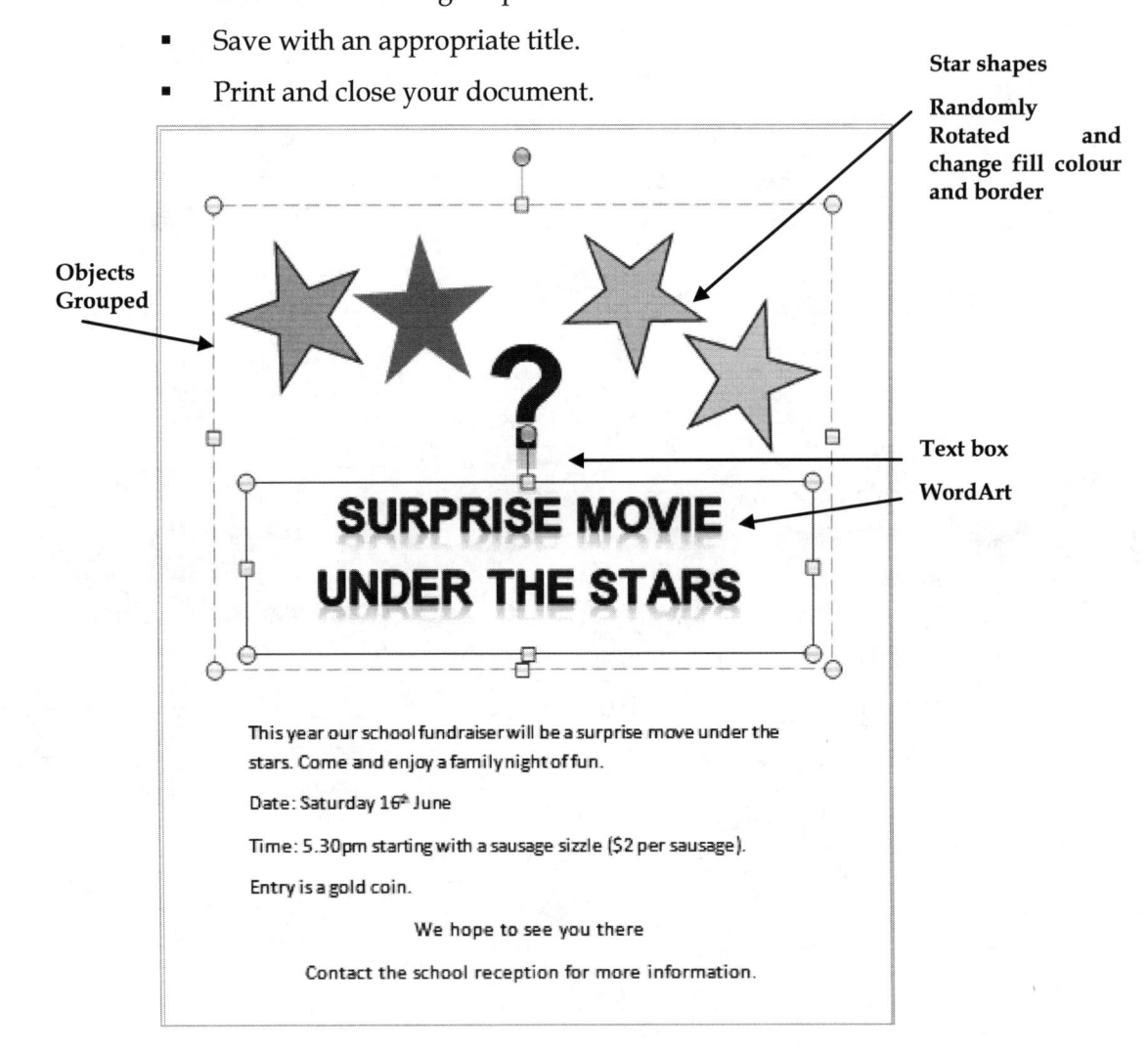

Consolidation task 4

In this task you insert and align shapes and WordArt to create an advertisement.

- Create a blank document.
- Insert the following shapes and text boxes into the document.
- Save with an appropriate title.
- Print and close your document.

Star shapes

Randomly Rotated and change fill colour and border

Objects Grouped

Text box

WordArt

SURPRISE MOVIE UNDER THE STARS

This year our school fundraiser will be a surprise move under the stars. Come and enjoy a family night of fun.

Date: Saturday 16th June

Time: 5.30pm starting with a sausage sizzle ($2 per sausage).

Entry is a gold coin.

We hope to see you there

Contact the school reception for more information.

Consolidation task 5

Create the following company logo using shapes and alignment

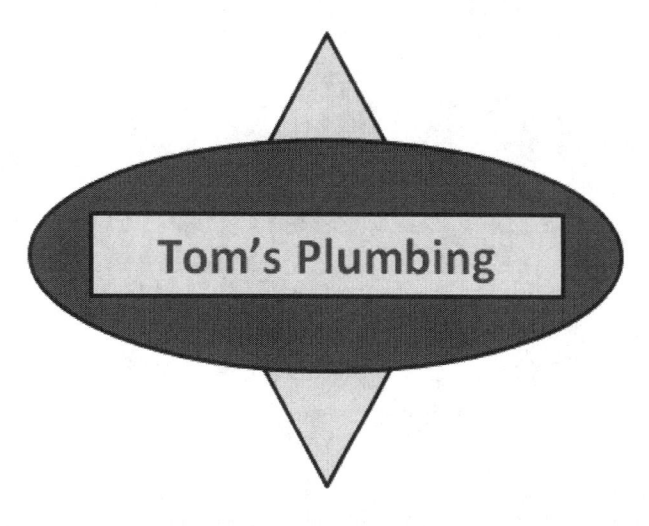

Here are the shapes used in the above logo:

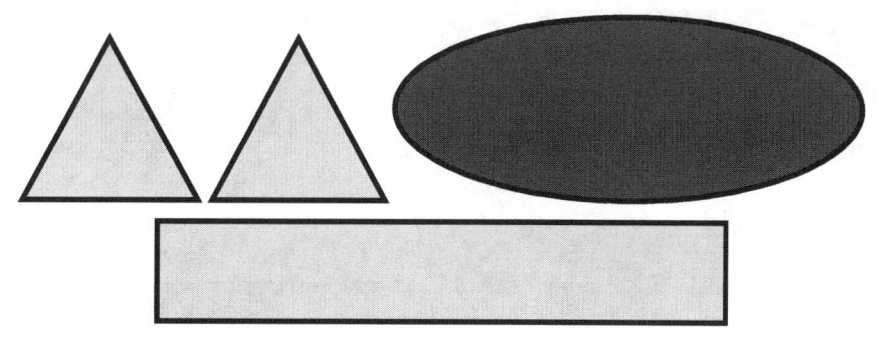

- Group the objects.
- Save the logo with an appropriate title.
- Open *Estimate form vs1*.
- Copy and paste it into the top of the estimate form (you may need to resize the logo – hint: **make sure** the items are grouped to do this).
- Save both documents.
- Print a copy of your estimate form.
- Close both documents.

Topic 5 – Complex mail merge

In this topic you commence working with complex mail merge features.

Mail merge for form (standard) letters

Merging involves bringing together two files: a file that contains the standard text of a letter, and a file that contains the address information of the multiple recipients. The letter is known as the **main document**, and the address file is known as the **data source**.

In order that the address information from the data source is inserted into each letter, the **main** document (i.e. the letter) includes **merge fields**. These fields correspond to the information held in the data source. These fields appear surrounded by << >> brackets.

When the two files are brought together, or **merged**, a third document is produced. This third document holds all of the (form) letters that are generated.

There are several ways that merging can be achieved in Word. In this course you are shown a process where merge fields are added directly to your main document using the **Mailing ribbon**.

Hands-on exercise 7

In this exercise you practise creating a standard letter (from a handwritten draft) to promote a new student textbook. This document is your **main document**.

- Print out the following document for reference:
  Org style guide – letter standard.

- In a **new** blank document, type the following letter. Follow your style guide for the letter layout. Check you have setup the following as requested:

    - Margins and page size.

    - Font and font size.

    - Line spacing.

- Space before/after paragraphs.

> Date
>
> (Leave space for college name & address.)
>
> Dear
>
> We are pleased to announce that our new textbook Successful Business Writing is now available. We have written this book based on office practice in Australia and we have consulted Australian companies in a range of industries. It contains guidelines and sample letters for all business situations.
>
> Successful Business Writing is being offered at a reduced rate of $20 for this term only. We look forward to receiving your order.
>
> Yours sincerely
>
> Megan Sullivan
> Director

- Spell and grammar check your document.
- **Save** your document as *Booksales letter*.

Creating a data source

The **data source** can simply be a document that holds a **table** of data or an Excel worksheet. The table/worksheet can hold all of your name, address and additional details efficiently.

When creating a data source, the first row of the table/worksheet contains your **merge field names**, i.e. labels for your variable data such as FirstName, LastName.

> *As an aside* … *When creating your own data source it is recommended that you do not include spaces in the merge field names.*

Each row of the table then becomes a merge record: one row being used for each form letter created as part of the merge process.

> *Additional info* … *You should avoid adding any formatting to the table being used as a data source. Let the text wrap naturally in the cells, e.g. do not press* Enter *between the words just because your column width is narrow.*

Hands-on exercise 8

In this exercise you create your data source using Excel.

- Open Excel, then select **Blank workbook**.
- Type the data shown in the worksheet. Do not include any formatting (formatting can cause merge errors).
- Don't resize any columns.
- **Save** your workbook as *Booksales data*.
- **Exit** Excel.

Additional info... A new record can be added to the data source at a later date by editing your worksheet. Likewise, a new field can be added to the data source by adding another column. Equally by deleting a row or column data can be removed.

Title	FirstName	LastName	College	Street	Suburb	State	Code
Mrs	Georgia	Dunn	Armidale College	23 Main Street	ARMIDALE	NSW	2550
Mr	Peter	Trigg	West Perth College	90 Prospect Place	WEST PERTH	WA	6005
Mr	Michael	Picton	Dandenong College	9 Mount Road	DANDENONG	VIC	3175
Miss	Kerry	Sargent	Gold Coast College	4 River Street	COOLANGATTA	QLD	4225
Mr	Jake	Gotts	Newcastle College	30 Pacific Street	NEWCASTLE	NSW	2300
Mrs	Lucy	Jones	North Queensland College	340 Tully Street	TOWNSVILLE	QLD	4810

Commencing the merge

Once you have created your main document and data source you can begin the merge process. Using the Mailing ribbon you:

Step 1 – nominate your letter as a form letter

Step 2 - attach your data source

Step 3 - insert your merge field

Step 4 – preview your merge letters

Step 5 – merge your letters.

How to: Nominate your letter

1. Display your main document.
2. Display the Mailings ribbon, click on the **Start Mail Merge** button, then click on **Letters** (Start Mail Merge group).

How to: Attach your data source

1. Display your main document.
2. Display the Mailings ribbon, click on the **Select Recipients** button, then click on **Use an Existing List...** (Start Mail Merge group).
   The Select Data Source dialogue box is presented.
3. Select the storage location of your data source.
   Click on the data source, then click on **Open**.
4. If you are using Excel, the Select Table dialogue box is presented.
5. Click on the appropriate worksheet, then **OK**.
   The data source is attached to your main document.

How to: Insert merge fields

1. Position your insertion point where you need a merge field.
2. Display the Mailings ribbon, click on the **Insert Merge Field** down-arrow, then click on the required field (Write & Insert Fields group).
   Remember to put punctuation as required around fields, e.g. leave a space between first name and surname.

   ```
   «FirstName» «LastName»
   «Company»
   «Address1»
   «Suburb» «State» «PostCode»

   Dear «FirstName»
   ```

3. **Save** your main document after you have inserted the merge fields.

Hands-on exercise 9

In this exercise you practise Steps 1-3 of the merge process (nominate your letter, attach your data source and insert merge fields).

- Display your main document (*Booksales letter*).

First, you nominate your letter.

- Display the Mailings ribbon, click on the **Start Mail Merge** button, then click on **Letters** (Start Mail Merge group).

Next, you attach your data source.

- From the Mailings ribbon, click on the **Select Recipients** button, then click on **Use an Existing List...** (Start Mail Merge group). The Select Data Source dialogue box is presented.
- Locate and select your data source *Booksales data*, then click on **Open**. Select Sheet1$ if not already selected, click on **OK**.
- The data source is attached to your main document.

Next, you insert your merge fields.

- Position your insertion point where the address is required.
- From the Mailings ribbon, click on the **Insert Merge Field** down-arrow, then click on the **Title** field (Write & Insert Fields group). If the fields are not available then the data source has not been attached.
- Press the Spacebar
- Click on the **Insert Merge Field** down-arrow, then click on the **FirstName** field.
- Press the Spacebar
- Insert **LastName** field.
- Press Enter
- Repeat this process to add the remaining address fields. Remember your punctuation.
- Position your insertion point after Dear and insert the **FirstName** field.

Dear «FirstName»

- **Save** your changes.

Completing your merge

Finally, you are ready to merge together the main document and the data source. You can preview your output to ensure the letters to be produced are as expected, then you can merge to a file for later printing or merge directly to the printer. It is recommended that you merge to a file to allow final checking or individual tweaking, and to allow you to print off larger merge files in smaller chunks (to minimise printer hiccups).

How to: Preview your merge output

1. Display the Mailings ribbon, then click on the **Preview Results** button (Preview Results group).
2. Note the first record from your data source is displayed in the letter.
3. To view other records, click on the **Next Record** ▶, **Previous Record** ◀ buttons.
4. Click again on the **Preview Results** button to switch off the preview feature. 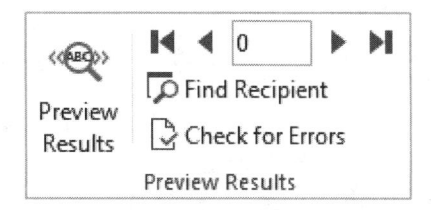

How to: Merge to a new document

1. Display the Mailings ribbon, click on the **Finish & Merge** button, then click on **Edit Individual Documents** (Finish group). The Merge to New Document dialogue box is presented.

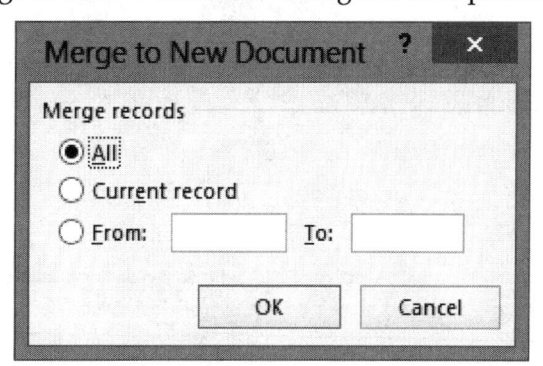

2. Click on **All** to merge all records in the data source; click on **Current Record** to merge only the previewed record; or click on **From/To** and type required merge record numbers (i.e. rows in the data source table).
3. Click on **OK**.
   A new document is presented with your merged letters.
   The document is called *Letters1*.
4. Scroll through the letters presented.

Hands-on exercise 10

In this exercise you practise Steps 4-5 of the merge process (preview and merge).

First, you preview your merge result.

- Ensure your letter is displayed.
- Display the Mailings ribbon, then click on the **Preview Results** button (Preview Results group).
- Note the first record from your data source is displayed in the letter.
- To view other records, click on the **Next Record** ▶, **Previous Record** ◀ buttons.
- Click again on the **Preview Results** button to switch off the preview feature.

Next, you merge to a new document, i.e. bring together the letter and data into a third document (the output).

- From the Mailings ribbon, click on the **Finish & Merge** button, then click on **Edit Individual Documents** (Finish group). The Merge to New Document dialogue box is presented.
- Click on **All** to merge all records in the data source.
- Click on **OK**.
  A new document is presented with your merged letters.
  The document is called *Letters1*.
- Scroll through the letters presented.
- **Close** your output document without saving (*Letters1*).
- **Save** and **close** your main document *Booksales letter*.

Creating labels

In an earlier course you learned the basic steps for creating labels. Here, the process of creating labels is revisited, and you also learn how to produce custom address labels.

Hands-on exercise 11

In this exercise you review generating labels to accompany the document *Booksales letter*. (You can print on plain paper.)

- Create a **new** blank document. This is your main document.
- Display the Mailings ribbon, click on the **Start Mail Merge** button, then click on **Labels** (Start Mail Merge group). The Label Options dialogue box is presented.
- Enter these label options: **Label vendor** Avery A4/A5 labels and **Product number** J8159. Click on **OK**.
- Your (blank) labels document is presented in a table layout.

- Click on the **Select Recipients** button, then click on **Use Existing List** (Start Mail Merge group). The Select Data Source dialogue box is presented.

- Locate and select the Excel workbook *Booksales data*, then click on **Open**. The data source is attached to your main document and the <<Next Record>> field is inserted in each label except the first.

- Ensuring your insertion point is located in the first label, click on the **Insert Merge Field** down-arrow, then click on the **Title** field.

- Press the `Spacebar`

- Click on the **Insert Merge Field** down-arrow, then click on the **FirstName** field.

- Press `Enter`

- Repeat this process to add the remaining address fields. Remember your punctuation.

- Select the table and reduce the font size if necessary to ensure Title, FirstName, LastName appears on one line.

- Select the table and remove any paragraph spacing.

- From the Mailings ribbon, click on the **Update Labels** button (Write & Insert Fields group). The merge fields are replicated in each label.

- **Save** your main document as *Booksales labels*.

- Preview and merge all records as previously (your output document will be *Labels..*).

- **Close** your output document without saving.

- **Save** and **close** your main document (*Booksales labels*).

Creating custom labels

The label stationery that you need to print onto may not correspond to any of the label products available in the Label Options dialogue box. If this is the case, you can create custom labels by selecting the exact measurements your labels require.

How to: Create custom labels

1. Create a **new** blank document. This is your main document.

2. Display the Mailings ribbon, click on the **Start Mail Merge** button, then click on **Labels** (Start Mail Merge group).
   The Label Options dialogue box is presented.

3. Click on any **Label vendor/Product number** you can use as a base (i.e. the dimensions come close), then click on **New Label**.
   The Label Details dialogue box is presented.

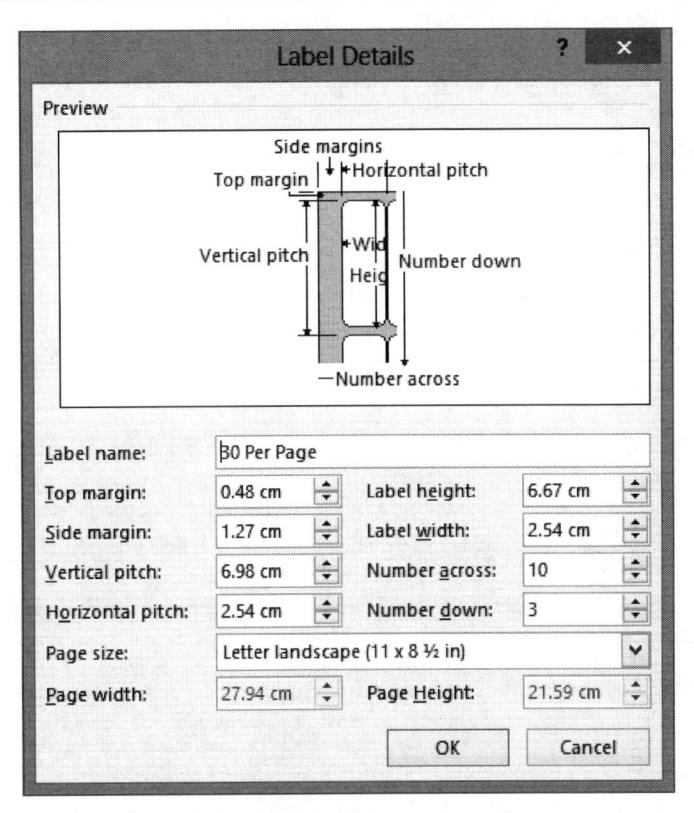

4. Type a descriptive **Label name**.

5. Adjust the measurements as necessary.

6. Click on **OK**.
   Note that your new label name is displayed.

7. Click on **OK**.

8. Select your data source, insert the required merge fields for your labels, then perform the merge following the usual steps. (Don't forget to Update Labels.)

Hands-on exercise 12

In this exercise you practise creating custom ID labels. Your data source will be an Excel worksheet.

- Create a **new** blank document. This is your main document.

- Display the Mailings ribbon, click on the **Start Mail Merge** button, then click on **Labels** (Start Mail Merge group). The Label Options dialogue box is presented.

- Enter these initial label options: **Label vendor** Avery A4/A5 labels and **Product number** L7084. Click on **New Label**. The Label Details dialogue box is presented.

- Type the **Label name:** Name labels.

- Adjust the **Top Margin** to 1.7 cm, and the **Side Margin** to 0.8 cm.

- Click on **OK**.
  Note that your new label name is displayed.
  (Note: If there is already a label of this name select **Yes** to overwrite it.)

- Click on **OK**.

- Click on the **Select Recipients** button, then click on **Use Existing List** (Start Mail Merge group). The Select Data Source dialogue box is presented.

- Locate and select the Excel workbook *Mailing list*, then click on **Open**. The **Select Table** dialogue box is presented.

- Ensure **Customers** is selected, then click on **OK**.
  ('Customers' is a named sheet in the Excel workbook.)

- Insert fields for FirstName, LastName and College underneath.

- From the Mailings ribbon, click on the **Update Labels** button (Write & Insert Fields group). The merge fields are replicated in each label.

- **Save** your main document as *Custom labels*.

- Merge all records as previously.

- **Close** your output document without saving.

- **Save** and **close** your main document (*Custom labels*).

Merging only some of your data

It is generally recommended that you create a single data source containing all the information needed for any number of merges. As the data is only stored in one place it can be easily maintained and updated. Selected data can then be extracted from the data source using various criteria or questions.

> *For example ...* You can send a personalised letter to your Queensland customers only, extracting these names and addresses from a national data source of all your customers.

It is also possible to select your data using more than one criteria (or question).

> *For example ...* You may want to extract all customers who live in Queensland **or** in South Australia.

How to: Set merge criteria

1. Create a main document with the data source attached and the merge fields inserted.

2. Display the Mailing ribbon, then click on the **Edit Recipient List** button (Start Mail Merge group). The Mail Merge Recipients dialogue box is presented.

3. Click on **Filter** (bottom of dialogue box). The Filter and Sort dialogue box is presented.

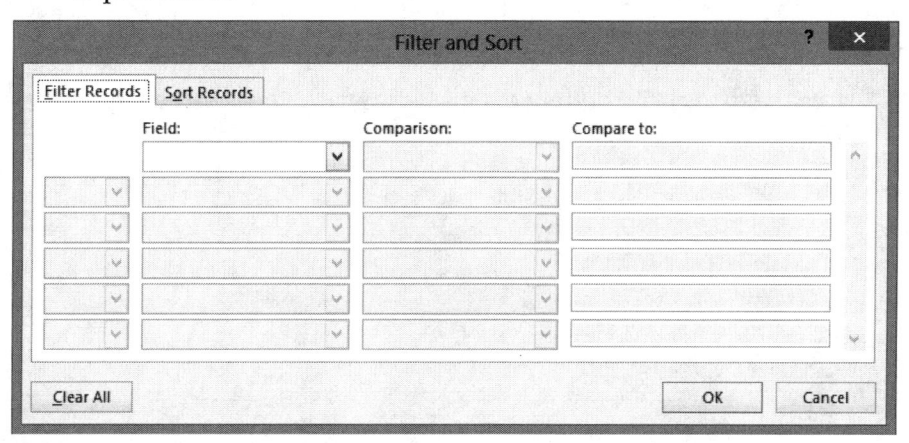

4. Ensure the **Filter Records** tab is selected.
5. Click on the first **Field** down-arrow, then click on the field you want to use as a selection criteria, e.g. State.
6. Click in the **Comparison** box, then click on a comparison phrase, e.g. Equal to.
7. Click in the **Compare to** box, then type the text or number that matches the records you require, e.g. QLD.
8. To specify another set of criteria (optional), click on **And** or **Or**, then complete the next set of Field, Comparison and Compare boxes. For example, **Or** State **Equal to** SA.
9. Click on **OK**. The Mail Merge Recipients dialogue box is presented.
10. Click on **OK**.
11. Complete the merge following the usual steps.

Hands-on exercise 13

In this exercise you merge using selection criteria.

- **Open** the document *Convention letter*.
  This letter is the main document for a letter merge.
- Commence a letter merge.
- Select the data source *Convention data*. (Also a Word document.)
- Insert the following merge fields

\<Today's date>

«Title» «FirstName» «LastName»
«Organisation»
«Street»
«Suburb» «State» «PCode»

Dear «FirstName»

It was such a pleasure to have your group as our guest in «ConventionMonth». Not only did we enjoy having «Organisation» in our hotel, but also getting to work with you was an added benefit. You are so professional and organised that you make us look good!

«FirstName», if there's anything I can do to provide more assistance in the future please do not hesitate to call.

Yours sincerely

Joanne Keen
Convention Services Manager

- Display the Mailing ribbon, then click on the **Edit Recipient List** button. The Mail Merge Recipients dialogue box is presented.
- Click on **Filter** (bottom of dialogue box). The Query Options dialogue box is presented.
- Ensure the **Filter Records** tab is selected.
- Click on the first **Field** down-arrow, then click on **State**.
- Ensure the **Comparison** box displays **Equal to**.
- Click in the **Compare to** box, then type the text QLD.
- To specify another set of criteria, click on **And**, and select **Or**.
- Click on the first **Field** down-arrow, then click on **State**.
- Ensure the **Comparison** box displays **Equal to**.
- Click in the **Compare to** box, then type the text NSW.
- Click on **OK**. The Mail Merge Recipients dialogue box is presented.
- Click on **OK**.
- Complete the merge for all records to a new document following the usual steps. Remember the merge fields are already inserted.
- Four letters are extracted. Review these letters.
- **Close** the output document without saving.
  Your main document (*Convention letter*) is presented.
- **Save** your main document, and leave open.

As an aside ... There is a short cut when you only require **single** extraction criteria. Click on the down-arrow beside a field heading and select from the presented criteria, e.g. if you want your letters to go only to your Queensland clients, click on the down-arrow beside the State field heading and select QLD. This is particularly useful for True/False requirements.

Removing your mail merge selection criteria

Once criteria have been established, you may want to remove them, e.g. you later want to perform a merge using all the records.

How to: Remove selection criteria

1. **Open** a main document with the data source attached and the merge fields inserted.
2. Display the Mailing ribbon, then click on the **Edit Recipient List** button (Start Mail Merge group). The Mail Merge Recipients dialogue box is presented.
3. Click on **Filter** (bottom of dialogue box).
4. Ensure the **Filter Records** tab is selected.
5. Click on **Clear All**.
6. Click on **OK**.
   You return to the Mail Merge Recipients dialogue box.
7. Click on **OK**.
8. **Save** your change to the main document.

Hands-on exercise 14

In this exercise you practise removing selection criteria previously saved with a merge.

- Ensuring the *Convention letter* is displayed, click on the **Edit Recipient List** button. The Mail Merge Recipients dialogue box is presented.
- Click on **Filter** (bottom of dialogue box). The Query Options dialogue box is presented.
- Ensure the **Filter Records** tab is selected.
- Click on **Clear All**.
- Click on **OK**.
  You return to the Mail Merge Recipients dialogue box.
- Click on **OK**.
- **Save** your main document, and leave open.

Using a Fill-in field in a merge

In addition to merge fields, other Word fields can be added to a main document to include custom data that is not stored in the data source, e.g. a personal greeting.

Earlier in this text, you saw how a Fill-in field can be used to prompt for changing information. When used in a mail merge, a **Fill-in** field displays a prompt as Word merges *each* data record with the main document. Your response to the prompt is printed in the letter or other main document.

For example ... You can use a Fill-in field to add personal greetings to your merge letters.

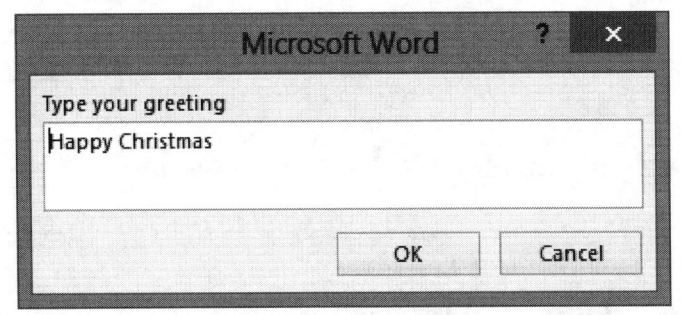

[Dialogue box: Microsoft Word — Type your greeting: Happy Christmas — OK / Cancel]

While merging you cannot see your main document, therefore in the above example you don't know who the letter is for. A better prompt would be:

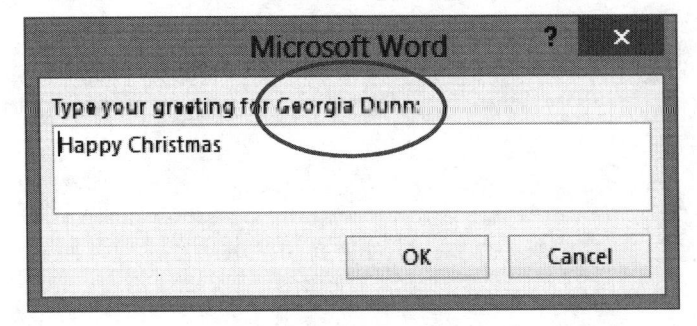

[Dialogue box: Microsoft Word — Type your greeting for Georgia Dunn: (circled) — Happy Christmas — OK / Cancel]

Dialogue box with an edited Fill-in field which displays details from the record being merged

In order to incorporate names into your prompt you need to insert merge fields within the Fill-in field, e.g. FirstName, LastName.

As an aside ... Inserting one field inside of another is referred to as **nesting**.

How to: Insert a Fill-in field into a main document

1. Position your insertion point in the main document where you want the additional information to appear.

2. Display the Mailings ribbon, then click on the **Rules** button (Write & Insert fields group).

3. Click on **Fill-in**.
   The Insert Word Field: Fill-in dialogue box appears.

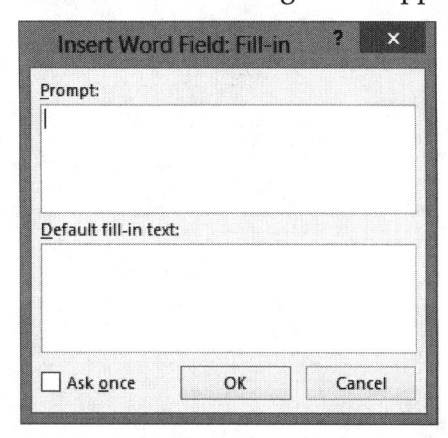

4. Type your prompt in the **Prompt** box, e.g. Type your greeting:

5. Type the **Default fill-in text** (optional), e.g. Happy Christmas

6. Click on **OK**.
   A confirmation of your prompt with the default text appears.

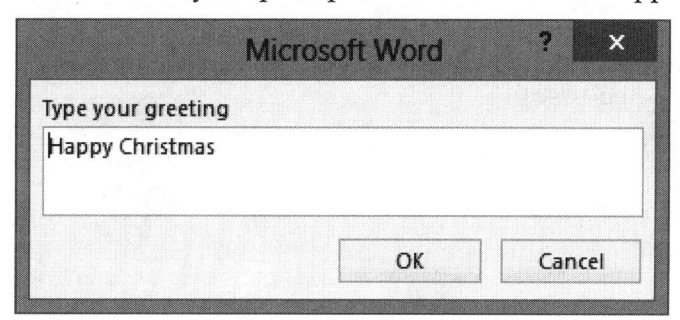

7. Click on **OK**.

8. You are returned to the main document.
   Only the default text appears.

How to: Edit a Fill-in field to include merge fields

1. Press Alt F9 to your field codes.

   { FILLIN "Type your greeting here:" \d "Happy Christmas" }

2. Click in the prompt text where the merge fields are to appear, e.g. after the text: greeting

3. Click on the **Insert Merge Field** button (Write & Insert Fields group).

4. Insert the required fields, e.g. FirstName, LastName.

5. Press Alt F9 again to re-display the field results.

6. Continue your merge in the usual manner.
The prompt – that you complete as required – appears for each record in the database.

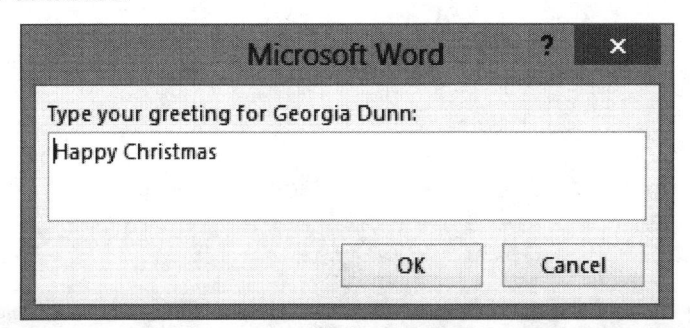

Hands-on exercise 15

In this exercise you customise a merge using a Fill-in field. The field will enable you to add a personal greeting to each order confirmation that you send to customers.

- **Open** the document *Order confirmation*.
- Commence a letter merge.
- Select *Accounts data* as the data source.
- Insert the following merge fields.

Order Confirmation			
Attention:	«Attention»		
College:	«College»	**Date Received:**	(Today's date)
Street:	«Street»		
Suburb:	«Suburb»		
State:	«State»		
Post Code:	«Pcode»		

Next, you insert the Fill-in field.

- Position your insertion point beneath the last sentence in the document.
- Click on the **Rules** button (Write & Insert fields group), then click on **Fill-in**.
  The Insert Word Field: Fill-in dialogue box appears.
- Type the following prompt in the **Prompt** box: Type your greeting here:
- Type the **Default fill-in text**: Thank you for your order.
- Click on **OK**.
  A confirmation of your prompt with the default text appears.

Topic 5 – Complex mail merge

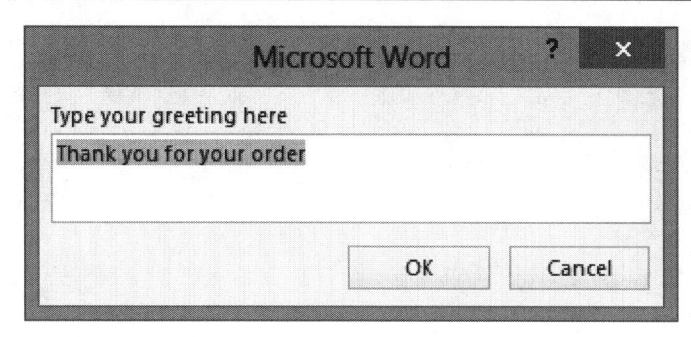

- Click on **OK**.
- You are returned to the main document.
  Only the default text appears (Thank you for your order).

Next, you edit your Fill-in field to include merge fields. The merge fields will display the name of the recipients of each letter.

- Press `Alt` `F9` to display your field codes.

`{ FILLIN "Type your greeting here" \d "Thank you for your order" }.`

- In the Fill-in field select the word 'here'. Type the word 'for'.
- Press the `Spacebar`.
- Click on the **Insert Merge Field** button (Write & Insert Fields group).
- Insert the field: **Attention**.

`{ FILLIN "Type your greeting for { MERGEFIELD Attention }" \d "Thank you for your order" }.`

- Press `Alt` `F9` again to re-display the field result.
  The default text appears.
- **Save** your changes.
- Merge all records to new document. The prompt appears, with name fields for each record in the database. For each record, do the following:

Georgina Dunn	Click on **OK** to accept the default greeting.
Peter Trigg	Type the following greeting: Thank you for your first order. Click on **OK**.
Michael Pictone	Type the following greeting: Thank you for your regular orders. Click on **OK**.
Kerry Sergeant	Click on **OK** to accept the default greeting.
Jake Gott	Type the following greeting: Please call our Accounts Department. Click on **OK**.
	Merge all remaining records with messages of your choice.

- Scroll through the letters created noting the inserted messages.
- **Close** your output document without saving.

- **Save** your main document (*Order confirmation*).
- **Close** your document.

As an aside ... It is not recommended that you use this approach if your data source holds more than 20 or 30 records!

Using an If field in a merge

An **If** field (**If...Then...Else**...) allows you to include additional information in the main document only *if* a certain condition is met.

For example ... Include a message to local customers (from MELBOURNE) 'Please visit our shop for a discount'. To all other customers, 'Please visit our website for a discount'.

How to: Insert an If field in a merge

1. Position your insertion point in the main document where you want the additional information to appear.

2. Display the Mailings ribbon, then click on the **Rules** button (Write & Insert fields group).

3. Click on **If...Then...Else**.
   The Insert Word Field: IF dialogue box is presented.

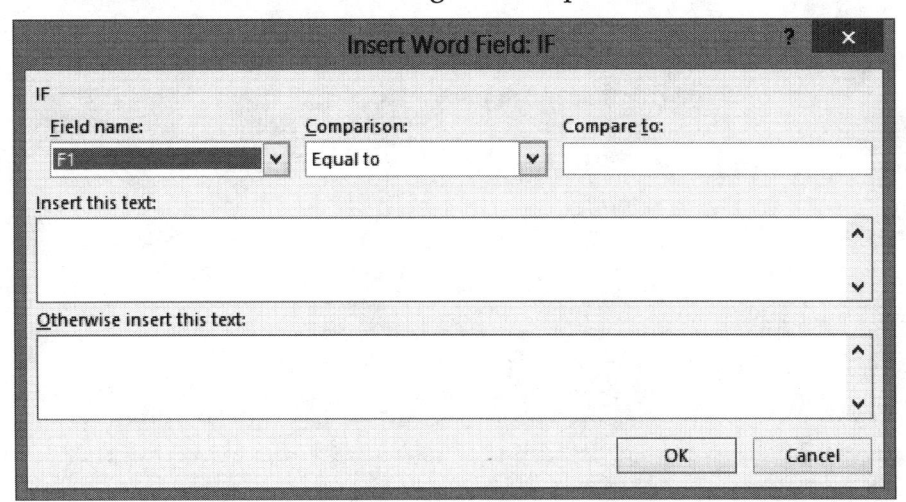

4. Click on the **Field name** down-arrow, then click on the required field, e.g. Suburb.

5. Select your **Comparison** field, e.g. Equal to

6. Click on the **Compare to** box and type your comparison, MELBOURNE.

7. Click in the **Insert this text** box and type the required text, e.g. Please visit our shop for a discount.

8. Click in the **Otherwise insert this text** box and type the required text, e.g. Please visit our website for a discount.

9. Click on **OK**. You are returned to the main document.

10. Continue your merge following the usual steps.

Topic 5 – Complex mail merge

Hands-on exercise 16

In this exercise you insert an **If** field into a merge letter to inform customers of a local or national telephone number. The telephone number given in the letter is dependent on the customer's location.

In this exercise it has been assumed that the sender of the letter is located in Townsville, QLD.

First, you create your main document.

- Create a **new** blank document.
- Type the following letter (use your standards guide for the letter layout). Leave some space beneath the date for name and address details to be included. A Word field will be included at the end of the second paragraph.

> Date
>
> Dear
>
> Thank you for your recent enquiry. Please find enclosed a brochure that I think will answer all of your questions.
>
> For further details feel free to
>
> Sincerely
>
> Susan Poole
> Marketing Manager

- Spell and grammar check your document.
- **Save** your document as *Enquiry letter*.
  Leave your letter open on the screen.
- Commence a letter merge.
- Select the data source *Enquiry data*. (A Word document.)
- Insert merge fields for the address and salutation.

Next, you insert a Word field to determine the contact telephone number to be quoted. If the customer lives in Townsville a local number will be given. If the customer does not live in Townsville, then a national number will be given.

- Click your insertion point at the end of the second paragraph (after the word 'to').
- Display the Mailings ribbon, then click on the **Rules** button (Write & Insert fields group).

- Click on **If...Then...Else**.
  The Insert Word Field: IF dialogue box is presented.

- Click on the **Field name** down-arrow, then click on **Suburb**.

- Ensure the **Comparison** box displays **Equal**.

- Click on the **Compare to** box and type: TOWNSVILLE
  (Note: Use capitals - the data in the data source is in capitals.)

- Click in the **Insert this text** box and type:
  contact your local office on 07 4756 6789.

- Click in the **Otherwise insert this text** box and type:
  contact our national office on 02 9967 8789.

- Click on **OK**. You are returned to the main document.

- Displayed in the field is the text required if the condition is not met, i.e. contact your national office ....

- Complete your merge of all records to a new document.

- Review your output letters re the **If** statement (TOWNSVILLE = local).

- **Close** your output document without saving.
  Your main document (*Enquiry letter*) is presented.

- **Save** your main document.

- **Close** your document.

Hands-on exercise 17

In this exercise you insert an **If** field into a merge letter to inform customers of a gift voucher they are eligible to receive. The amount of the gift voucher is dependent on the value of their last order.

First, you create your main document.

- Create a **new** blank document.

- Type the following letter (use your standards guide for the letter layout). Leave space beneath the date for name and address details to be included. A Word field will later be included after the $ sign in the body of the letter.

> Date
>
> Dear
>
> Thank you for your order. As a valued customer we would like to offer you a $ gift voucher to thank you for your recent support. Please call into your local branch to collect your voucher.
>
> Sincerely
>
> James Strong
> Promotions Manager.

- Spell and grammar check your document.
- **Save** your document as *Gift promotion*.
  Leave your letter open on the screen.
- Commence a letter merge.
- Select the data source *Gift promotions data*. (A Word document.)
- Insert merge fields for the address and salutation.

Next, you insert a Word field to determine the value of the gift voucher offered. If a customer spent $50 or more on their last order, they will be eligible for a $15 gift voucher. If they spent less than $50 they will be eligible for a $5 gift voucher.

- Click your insertion point after the $ sign.
- Click on the **Rules** button (Write & Insert fields group).
- Click on **If…Then…Else**.
  The Insert Word Field: IF dialogue box is presented.
- Click on the **Field name** down-arrow, then click on **OrderValue**.
- Click on the **Comparison** down-arrow, then click on **Greater than or equal**.
- Click in the **Compare to** box and type: 50
- Click in the **Insert this text** box and type: 15
- Click in the **Otherwise insert this text** box and type: 5
- Click on **OK**.
  You are returned to the main document.
  Displayed in the field is the text that would be inserted if the condition is not met, i.e. 5.
- Apply **Bold** to the $ sign and the Word field.
- Complete your merge of all records to a new document.
- Review your output letters.
- **Close** your output document without saving.
- **Save** your main document (*Gift promotion*).
- **Close** your document.

Hints & tips

If you need to delete a merge field drag over the merge field and press `Delete`.

Unless you make individual changes to letters in your merge output, there is no need to save the output. It can always be regenerated from your main document and your data source. The main document retains the connection with your nominated data source. It might be worth keeping the output from a large merge until the documents are in the post!

*In your main document, click on the **Highlight Merge Fields** button (Write & Insert Fields group) to shade the merge fields. This is helpful to see where the merge fields are.*

What does this dialogue box mean? It is presented when I re-open my main document.

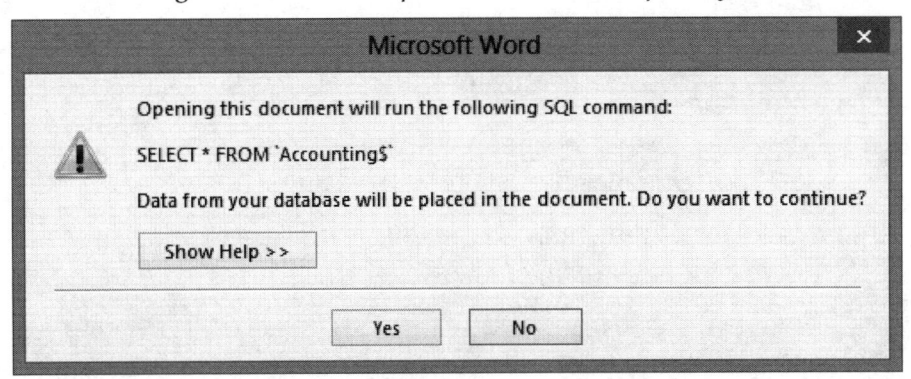

> **Microsoft Word**
>
> Opening this document will run the following SQL command:
>
> SELECT * FROM `Accounting$`
>
> Data from your database will be placed in the document. Do you want to continue?
>
> [Show Help >>]
>
> [Yes] [No]

When you save a main document a link to the selected data source is also saved. When you re-open the main document it remembers the data source it is connected to and asks if you want to retain this connection.

Terms & concepts review

- Does the data source in a mail merge have to be a Word document?

  _____

  _____

- You are performing a mail merge to send a letter to all customers who live in NSW. This information is stored in the data source. Would you set merge criteria using a Filter or insert a Fill-in field?

  _____

  _____

  _____

Topic 6 – Working with long documents

In this topic you look at a number of techniques for working with long documents. These include:

- consistency and organising your text using heading styles and outlining
- numbering your document headings
- building a table of contents and index
- importing text, numeric data and graphics.

As your documents become more complex it is worth reviewing document design and layout principles to ensure your documents are readable and well structured.

Text presentation

Text appearance and presentation contribute enormously to producing readable and well-structured documents.

Listed below are a number of formatting suggestions that you can use to improve your text presentation.

- Don't use too many fonts and font sizes in a document as this reduces readability and makes the document look disjointed.

- Try using serif fonts for large amounts of text, e.g. Times New Roman and Century Schoolbook. Serif fonts have short lines that cross the ends of most characters. The short lines (serifs) help to guide the eye across the page which makes text easier to read.

- Try using sans serif fonts for headings and shorter documents, e.g. Arial and Calibri. Sans serif fonts have no serifs to guide the eye.

  Standard fonts, e.g. Times New Roman and Arial are also good choices because they are found in all word processing programs. So, when you send a document electronically rather than on paper, you can be sure the recipient can print it the way you intended it to look.

- Use bold or italic to emphasise words, e.g. keywords. However, do not overuse as this makes text harder to read.

- Avoid too much underlining, as the line can blend in with the text, which again makes text harder to read.
- Avoid capitals. Lots of capital letters make your text 'unfriendly' and hard to read.
- Avoid using a double space between sentences. A single space is sufficient with modern word processing.

These are general points to consider when creating professional-looking business documents. However, fancy posters and advertising can challenge design choices, and can often break the rules!

Document design

There are three basic rules of thumb for good document design and layout:

- keep the design simple;
- keep the design consistent; and
- add contrast.

Simplicity

With a simple design the reader gets the message immediately. Limit the number of elements on a page, e.g. limit fonts, decorative elements and pictures.

Consistency

Consistency in design helps a reader to move through a document more easily and to understand quickly how information is organised. Be consistent with the size of headings, spacing between paragraphs, spacing between sentences and indent measurements, and bullet design.

Contrast

Contrast catches the reader's eye and helps draw it to what is important. White space helps to create contrast, i.e. the parts of your page that remain unprinted.

Filling a page with information can overwhelm your audience and distract them so that they fail to understand your message (or simply decide that it is easier to ignore your message). Therefore, give your layout room to breathe by using white space, e.g. space around headings, around pictures and making sure margins are not too small.

Picture placement

For an effective page layout with pictures, consider your picture placement.

Generally, a reader scans a page from the top-left corner down to the bottom-right corner. Clever picture placement can be used to lead the reader's eye across the page, enhancing readability and making information easier to digest.

A picture or title is often placed in the top-left corner so that the reader's eye is drawn into the page. Company logos are frequently placed alongside a title for immediate identification, or in the bottom-right corner.

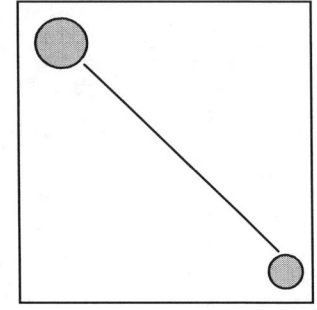

The bottom-right corner of a page is the last place that the eye rests as it scans the page. So, a logo that has been placed in the bottom-right corner is likely to form part of the final impression left with the reader.

Consistency when using styles

Using **styles** you can ensure a consistent and professional appearance for your documents. A style is created by bringing together a number of formatting characteristics and giving that set of formatting characteristics a name.

> *For example ...* Instead of applying bold, a font, and a font size to each heading in a document (three actions), you can save these formatting characteristics into a single style. Then, you simply use one action to apply the style.

If you update any of the formatting characteristics in a style, all instances of the style are updated.

Word supplies numerous built-in **'quick'** styles for elements in a document. These are organised in **style sets**. You can create your own styles if you have particular corporate or personal requirements.

Styles fall into five categories: **paragraph**, **character**, **linked** (elements of paragraph and character), **table** and **list**. Paragraph styles control the appearance of an entire paragraph, whereas character styles control only selected text (usually selected words within a paragraph). Table styles control the appearance of a table, such as borders, shading and fonts. List styles control the appearance of alignment, numbering, bullet characters and fonts displayed in lists.

Applying a quick style

Text in a new document uses (by default) the **Normal** style. Use the Quick Styles Gallery to apply a different built-in style. Styles can be applied in a number of ways.

How to: Apply a quick style using the Quick Styles Gallery

1. Click in a paragraph, or select the required text.
2. Display the Home ribbon, point to any option in the **Quick Styles Gallery** (Styles group). The style is previewed in your paragraph(s). Click on the **More** button to display the full gallery of styles.
3. Click on the required style to apply.

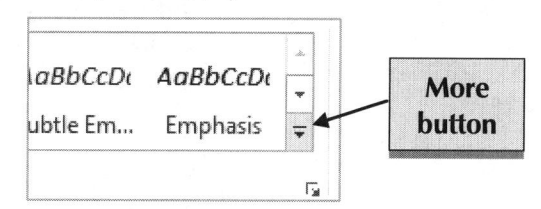

How to: Apply a quick style using the Styles task pane

1. Click in a paragraph, or select the required text.
2. Display the Home ribbon, locate the Styles group, then click on the dialogue box launcher ~or~
   The Styles task pane is presented.
3. Click on the required style.

> *As an aside ...* This task pane is useful as it identifies the type of style, e.g. paragraph style ¶, character style **a**, or a style that has properties of both (linked style ¶a). Also if you point to each style you get full details of what the style comprises.

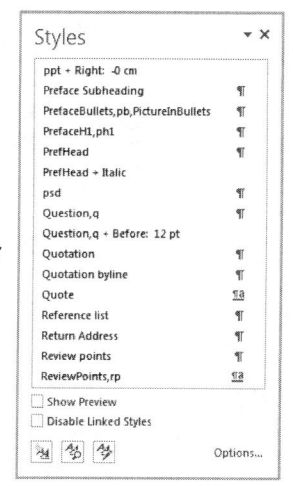

How to: Remove quick styles

1. Select the required text.
2. Display the Home ribbon, in the **Quick Styles Gallery,** click on the **More** button, then click on **Clear Formatting**.

Updating a quick style

When required, any style can be updated. Updating a style is the quickest way to change formatting throughout a document. When a style is updated, all text with the selected style is immediately changed to the new look.

> *For example ...* *You have just completed formatting a 40 page document when you decide to change the appearance of all major headings.*

For simple changes update the style by example.

How to: Update a quick style by example

1. Apply your formatting changes to any text formatted with the existing style.
2. Select the text.
3. Display the **Styles** task pane.
4. Point to the style in the task pane. A down-arrow appears beside the style. Click on the down-arrow. 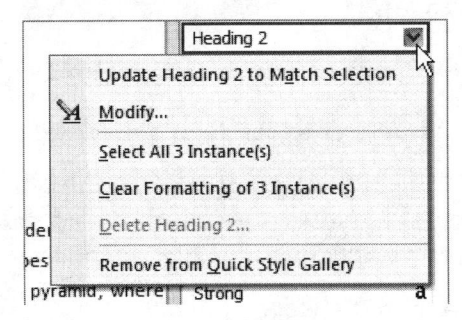
5. Click on Update 'style name' to Match Selection.
6. All occurrences of the style in the document are updated to reflect the changes

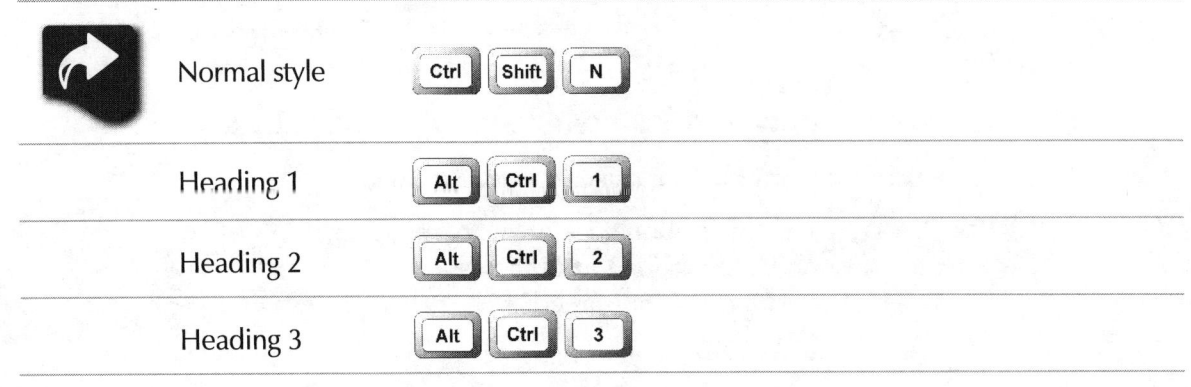

Normal style	Ctrl + Shift + N
Heading 1	Alt + Ctrl + 1
Heading 2	Alt + Ctrl + 2
Heading 3	Alt + Ctrl + 3

Topic 6 – Working with long documents

Hands-on exercise 18

In this exercise you apply heading styles to a document and then use Outline view to explore the document.

- **Open** the document *SuperFood annual report*.
- Click on the heading: The Managing Director's Report, then apply the **Heading 1** style.
- Apply the **Heading 2** style to the next three headings:

    Focusing on our Customers' Needs
    Ensuring Quality
    Food Safety

- (Hint: You can use the repeat key `F4` once you have applied the selected style for the first time.)
- Click on the next heading: Feeding More Australians, then apply the **Heading 1** style.
- Apply the **Heading 2** style to the next three headings:

    New Stores
    Electronic Shopping Services
    Magazine Initiative

- Click on the heading: SuperFood Initiatives, then apply the **Heading 1** style.
- Apply the **Heading 2** style to the next four headings:

    SuperPetrol
    New Outlets
    SuperMetro
    SuperElectronic

- Click on the next heading: Our New Technology, then apply the **Heading 1** style.
- Apply the **Heading 2** style to the next four headings:

    New Warehouse Technology
    Construction of Warehouses
    Flavoursome Fruits
    Supermarket Merchandising Systems

- Click on the heading: This Year's Highlights, then apply the **Heading 1** style.
- **Save** your changes.

Working with heading styles and outlining

You have already seen how useful heading styles can be when you want to create consistent formatting in a document. However, you may not know that Word automatically applies an outline level to text each time you apply a heading style.

As a result, you then have the option of using **Outline** view to display the heading structure of a document.

Using Outline view:

- gives you an overall impression of the flow of your topics or chapters
- shows you at a glance which topics are subordinate to others
- makes it easier to reassign a heading level or reorganise the order of your topics.

> *For example ...* The document below is formatted with the heading styles 1, 2 and 3. In Outline view you can choose to display only these three levels.

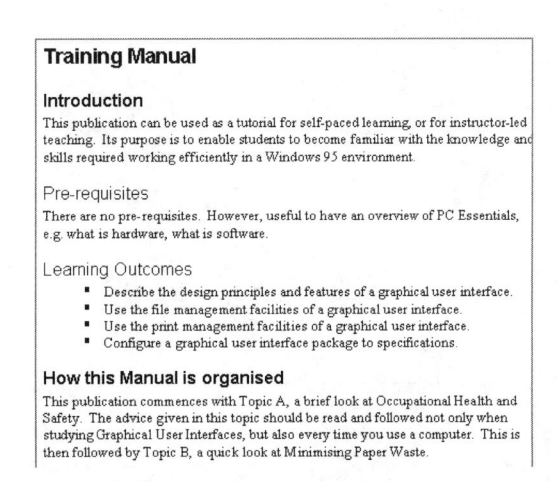

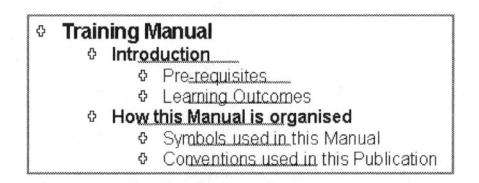

Document in Print Layout view

Same document in Outline view displaying levels 1-3 only

How to: Display Outline view

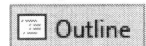

1. Display the View ribbon, then click on the **Outline** button (Views group).
2. Outline view is displayed and the **Outlining** ribbon presented.

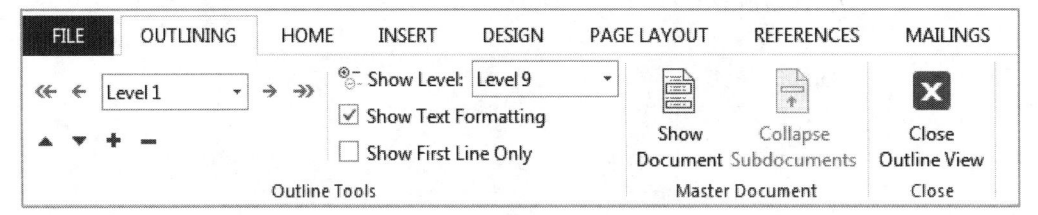

How to: Display your required headings

1. Click on the required button (Outlining ribbon, Outline Tools group):

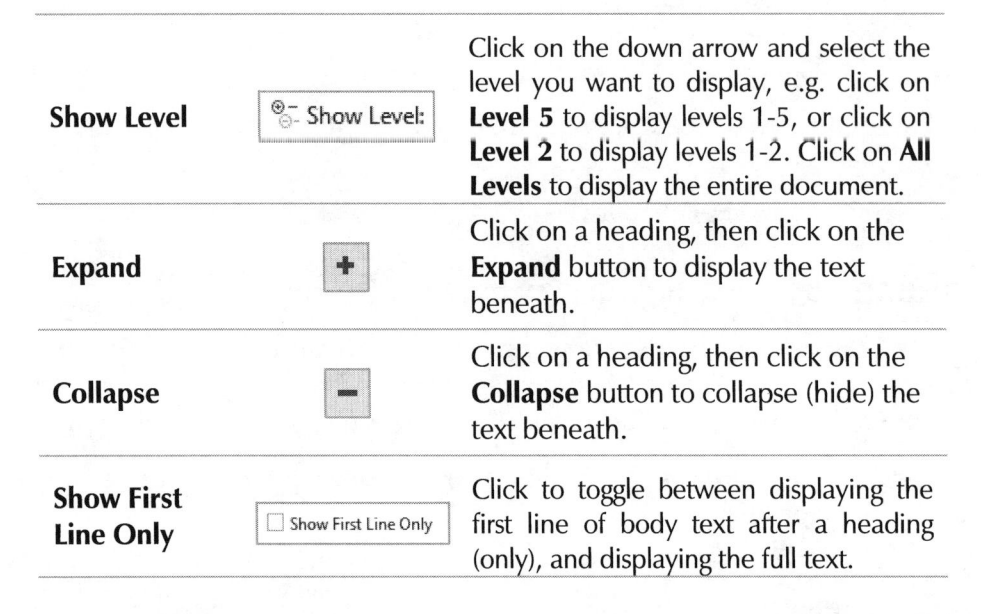

Show Level	Show Level:	Click on the down arrow and select the level you want to display, e.g. click on **Level 5** to display levels 1-5, or click on **Level 2** to display levels 1-2. Click on **All Levels** to display the entire document.
Expand	+	Click on a heading, then click on the **Expand** button to display the text beneath.
Collapse	−	Click on a heading, then click on the **Collapse** button to collapse (hide) the text beneath.
Show First Line Only	Show First Line Only	Click to toggle between displaying the first line of body text after a heading (only), and displaying the full text.

2. Click on the **Close Outline View** button to exit.

Managing your documents with Outline view

Outline view makes it easy for you to determine whether a heading level is suitable and to change a heading level if necessary. Outline view is also a useful tool for moving large sections of your document around. As you move a heading, all subordinate headings and text move as well.

How to: Change a heading level

1. Display the document in Outline view and click on the required heading.
2. Click on the required button (Outlining ribbon, Outline Tools group).

Promote	←
Demote	→
Promote to Heading 1	⇐
Demote to Body Text	⇒

Hands-on exercise 19

In this exercise you use Outline view to explore the document.

Now, with the heading styles applied from the last exercise, you look at your document in Outline view, collapsing and expanding the heading levels to view the structure of your report.

- Go to the top of the document.

- Click on the **Outline** button (View ribbon, Views group).
  Outline view is displayed and the Outlining ribbon is presented.

- Click into the heading: The Managing Director's Report.
  Notice the heading level listed in the Outline Level.

- Click into the body of the text, (one of the dot points below).
  Notice the Outline Level.

- Click on the **Show Level** down-arrow (Outline Tools group), then click on **Level 2**. The document collapses to display only headings at levels 1 and 2.

- Note that although the headings are left aligned in the document in Print Layout view, they are indented in Outline view to indicate their heading level.

- Also note that a plus on the left of the text is an outline symbol that identifies headings with sub-text (a minus would identify a heading with no sub-text). The grey wavy line under a heading indicates that there is hidden sub-text.

- Click on the **Show Level** down-arrow, then click on **Level 1**.
  The document collapses to display only headings at level 1.

- Click on the heading: Feeding More Australians, then click on the **Expand** button.

- Click on the heading: New Stores, then click on the **Expand** button.
  The small circles indicate body text, i.e. this text is not a heading.

- With your insertion point still on the heading: New Stores, click on the **Collapse** button.

- Click on the **Show Level** down-arrow, then click on **All Levels**.
  The entire document - including body text – becomes visible.

- Click on the **Show First Line Only** option (remove the tick).
  All headings are displayed along with the first line of each paragraph of body text.

- Click on the **Show Level** down-arrow, then click on **Level 2**.

- Click on the heading: Ensuring Quality, then click on the **Expand** button.
  Notice that the **Show First Line Only** option is still activated.

- Tick the **Show First Line Only**.

- With your insertion point still on the heading: Ensuring Quality, click on the **Collapse** button.

- Leave your document open on the screen in Outline view.

How to: Move a heading

1. Display the document in Outline view and click on the required heading.

2. Click on the required button (Outlining ribbon, Outline Tools group).
   (When you move a heading, the associated minor headings and text are also moved.

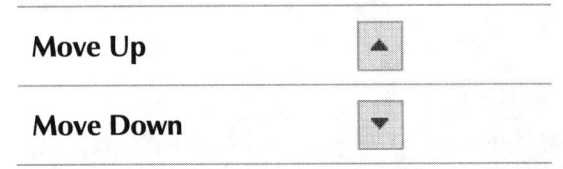

Move Up	▲
Move Down	▼

Hands-on exercise 20

In this exercise you practice using Outline view to modify a document's structure.

- Using the document *SuperFood annual report*, ensure you are in Outline view. Display Level 1 headings.

- Go to the bottom of the report.

First, you move a topic and demote it to a lower heading level.

- Click on the heading: This Year's Highlights
  This heading displays a plus symbol to the left indicating it has associated sub-text.

- Click on the **Move Up** button until the heading is positioned beneath the heading and associated text: The Managing Director's Report
  The heading and its associated sub-text are relocated.

- Click on the **Expand** button to view the associated sub-text.

- Click on the **Collapse** button to hide the sub-text again.

- Click on the **Demote** button.
  The heading becomes a level 2.

- Display the Level 2 headings to view the new structure.

Next, you change the heading: Focusing on our Customers' Needs to a level 1. Then, you relocate this entire topic.

- Click on the heading: Focusing on our Customers' Needs

- Click on the **Promote to Heading 1** button (before you click on the button, hover over the double arrow and notice its label).
  The heading becomes a level 1.

- Display Level 1 headings.

- With your insertion point still in the heading 'Focusing on our Customers' Needs', click on the **Move Down** button until the topic is under the heading: SuperFood Initiatives

- Display Level 2 headings.
  Notice that the lower heading levels have moved also.

Finally, you make some minor changes to the report.

- Click on the heading: Magazine Initiative.

- Click on the **Move Down** button until the heading is the last item in the section on SuperFood Initiatives.

- Click on the heading: New Outlets, then click on the **Demote** button to make this heading a level 3.

- Click on the heading: Construction of Warehouses, then click on the **Demote** button to make this heading a level 3.

- Edit the heading: SuperFood Initiatives to read: Our Initiatives

- Change back to Print Layout view.

- **Save** your changes.

Hints & tips

If you find heading formatting (such as large fonts) distracting to look at, de-select the Show Text Formatting option (Outline Tools group).

You can also move a heading (and text) by dragging the heading's outline symbol (e.g. +) up or down. As you drag, Word displays a horizontal line. Release the mouse when this line is where you want the text moved to. To change the level of a heading, you can drag the outline symbol to the left or the right.

Numbering your headings automatically

If you have used Word's built-in heading styles you can also use these styles to automatically number headings. Numbered headings are frequently used in legal contracts or regulation documents to enable specific sections to be quickly identified.

For example ...

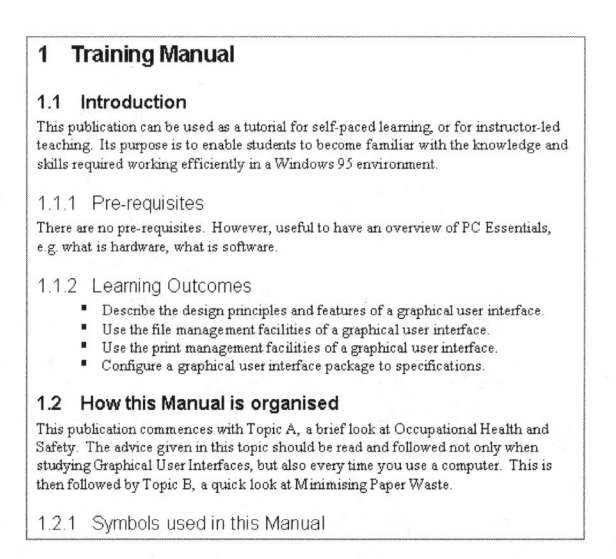

> **1 Training Manual**
>
> **1.1 Introduction**
> This publication can be used as a tutorial for self-paced learning, or for instructor-led teaching. Its purpose is to enable students to become familiar with the knowledge and skills required working efficiently in a Windows 95 environment.
>
> 1.1.1 Pre-requisites
> There are no pre-requisites. However, useful to have an overview of PC Essentials, e.g. what is hardware, what is software.
>
> 1.1.2 Learning Outcomes
> - Describe the design principles and features of a graphical user interface.
> - Use the file management facilities of a graphical user interface.
> - Use the print management facilities of a graphical user interface.
> - Configure a graphical user interface package to specifications.
>
> **1.2 How this Manual is organised**
> This publication commences with Topic A, a brief look at Occupational Health and Safety. The advice given in this topic should be read and followed not only when studying Graphical User Interfaces, but also every time you use a computer. This is then followed by Topic B, a quick look at Minimising Paper Waste.
>
> 1.2.1 Symbols used in this Manual

As an aside ... *The numbering will automatically adjust when headings are moved or the heading level changes.*

How to: Number headings automatically

1. Ensure your document uses the Word's built-in heading styles (Heading 1, Heading 2, etc…).
2. Click on a heading.
3. Display the Home ribbon, then click on the **Multilevel List** button (Paragraph group). A gallery of options is presented.
4. Click on any of the following options:

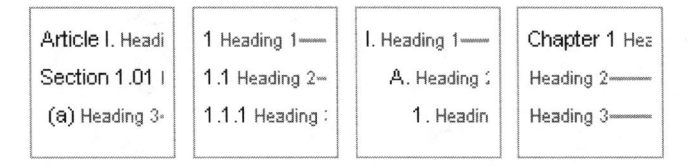

Article I. Headi	1 Heading 1	I. Heading 1	Chapter 1 Hea
Section 1.01	1.1 Heading 2	A. Heading 2	Heading 2
(a) Heading 3	1.1.1 Heading	1. Headin	Heading 3

As an aside ... *You can be in any view when you apply heading numbering.*

How to: Adjust your numbering format

1. Display the Home ribbon, then click on the **Multilevel List** button (Paragraph group). A gallery of options is presented.
2. Click on **Define New Multilevel List** (bottom of gallery).
   The Define new Multilevel list dialogue box is presented.

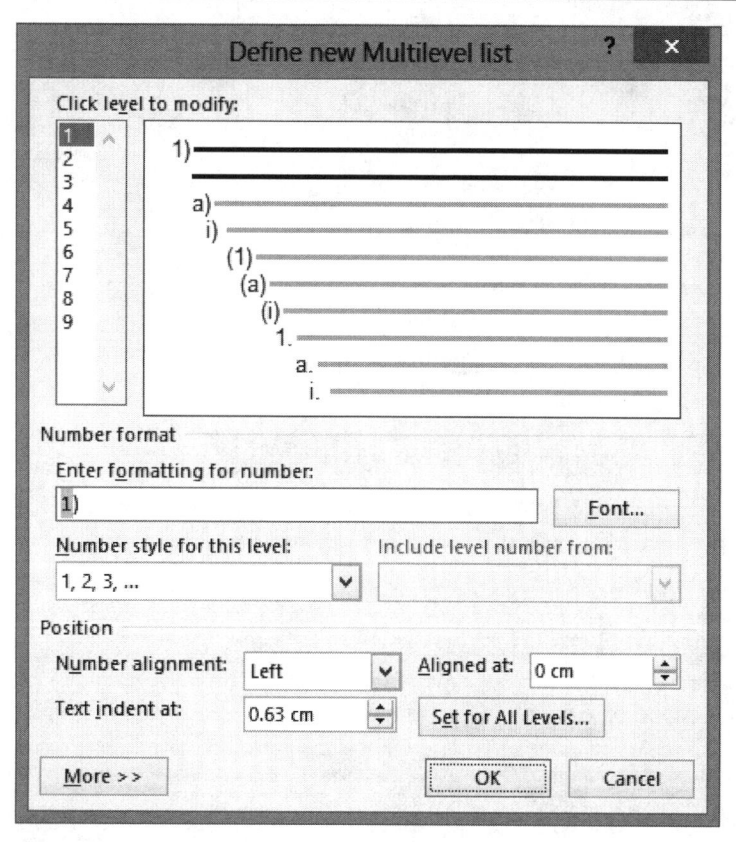

3. Make your adjustments.
4. Click on **OK**.

Hands-on exercise 21

In this exercise you apply automatic heading numbering. Then, you will note how this numbering changes when you edit your document.

- Using the document *SuperFood annual report*, ensure you are in Print Layout view.
- Go to the top of the document.
- Click on the heading: The Managing Director's Report
- Display the Home ribbon, then click on the **Multilevel List** button (Paragraph group). A gallery of options is presented.
- Click on this option:

   Article I. Headi
   Section 1.01 I
   (a) Heading 3

- Scroll through your document to view this numbering.

Next, you apply a different numbering outline.

- Ensure your insertion point is in a heading.
- Display the Home ribbon, then click on the **Multilevel List** button (Paragraph group). A gallery of options is presented.
- Click on this option:

> 1 Heading 1
> 1.1 Heading 2
> 1.1.1 Heading 3

- Scroll through your document to view this numbering.

Next, you edit your report in Outline view and observe how the numbering adjusts automatically.

- Display your document in Outline view, click on the **Show Level** down-arrow, then select **Level 3**.

- Click on the heading: Flavoursome Fruits

- Click on the **Move Up** button until the topic is under the heading: Our Initiatives, as a new point 3.4.

- Click on the heading: New Stores

- Click on the **Promote** button.
  The heading becomes number 3 and all headings are re-numbered.

- Click on the heading: SuperMetro

- Click on the **Move Up** button, until the topic is under the heading: New Stores, as a new point 3.1.

- Click on the heading: SuperElectronic

- Click on the **Move Up** button, until the topic is under the heading: New Stores, as a new point 3.2

- Click on the heading: Electronic Shopping Services

- Click on the **Demote** button.
  The heading becomes point 3.2.1

- Display your document in Print Layout view.

- **Save** your changes.

Next, you customise the position of a numbered heading.

- Go to the top of the document.

- Click in heading 1 (The Managing Director's Report).

- Display the Home ribbon, then click on the **Multilevel List** button (Paragraph group).

- Click on **Define New Multilevel List...**
  The Define new Multilevel list dialogue box is presented.

- Click next to the 1 in **Enter formatting for number**.

- Type a full stop.

- Click on **OK**.

- Scroll through your document and observe the changes to the level 1 headings.

- **Save** your changes.

Creating a table of contents

A table of contents is an important part of any report-style document. You can quickly generate a table of contents if Word's built-in heading styles have been used in the document (i.e. Heading 1, Heading 2, etc.).

When you create a table of contents, Word searches for the headings, sorts them by heading level, then references their page numbers.

How to: Build an automatic table of contents

1. Ensure your document has Word's built-in heading styles applied.
2. Click your insertion point where you want the table of contents inserted, e.g. at the top of the document.
3. Display the References ribbon, then click on the **Table of Contents** button (Table of Contents group). A gallery of options is presented.
4. Click on the required **Built-In** option (**Automatic Table 1** or **Automatic Table 2**) ~or~
   Click on **Insert Table of Contents...** The Table of Contents dialogue box is presented.

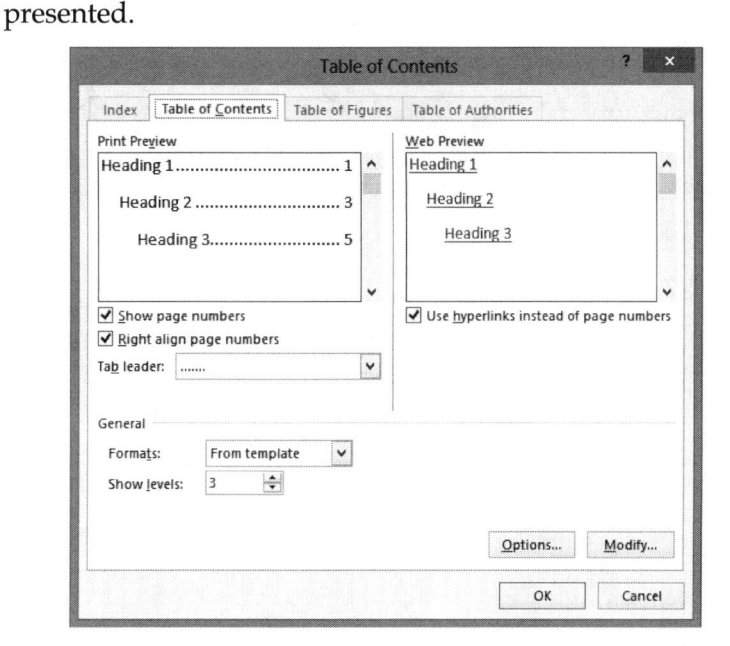

5. Click on the required 'look' from the drop-down list of **Formats**.
   Note how the table of contents is displayed in the **Print Preview** and **Web Preview** boxes.
6. By default, the table of contents displays heading levels 1 to 3. You can change the number of levels displayed using the **Show levels** box.
7. Click on **OK**.

Hands-on exercise 22

In this exercise you generate an automatic table of contents.

- Using the document *SuperFood annual report*, ensure you are in Print Layout view.
- Go to the top of the document.
- Insert a page break after the document heading.

- Go to page 1 and position your insertion point under the document heading.
- Display the References ribbon, then click on the **Table of Contents** button (Table of Contents group). A gallery of options is presented.
- Click on the required **Built-In** option **Automatic Table 2**.
- Scroll up to view your table of contents.
- Note if you point to the table of contents it is shaded. This simply indicates a field has been used to generate the table. The shading does not print.
- Note also that the document heading at the top of the document is not included in the table of contents. This is because it is not formatted with a heading style. (It is formatted with a style called Title.)
- **Save** your changes.

As an aside ... Hold `Ctrl` and click on a page number listed in a table of contents to go directly to that item.

Updating your table of contents

If you continue working on your document after you have built your table of contents, and you then add or delete pages or headings, the information in your table of contents will be out-of-date. However, your table of contents can be simply updated.

How to: Update a table of contents

1. Click into the table of contents, then click on the **Update Table** button (Reference ribbon, Table of Contents group). The Update Table of Contents dialogue box is presented.

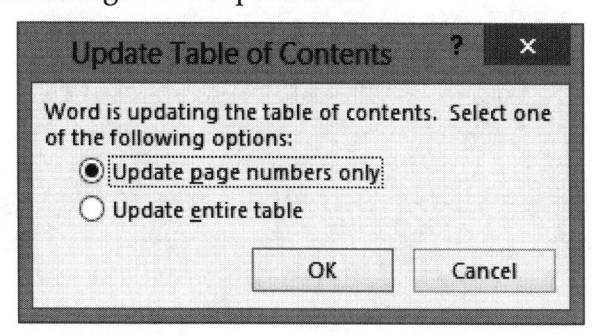

2. If you have only moved text to a different page, click on **Update page numbers only**. If you have changed or added to your document headings, click on **Update entire table**, then click on **OK**.

   Press `Alt` `F9` to view your table of contents field.

   Press `F9` to update your table of contents.

Hints & tips

What if I see "Error! Bookmark not defined" instead of my page numbers?
You need to update your table of contents because the heading text has changed or has been deleted.

Hands-on exercise 23

In this exercise you update your table of contents.

First, you make some changes to your report.

- Using the document *SuperFood annual report*, locate the heading in the report: Focusing on our Customers' Needs. (Hint: Hold `Ctrl` and click on the heading in the table of contents to go directly to that item.)

- Edit the heading to read: Customer Needs Focus

- Display your document in Outline view, and display level 1 headings.

- Click on the heading 'Customer Needs Focus' then click on the **Move Up** button until this heading is under the heading: The Managing Director's Report.

- Return to Print Layout view.

- Go to the top of the document.

- Click on the table of contents.

- Display the Reference ribbon, then click on the **Update Table** button. The Update Table of Contents dialogue box is presented.

- Click on **Update entire table**, then click on **OK**.

- Observe the changes to your table of contents.

- **Save** your changes and **Close** your document.

Consolidation task 6

In this task you practise generating and updating a table of contents.

First, you will apply a number of heading styles.

- **Open** the document *Evergreen annual report*.
  This is a five page document.

- At the top of page 2, apply the **Heading 1** style to the heading:
  Managing Director's Review

- Apply the **Heading 2** style to the following headings:

  Transformation over the last three years
  Evergreen values
  Evergreen in a strong position
  Looking forward
  Opportunities for Evergreen Energy

- On page 3, apply the **Heading 3** style to the following headings:

  Leadership
  Respect
  Focus
  Performance
  Persistence

- Go to the top of the document.

- Insert a table of contents using **Automatic Table 1** under the document heading.
- Change the colour of the 'Contents' heading to green.
- **Save** your changes.

Next, you add a page break and edit a heading.

- Locate the heading: Transformation over the last three years
  (Hint: You can jump to the heading from the table of contents).
  Insert a page break before it.
- Edit the heading to read: Transformation over the previous three years
- Return to the table of contents.
- Update the table of contents.
- Observe the changes to your table of contents.
- **Save** your changes.
- **Close** your document.

Adding a header & footer

One of the most powerful Word features available when working with multi-page documents is headers and footers. These can be used for further information and to direct the reader, e.g. using page numbers. Word offers a variety of pre-designed layouts for headers and footers, or you can create your own and align text using pre-existing tab stops at the centre and far right.

How to: Add a pre-set header & footer

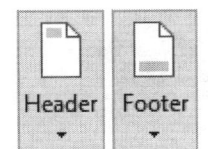

1. Display the Insert ribbon, then click on the **Header** or **Footer** button (Header & Footer group). A gallery of options is presented.
2. Click on the required option. Your header/footer is displayed. The insertion point is located in an area of your document reserved for your header/footer, and the body of the document appears greyed. A new Design ribbon is displayed with Header and Footer Tools.
3. Click on any of the '**Type text**' markers and insert your own text. 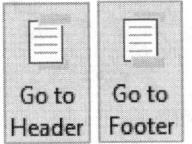
4. Click on the **Go to Header/Go to Footer** buttons (Navigation group) to move between header/footer.
5. Click on the **Header/Footer** buttons to re-display the gallery options (Header & Footer group – start of ribbon). 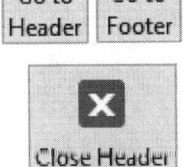
6. Click on the **Close Header and Footer** button to exit.

How to: Add your own header & footer

1. Display your document and double-click on the header or footer area (even if blank).
2. Your header/footer is displayed. The insertion point is located in an area of your document reserved for your header/footer, and the body of the document appears greyed. A new Design ribbon is displayed with Header and Footer Tools. Type or insert your details.
3. Click on the **Go to Header/Go to Footer** buttons (Navigation group) to move between header/footer.

4. Click on the **Close Header and Footer** button to exit.

As an aside …You can also double-click in the document area to exit a header or footer.

How to: Display/edit a header & footer

1. Display the Insert ribbon, then click on the **Header** or **Footer** button (Header & Footer group).

2. Click on the Edit Header/Edit Footer option.
   Your header/footer is presented and the Design ribbon displayed.

As an aside …You can also double-click on an existing header and footer area to edit.

How to: Insert a page number

1. Display the header or footer and position your insertion point.

2. Click on the **Page Number** button (Design ribbon, Header & Footer group). A number of position options are presented.

3. Point to the required position, e.g. Bottom of Page, then click on the required option.

How to: Remove a header & footer

1. Display the Insert ribbon, then click on the **Header** or **Footer** button (Header & Footer group).

2. Click on the **Remove Header/Remove Footer** option.
   Your header/footer is removed.

As an aside … To remove you can also display, select any text and press `Delete`

Hands-on exercise 24

In this exercise you practise inserting a simple header and footer into a document.

- **Open** the document *SuperFood annual report*.

- Display the Insert ribbon, then click on the **Header** button (Header & Footer group).

- Scroll down the list and click on **Pinstripes**.

- Click into the title and type: SuperFood's Annual Report
  Note: the words 'SuperFood' may already be in the box.

- Double click into the document to close the header.

- Scroll through the document to see the header on every page.

Next you will add page numbers.

- Double-click into the header then click on the **Go to Footer** button (Navigation group).

- To match the style of the header, click on the **Footer** button.

- Scroll down and click on **Pinstripes.**

- Click on the *Type Text* box and press `Delete`.

- Double click back into the document to close the footer and scroll through the document to see the header and footers.

- **Save** your changes.
- **Close** your document.

Advanced headers & footers

Word allows you to insert a variety of fields to create headers and footers through **Quick Parts**. For example, if you are using an internal order form and a variety of people use the form, add the filename and path field to the footer so anyone can follow the path to print more copies. Another useful Quick Part field header is to include style fields. If your long document has been broken into many sections, often it is useful to show your document headings (or style references) in your header.

How to: Insert a filename field

1. Display the header or footer and position the insertion point.
2. On the Design tab (Header & Footer Tools), click on the **Quick Parts** button, then click on **Field** (Insert group).
   The Field dialogue box is presented.
3. Scroll down the **Field names** list and click on **FileName**.
   Note the **Description**.
4. Click on a **Format**, and click on **Add path to filename** if required.
5. Click on **OK**.

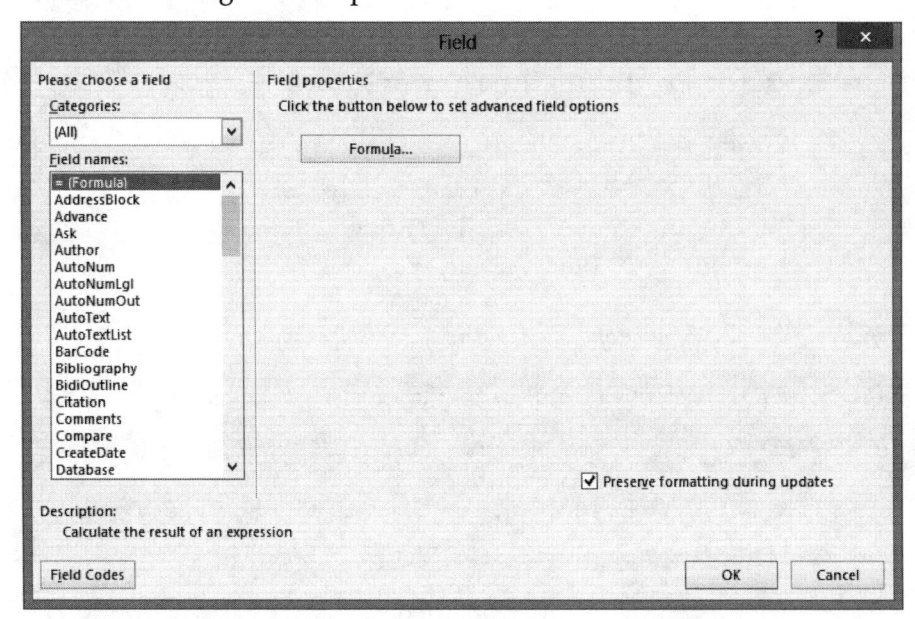

As an aside ... *Other useful fields to insert include CreateDate, PrintDate, SaveDate, Page and NumPages.*

How to: Insert a style reference field

1. Ensure you have inserted Styles and section/page breaks into your document. (This would usually be one of the last steps in preparing a long document).
2. Display the header or footer and position the insertion point.
3. On the Design tab (Header & Footer Tools), click on the **Quick Parts** button, then click on **Field** (Insert group). The Field dialogue box is presented.

4. Scroll down the **Field names** list, then click on **StyleRef**.
   A list of Styles is presented.

5. Click on the required style in the **Style name** list, then click OK.

6. Scroll through your document and check on the fields.

Hands-on exercise 25

In this exercise you practise adding the file name and path to a footer.

- Open *Estimate form vs1*.
- Display the footer and place your insertion point at the left of the footer.
- On the Design tab (Header & Footer Tools), click on the **Quick Parts** button, then click on **Field** (Insert group).
  The Field dialogue box is presented.
- Scroll down to find **FileName**.
- Under Field Options, click on Add path to file name.
- Click on **OK**.
- **Print** and **Save** your changes.
- **Close** your document.
- Follow the path listed on the bottom of the footer to ensure the path is correct.

As an aside ... Note when you are working on a network there could be different drives listed and the path name could be quite long.

Different headers & footers for document sections

In a longer document you may have areas that require a different header and/or footer.

For example ... A different header and/or footer for the executive summary before the body of the report. A different header and/or footer for the marketing pages, finance pages and personnel pages.

To achieve different headers and footers in different areas of a document you need to separate your document into sections. This is achieved by inserting **section breaks** to create separate 'compartments'. Once section breaks have been inserted, you can **unlink** the sections that require a different header and/or footer and enter the new information (or leave blank as required).

Note: If it's only the cover page that you need to be different from the other pages (in terms of its headers and footers), you can apply a **different first page** so that you don't have to create sections.

How to: Insert a section break for headers & footers

1. Position your insertion point in the text where you want the new section to begin. 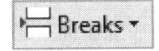
2. Display the Page Layout ribbon, then click on the **Breaks** button (Page Setup group).
3. Under Section Breaks in the list presented, click on the **Next Page** option.
4. Display the header or footer. Once sections are inserted, a marker appears on the left of the header or footer indicating the section number, e.g. Header – Section 1.  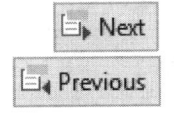
5. Click on the **Show Next / Show Previous** buttons to move between the sections (Design ribbon, Navigation group).

How to: Unlink a section header/footer

1. Display the header or footer.
2. When a header or footer is linked to the previous section, Word displays the **Same as Previous** marker on the right of the header or footer area. 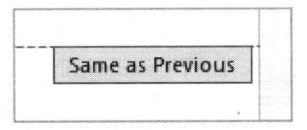 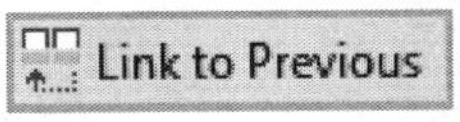
3. Click on the **Link to Previous** button (Design ribbon, Navigation group). (This button is lit up (active) until the section is unlinked.)
4. The **Same as Previous** marker is removed.
5. Your new header or footer information can now be entered without affecting the previous header/footer.

As an aside …You need to unlink a header and footer separately.

How to: Restart page numbering

1. Display the header or footer. 
2. Click on the **Page Number** button, then click on **Format Page Numbers** (Header & Footer group). The Page Number Format dialogue box is presented. 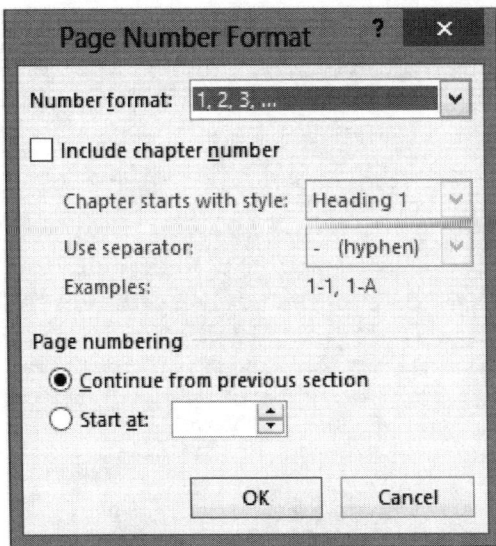
3. Click on the option **Start at**, and ensure the number is set to **1**.
4. Click on **OK**.

> ***As an aside*** *... Also use this dialogue box to change the format of your numbers, e.g. to roman numerals.*

Hands-on exercise 26

In this exercise you practice adding a cover page, inserting page breaks and inserting a style reference header.

- Open the document *SuperFood annual report.*

First we make the first page different.

- Double click into the footer of page one.
- In the Header & Footer Tools ribbon, click on the option **Different First Page** (Options group).
- Double click into the document and review your changes.
  The first page no longer has any header or footer but the rest of the document has remained the same.

Next, you include a cover page to the document.

- Go to page 1, then click into the heading.
- Display the Insert ribbon, then click on the **Cover Page** button (Pages group).
- To make the whole document match, click on **Pinstripes.**
- You will notice the cover page has inserted your report title.
- Delete the subtitle field.
- Insert today's date into the date field.
- Display the Developer tab and click on the **Properties** button (Controls group).
- Change the display of the date to: dddd, MMMM dd, yyyy
- Insert the company's name into the Company Name field.
- Insert your name into the Author field.
- Go to page 2 (table of contents) and notice the header and footer has been inserted as it is now the second page of the document, not page 1 (although the footer is displayed as page 1).

Next, you insert page breaks to then include the style reference in the header.

- Go to page 3.
- Place your cursor between the numbering and the heading:
  2. Customer Needs Focus
- Display the Insert ribbon, then click on the **Page Break** button (Pages group).
- Repeat so all of the headings with the style Heading 1 are on a new page.
- Your document is now 8 pages long.
- Go to page 3 and double click into the header.

- Remove the current field.
- Right align your header (`Ctrl` `R`).
- Display the Header & Footer Tools ribbon, then click on the **Quick Parts** button and select **Field...**.
- Scroll down in the Field Names list, then select **StyleRef**.
- Select **Heading 1** in the Style name list.
- Double click into the document.
- Scroll through your document to see the new headers.
- Notice your header for the table of contents page is listed as: The Managing Director's Report. The reason for this is the heading words or the table of contents words do not have the Heading 1 style.
- Highlight the words: Table of Contents.
- Apply the style Heading 1.
- Update the table of contents (page numbers only).
- Review your document.
- **Save** and **close** your document.

Topic 7 – Expanding and enhancing documents

Creating an index

An **index** is a detailed list which references document terms by page number. Long reference documents are easier to use when they contain an alphabetical index listing. These listings are usually found at the back of the document.

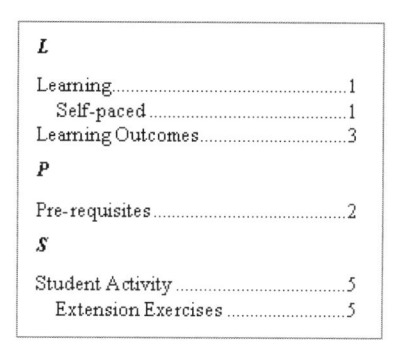

```
L
Learning.................................................1
    Self-paced........................................1
Learning Outcomes..............................3
P
Pre-requisites........................................2
S
Student Activity....................................5
    Extension Exercises.......................5
```

To create an index you must first mark the words or phrases you want to appear in the index. Once all of the entries have been marked, the index can be built. Word does this by collecting all the index entries, sorting them alphabetically, referencing their page numbers, and then displaying them in an index.

For example ...

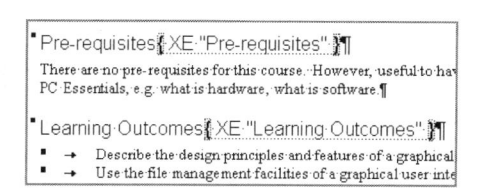

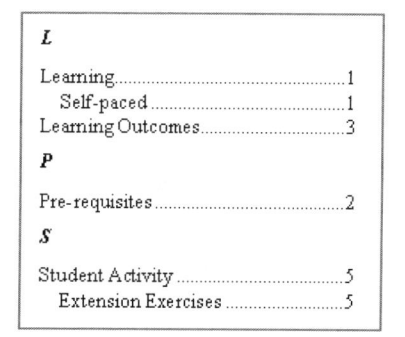

Index entries marked in a document, and part of an index displaying these entries

How to: Mark an index entry

1. Switch on the **Show/Hide** button (Home ribbon).
   Index entries are formatted as hidden text and cannot be seen unless you are displaying non-printing characters. (This button will be switched on automatically as you create an index entry if you do not switch at this point.)

2. Select the text to be used as an index entry, i.e. the words you want to appear in the index.

3. Display the References ribbon, then click on the **Mark Entry** button (Index group). The Mark Index Entry dialogue box is presented.

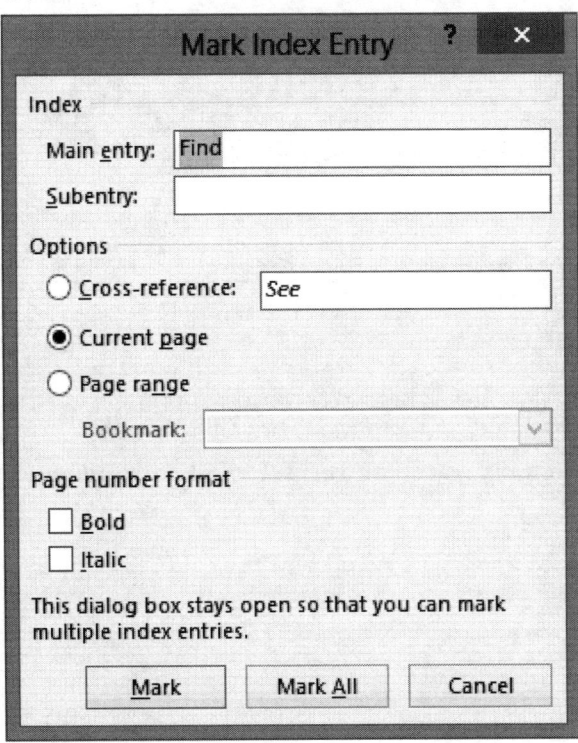

4. Your selected text is displayed in the **Main entry** box.
   (The text can be edited if necessary.)

5. Click on **Mark**.
   An index entry field is inserted in your document ~or~
   Click on **Mark All** to mark all occurrences of the selected text in your document.

6. The dialogue box remains open for you to mark additional entries. Click in your document and select the next entry, click back on the dialogue box, then repeat from step 4 above.

7. When your index entries are complete, click on **Close**.

How to: Create an index

1. Ensure you have marked index entries throughout your document.

2. Switch off the **Show/Hide** button.

3. Position your insertion point where the index is required – usually at the end of the document.

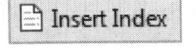

4. Display the References ribbon, then click on the **Insert Index** button (Index group). The Index dialogue box is presented.

Topic 7 – Expanding and enhancing documents

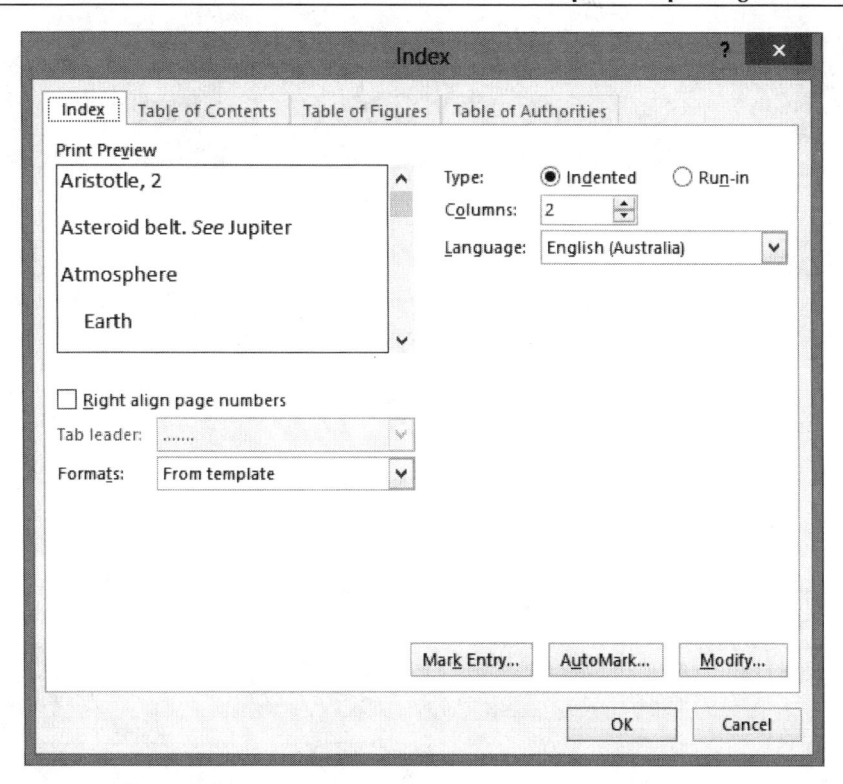

5. Select from the list of **Formats**.
6. Click on **OK**. Your index is presented.

How to: Update an index

1. Click in your index.
2. Display the References ribbon, then click on the **Update Index** button (Index group).

   ~or~

   Press **F9** to update your index.

Hands-on exercise 27

In this exercise you practise marking index entries and generating an index.

- **Open** the document *Evergreen annual report 2*, switch on the **Show/Hide** button.

- **Find** (Home ribbon) the following text: key objective

- Keeping the text selected display the References ribbon, then click on the **Mark Entry** button (Index group). The Mark Index Entry dialogue box is presented, and your selected text is displayed in the **Main entry** box.

- Edit the 'k' to an uppercase letter.
  This will make the entry uppercase in your index. It will not alter the word in your document.

- Click on **Mark**.
  An index entry field is inserted in your document.
  (Note that an index entry in your document is a field code which commences **XE**. If necessary, drag the dialogue box down by its Title bar to view your index entry.)

- The Mark Index Entry dialogue box remains open.
- Click back in your document and **find** the text: forestry
- Keeping the text selected, click back in the Mark Index Entry dialogue box. Your selected text is displayed.
- Edit the 'f' to an uppercase letter.
- Click on **Mark All**.
  This ensures that every occurrence of the word forestry is marked for inclusion in the index.
- Click back in your document and **find** the text: key strategies
- Keeping the text selected, click back in the Mark Index Entry dialogue box.
- Edit the 'k' to an uppercase letter, then click on **Mark All** as there are multiple occurrences of the text.
- Click back in your document and **find** all occurrences of the text: PEP
- Keeping the text selected, **Mark All** occurrences.
- Click back in your document, and **find** all occurrences of the text: growth opportunities. Click back in the Mark Index Entry dialogue box.
- Edit the 'g' to an uppercase letter, then click on **Mark**.
- Click on **Close**.
- **Save** your changes.

Next, you generate your index.

- Go to the end of the document and insert a page break.
- Type the text: Index
- Format the heading with the style: **Heading 1**.
- Press `Enter` to create a new paragraph.
- Switch off the **Show/Hide** button.
  (Leaving this button on can result in an inaccurate index because the display of field codes can push text onto different pages.)
- Display the References ribbon, then click on the **Insert Index** button (Index group). The Index dialogue box is presented.
- Select from the **Formats** drop-down list the format: **Formal**
- Click on **OK**.
  Your index is presented.

Now, you review your index.

- Note that all entries in the index have an initial capital.
- Note the multiple page references for the entries: forestry and key strategies
- Note that there is only one page reference for the entry: PEP
  This is because both entries appear on the same page.

Finally, you add more index entries and update your index once more.

- Mark the following entries for inclusion in your index:

- Magna Carta
- Suncore Power
- framework (mark all).
- Switch off your **Show/Hide** button
- Click in your index (final page), then click on the **Update Index** button (Index group).
- Note the changes to your index.
- **Save** your changes
- **Close** your document.

Hints & tips

What if I what to delete an index entry?

Switch on the **Show/Hide** button. Select the required index entry and press `Delete`. (When selecting, drag over the opening bracket { and the selection 'jumps' to include the end bracket.)

What if I want to delete my index?

Right-click on the index, then click on **Toggle Field Codes**. Select the field code, including the brackets, then press `Delete`.

What if I want an index heading to move to the top of a new column?

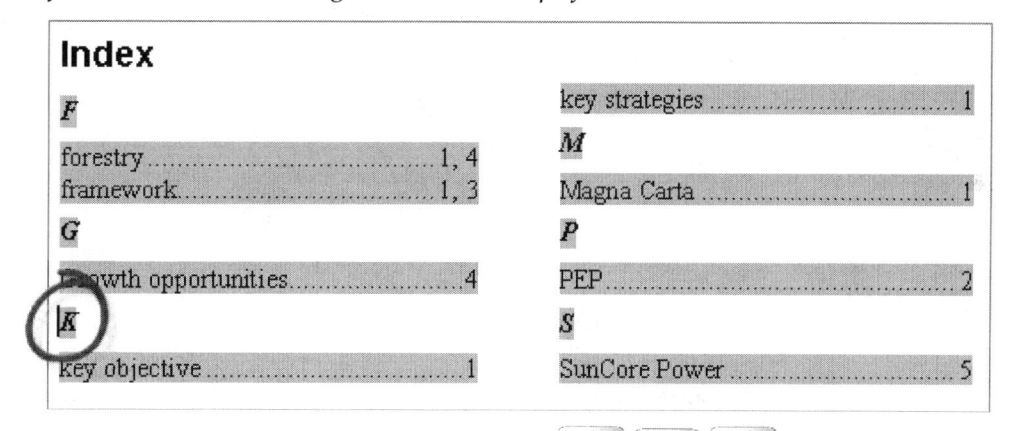

Index	
F	key strategies 1
forestry 1, 4	**M**
framework 1, 3	Magna Carta 1
G	**P**
growth opportunities 4	PEP 2
K	**S**
key objective 1	SunCore Power 5

Click at the start of the heading, then press `Ctrl` `Shift` `Enter`. This creates a column break.

Inserting footnotes and endnotes

Footnotes explain or provide references for text that appears in the body of a document. They are displayed at the bottom of the page where they appear. A footnote consists of two linked parts, the footnote reference in the body text [1], and the corresponding footnote text at the bottom of the page (see below example).

Endnotes operate in the same way but the corresponding endnote text is located at the end of the document.

---

[1] This is an example of footnote text. It is displayed above the footer but under the body text on the page.

How to: Insert a footnote

1. Click your insertion point where you want to insert the footnote reference.
2. Display the References ribbon, then click on the **Insert Footnote** button (Footnotes group).
3. The footnote reference is inserted and you are positioned in the Footnote area at the bottom of the page. Type your footnote text, then click in the document to continue.

How to: Insert an endnote

1. Click your insertion point where you want to insert the endnote reference.
2. Display the References ribbon, then click on the **Insert Endnote** button (Footnotes group).
3. The endnote reference is inserted and you are positioned in the endnote area at the end of the document. Type your endnote text, then click in the document to continue.

How to: Locate the next footnote

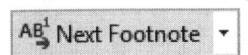

1. Display the References ribbon, click on the **Next Footnote** button (Footnotes group).

How to: Locate the next footnote

1. Display the References ribbon, click on the **Next Footnote** down-arrow, then click on **Next Endnote** (Footnotes group).

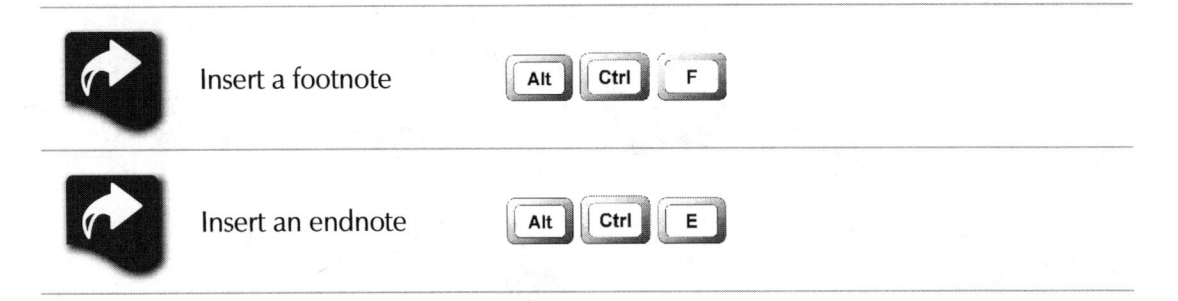

Insert a footnote **Alt** **Ctrl** **F**

Insert an endnote **Alt** **Ctrl** **E**

What if I want to delete a footnote or endnote?

Delete the footnote/endnote reference in the body text. This also deletes the footnote/endnote text.

```
Consolidation task 7
```

In this task you further practise marking index entries and generating an index.

- **Open** the document *SuperFood annual report 2*.

First, you create a number of index entries from the first page of this document.

- Locate and select the text: SuperDiscount division
- **Mark** this text as an index entry.
- Click back in your document, then locate and select the text: SuperPetrol
- **Mark** this text as an index entry.

- Click back in your document, then locate and select the text: supermarkets
- **Mark All** occurrences of this text as index entries.
- **Close** your dialogue box.

Next, you create index entries from the other pages of this document.

- Add six additional index entries from other pages of your report. (Print out these pages if this makes it easier for you to determine appropriate entries.)

Now, you generate your index.

- Switch off the **Show/Hide** button.
- Go to the end of the document and add a new page.
- On the new page, type the text 'Index' and apply the style **Heading 1.**
- Below your Index heading, insert an index using a format of your choice.
- Check that your index has the entries you expected.

Finally, you add more index entries and then update your index.

- Add three more index entries to your document.
- Return to your index, switch off the **Show/Hide** button, then update your index.
- **Save** your changes.
- **Close** your document.

Consolidation task 8

In this task you the new skills you have acquired with tables of contents, indices, and footnotes.

- **Open** the document *Biological engineering*.
- Review your document in Print Preview.

First, you create a table of contents for your document. Headings already have heading styles applied.

- Insert a new page between pages 1 and 2.
- Create a table of contents on the new page.

Next, you add a few index reference entries.

- On the first page of text, mark the following index references:
  - curriculum
  - electives
  - computers.
- On the remaining pages, mark the following index references:
  - internships
  - scholarships

- graduate program
- financial aid.

Next, you create an index for your document.

- Insert a new page at the end of the document.
- Create an index on this new page.
- **Save** your changes.
- **Close** your document.

Applying page borders and watermarks

Pages can be made more attractive with **borders** and **colour**, e.g. for flyers or invitations or just for the first page of a long document. **Watermarks** appear behind text and are useful to indicate that a document is a draft, should not be copied or is confidential.

How to: Apply a page border

1. Display the Design ribbon, click on the **Page Borders** button (Page Background group). The Borders and Shading dialogue box is presented. Ensure the **Page Border** tab is selected.

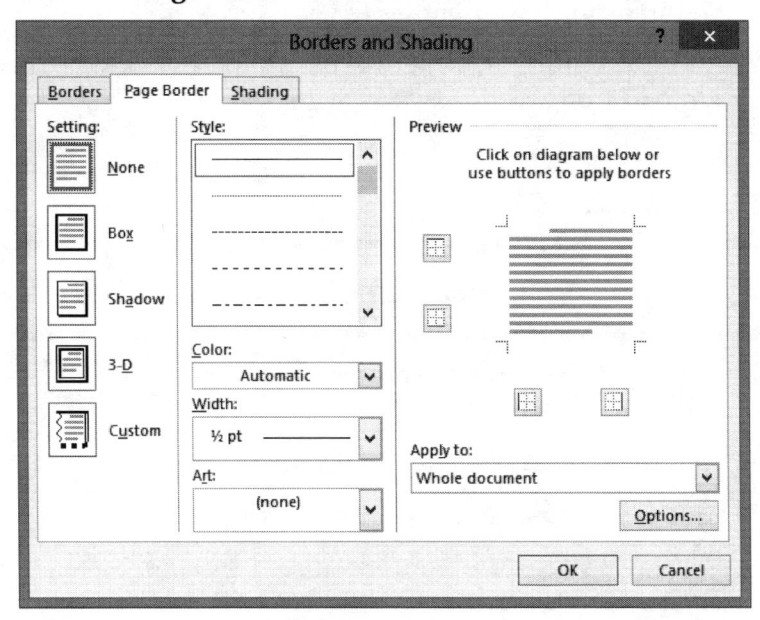

2. To design your page border, click on a combination of **Setting, Style, Color, Width** or use **Art**.

3. Click on **OK**.

*As an aside … To remove a border select a Setting of **None** from the dialogue box options.*

How to: Apply a page border for only the first page

1. Display the Design ribbon, click on the **Page Borders** button (Page Background group). The Borders and Shading dialogue box is presented.

2. Select the appropriate style, width and colour.

3. Click on the **Apply to**: drop-down box and select: **This section: First page only.**

4. To change the margin of the border, click on the **Options...** button and adjust the margin size.

Topic 7 – Expanding and enhancing documents

How to: Apply a watermark

1. Ensure you are working in Print Layout view.
2. Display the Design ribbon, click on the **Watermark** button (Page Background group). A gallery of watermarks is presented.
3. Click on the required option.

As an aside ... To remove a watermark select **Remove Watermark** from the gallery.

How to: Create a custom watermark

1. Display the Design ribbon, click on the **Watermark** button (Page Background group) then select **Custom Watermark...** The Printed Watermark dialogue box is presented.
2. In this dialogue box you are given the choice to a picture watermark or a text watermark.
3. To create a picture watermark, click on the **Select Picture...** button and select an appropriate picture (for example, company logo).
4. To select different text click on the Text drop-down box and select one of the choices.

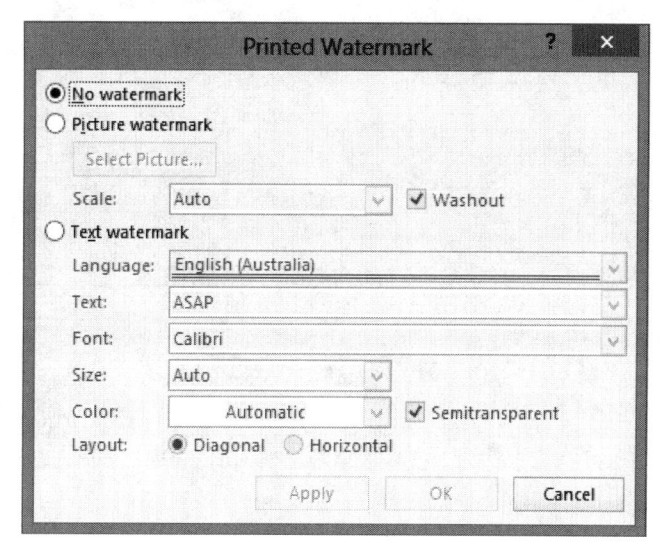

Building long documents by importing data

Complex documents may need to use information from other files. This information may include other text, pictures, charts or spreadsheet data.

For example ... To create an Annual Report you may need to import text from other documents, scanned images, or numerical/graphical spreadsheet data.

Inserting a text file

Word allows you to insert the contents of one file directly into another. The file does not need to be a Word document.

How to: Insert a file

1. Click in your document where you want to insert the text.
2. Display the Insert ribbon, click on the **Object** down-arrow, then click on **Text from File** (Text group). The Insert File dialogue box is presented.

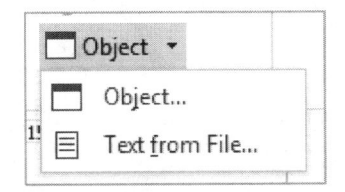

3. Locate and click on the required file.
4. Click on **Insert**.

Hands-on exercise 28

In this exercise you practise inserting a text file.

- **Open** the document *Operating statement*.
- Go to the end of the document.
- Press Ctrl Enter to insert a page break.
- Display the Insert ribbon, click on the **Object** down-arrow, then click on **Text from File** (Text group). The Insert File dialogue box is presented.
- Locate and click on the file: *Operating statement 2*.
- Click on **Insert**.
  The file is inserted.
- Apply the styles used on the first page of the document to the newly inserted text so that the new text is consistent with the rest of the document.
- **Save** your changes.

Inserting a picture file

You can also insert a graphic file from another program and location, e.g. company logo or scanned photographs

How to: Insert a picture file

1. Click in your document where you want to insert a picture.
2. Display the Insert ribbon, then click on the **Picture** button (Illustrations group). The Insert Picture dialogue box is presented.
3. Locate and click on the required picture.
4. Click on **Insert**.
5. Click to select the picture before resizing, etc.

Hands-on exercise 29

In this exercise you practise inserting graphic files.

- Using the document *Operating statement*, go to the top of the document.
- Display the Insert ribbon, then click on the **Picture** button (Illustrations group). The Insert Picture dialogue box is presented.
- Locate and click on the picture file: *Greg*
  (This is a scanned photograph located with your exercise files.)
- Click on **Insert**.
  The picture is inserted in line with the heading in your document.
- Apply **Text Wrapping** of **Square** (Format ribbon, Arrange group).

Next, you insert another scanned picture.

- Position your insertion point above the name Greg Chambers, where his signature would normally go.
- Insert the picture file: *G C signature*
  This is a scanned signature.
- With the object selected, drag out diagonally on the bottom-right sizing handle to increase the size of the object.
- **Save** your changes.

Hands-on exercise 30

In this exercise you practise copying an Excel chart into Word.

- Using the document *Operating statement*, go to the end of the document.
- **Start** the program Excel.
- **Open** the workbook *Profit*.
- Click on the chart object to select it.
- Click on the **Copy** button (Home ribbon).
- **Close** the workbook *Profit*.
- Display the *Operating statement* document in Word.
- At the end of the document click on the **Paste** button.
  The chart object is copied into the document.
  This is known as an embedded object.
- **Save** your changes.

Importing data from other sources

When you have data in Excel that is frequently changing, and this data is also being incorporated into a Word report, the data can be **linked**. Linking ensures that any changes made to the data in Excel are also automatically updated in your Word document (the next time you open the document or any time the Excel data changes while the Word document is open).

Linking to an Excel workbook

When you link a workbook to Word, the active worksheet's work area appears in Word even though the entire workbook is actually linked.

How to: Link an Excel file

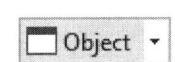

1. In a Word document, position your insertion point where require the linked object.
2. Display the Insert ribbon, click on the **Object** down-arrow, then click on **Object** (Text group). The Object dialogue box is presented.
3. Click on the **Create from File** tab.

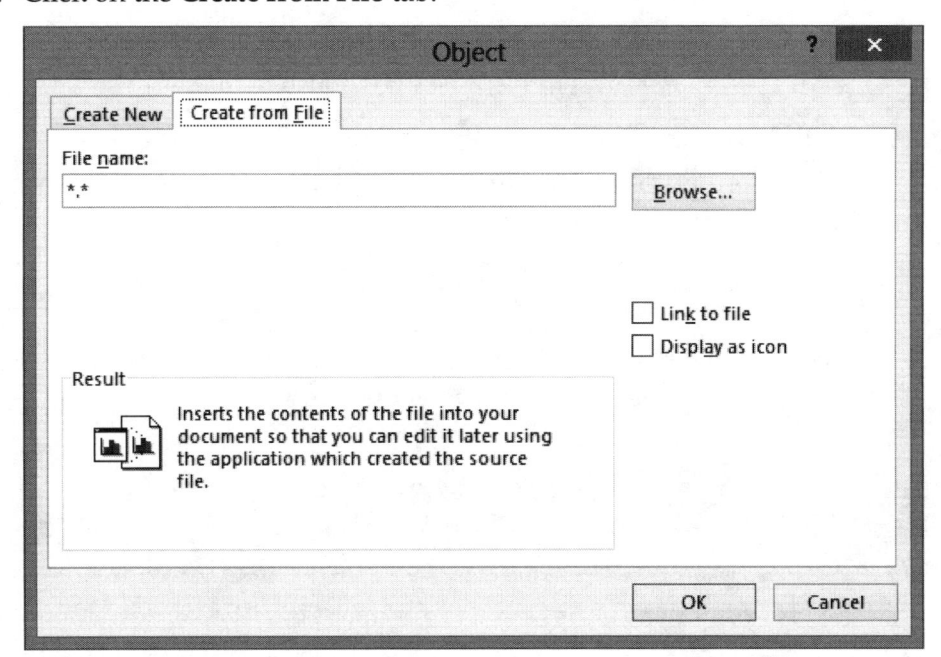

4. Type the **File name** ~or~
   Click on **Browse** to locate the required file, then click on **Insert**.
5. Select the **Link to file** option.
6. Click on **OK**.

Hands-on exercise 31

In this exercise you practise adding a linked spreadsheet to your Word report.

- Ensure the document *Operating statement* is open on your screen.
- Select the chart at the end of the document. Click on the border then press Delete.
- Switch to **Excel** and open the workbook *Profits data*.
- Review the data, then **close** the workbook.
- Display your *Operating statement* document and ensure the insertion point is located at the end of the document.
- Display the Insert ribbon, click on the **Object** down-arrow, then click on **Object** (Text group). The Object dialogue box is presented.
- Click on the **Create from File** tab.

- Click on **Browse** and locate the *Profits data* file, then click on **Insert**.
- Select the Link to file option.
- Click on **OK**.
  The linked data appears in your document.
- **Save** your changes.
- **Close** your document.

Then, you edit the data in Excel and view the result in Word.

- Open **Excel** and the workbook *Profits data*.
- Enter the following additional data.

  | XY250 | $ | 42,000 | $ | 61,000 |

- **Save** your changes.
- **Close** Excel.
- Re-open the Word document *Operating statement*.
  The following message is presented.

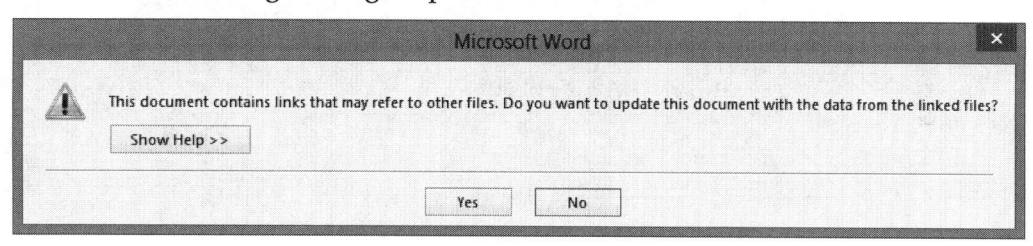

- Click on **Yes**. Review your updated data.
- Also, double-click on your linked data and note that the Excel worksheet is displayed. The link has a 'pointer' to the external file.
- Close Excel.
- **Save** your changes.
- **Close** your document.

Hints & tips

*To link **selected** Excel data into Word, you can use **Copy** and **Paste Special** (click on the **Paste** down-arrow). However, this limits the link to the selected cells only, and if you add more rows/columns the work area of the link does not change.*

If the file location of your linked data changes, the link will no longer work.

You can update a link manually without close/opening a file. Select the linked data and then press [F9].

Terms & concepts review

- Explain the connection between styles and Outline view.

- Name two benefits of working in Outline view.

- What must you have used in your document for Word to be able to automatically generate a table of contents?

- What does 'linking' data mean?

Consolidation task 9

In this task you attractively format and structure a very plain document.

- **Open** the document *Growth statement*.
- At the end of the document, insert the file: *Results*
- Format the document attractively incorporating the following:
  - Apply heading styles to format the text and increase readability.
  - Insert the picture file *Greg* above the heading: Achieving Results …
- Insert a table of contents on its own page at the top of the document.
- Add suitable headings above the table of contents, e.g. Annual Report, Table of Contents. Format your headings with the style: Title.
- **Save your changes.**
- **Close your document.**

Topic 8 – Inserting charts and SmartArt

Inserting a chart object

In Word you can insert a chart object to display data in graphical form. When you insert a chart Word opens Excel which then displays a workbook with sample data. You then replace the sample data in Excel with your own information, and Word creates a chart.

How to: Create a chart

1. Click where you want to insert the chart.
2. Display the Insert ribbon, then click on the **Chart** button (Illustrations group). The Insert Chart dialogue box is presented.
3. Click on one of the charting options in the left pane, e.g. Column, Line, then click on one of the chart styles from the right pane, e.g. Clustered Column.

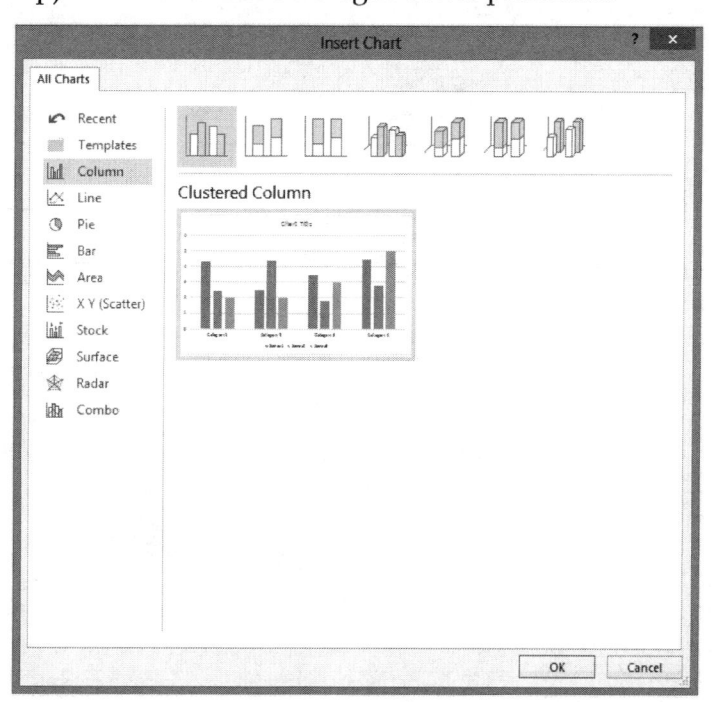

4. Click on **OK**.
   Word opens Excel which displays a workbook with sample data. Your chart is in the Word document, and your data is in an Excel worksheet. Two new ribbons are displayed in Word with Chart Tools (Design and Format). The Design ribbon is active.

5. To replace the sample data in the Excel worksheet, click on a cell and type the new text or numbers required. The chart in Word automatically updates with the new data. If you need to create a larger data area in Excel, drag the sizing handle in the bottom right corner until the area is the required size.

6. **Save** your document in the usual way and the (embedded) worksheet data is also saved. Closing the Word document also closes the Excel worksheet.

How to: Edit chart data

1. Click on the chart to activate the Chart Tools.
2. On the Design ribbon, click on the top half of the **Edit Data** button (Data group). Excel is re-displayed with your worksheet data.
3. Edit the data in the worksheet as previously (close Excel if you need to).

How to: Change your chart type

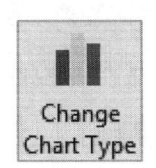

1. Click on the chart to activate the Chart Tools.
2. Click on the **Change Chart Type** button (Design ribbon, Type group). The Change Chart Type dialogue box is presented.

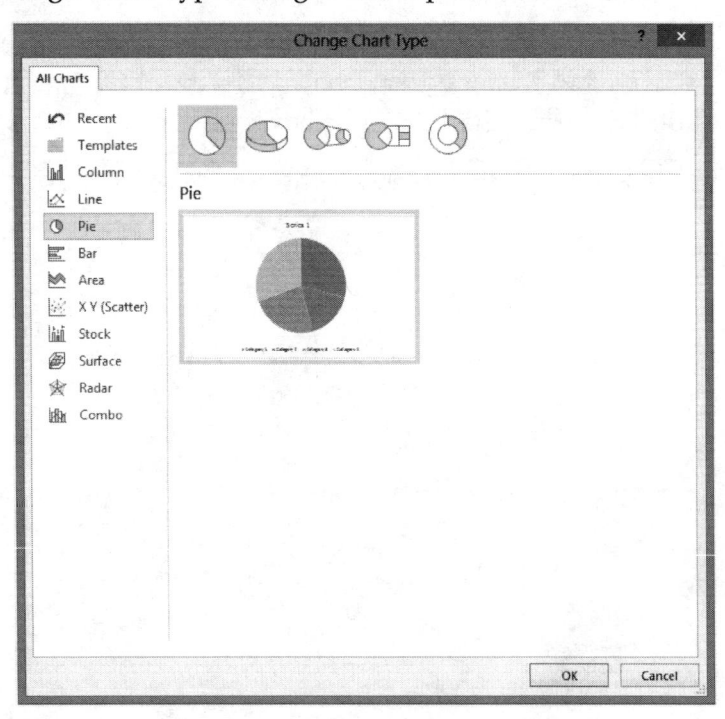

3. Click on the chart type required from the left pane, then click on a variation from the right pane.

4. Click on **OK**. The chart is updated.

Topic 8 – Inserting charts and SmartArt

Hands-on exercise 32

In this exercise you practice creating a chart to present numerical data.

- Create a new blank document.

- Display the Insert ribbon, then click on the Chart button (Illustrations group). The Insert Chart dialogue box is presented.

- Select the first Pie chart, then click on the OK button.

- Word opens Excel. As we have chosen the pie chart, the total must equal 100%. Type the following:

	A	B
1		Sales
2	1st Qtr	25
3	2nd Qtr	50
4	3rd Qtr	15
5	4th Qtr	10
6	Select	

- Notice the chart change when you type the numbers in.

- Display your Pie Chart in Word and ensure the Chart Tools/Design ribbon is visable.

- In Chart Layouts, click on Layout 1.

- How did the chart change?

Next we change the layout of the chart.

- Click on the **Change Chart Type** button.

- Choose a Clustered bar chart.

- How did your data change?

Next we change the layout of the bar chart by removing the title and changing the data label position

- Display the Chart Tools/Layout ribbon.

- Click on the **Chart Title** button (Labels group) and select **None.**

- Click away from your chart to go back into the document.

- Move your cursor before the chart and press Enter.

- Using WordArt, add a chart title: Sales

- Change the Text Wrap to be **In Line with Text** (Drawing Tools/Format ribbon, Arrange group)**.**

- Centre your title on the page horizontally.

- Click back into your chart to display the Chart Tools ribbons.

- Display the Chart Tools/Layout ribbon, then click on the **Data Labels** button (Labels group).

- Select Inside End.

- What changed in your chart?

- Click on the **Data Labels** button again and select **Center**.
- What changed in your chart?
- Click on the other options and choose the one you feel displays the information the best.

Finally we change the chart into a column chart, change the chart style and edit the data.

- Click on the **Change Chart Type** button (Chart Tools/Design ribbon, Type group).
- Select 3D Cylinder.
- How did your chart change?
- Firstly remove the Data labels as they are listed in the axes directly below the chart. (Chart Tools/Layout ribbon, Labels group, Data Labels button, None).
- Display the Chart Tools/Design ribbon and click on a Chart Style.
- Click on the Chart Styles More button and select a style with a black background.
- Click on the **Edit Data** button (Chart Tools/Design ribbon). Excel opens again with your data.
- Change the data to the following:

	Sales team 1	Sales team 2
May	1,432	2,414
June	2,323	3,223
July	2,141	2,233
August	3,655	4,231

- Extend the blue sizing handle to encompas all your data.
- Click back into Word.
- How has your chart changed?
- Is there information now missing that needs to be included in the chart?
- Change the labels and style of the chart.
- Add a legend to the new chart to show what the 2 different columns mean (Chart Tools/Layout ribbon, Labels group, Legend button).
- Save your document as *Sales team chart*
- Close your document.

Topic 8 – Inserting charts and SmartArt

Consolidation task 10

You have been asked to chart the sales for a new product gathered from 3 states.

- Create a new blank document
- Select a line chart.
- Enter the following data:

	NSW	VIC	SA
Jan-March	103	210	290
April-June	140	430	190
July-Sept	200	340	240
Oct-Dec	140	290	250

- Does a line chart effectively represent the data? Why? Why not?

_____

_____

_____

- Change the chart style to represent the data more effitively.
- Add/change any additional information (legend, labels, style).
- Looking at your chart:

    Which state sold the most in July – September?

    How much did SA sell in April – June?

    Which state sold the most in April – June?

- Save your chart as *Chart sales comparison by state*.
- Under the current chart, insert another chart with the same style (for example, if you chose bar, insert another bar chart).
- Using the same data above, change the data so months are at the top row and the state is in the first column.

	Jan-March	April-June	July-Sept	Oct-Dec
NSW	103	140	200	140
VIC	210	430	340	290
SA	290	190	240	250

- Review your chart.
- How is the information displayed differently?

_____

_____

- Which chart would you use if you were comparing sales per state throughout the year? Why?

  _____

  _____

- Add/change any additional information (legend, labels, style).
- Print your document.
- Close your document.

Consolidation task 11

In this exercise you create a pie chart to show your daily activities.

- What are your daily activities? (study, work, eat, watch tv, sleep)
- How much time do you spend doing these activities?

Activity	Time spent doing this activity
Total	24

- Create a pie chart to represent the above information.
- Format your chart and insert a relevant title.
- Save your document with an appropriate title.
- Print and close your document.

Creating an organisation chart using SmartArt

An organisation chart can be quickly and effectively incorporated into your document using **SmartArt**. SmartArt helps you to illustrate information and ideas with shapes, e.g. an organisation chart, steps in a process, cyclical information. Here you concentrate on an organisational chart.

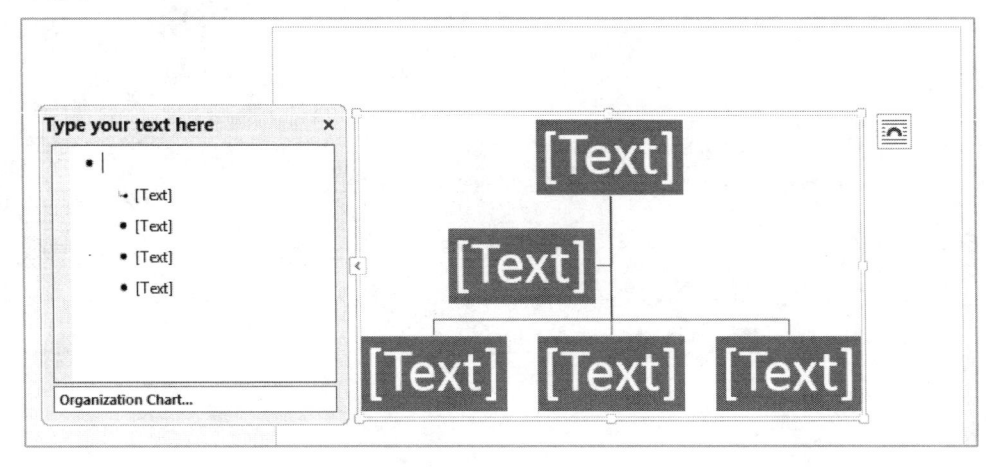

Organization Chart SmartArt with Text Pane to the left

Topic 8 – Inserting charts and SmartArt

How to: Insert an organisation chart

1. Click where you require the organisation chart.
2. Display the Insert ribbon, then click on the SmartArt button (Illustrations group). The Choose a SmartArt Graphic dialogue box is presented.
3. Click on the Hierarchy option in the left pane, then click on Organization Chart (first option) from the List in the right pane.

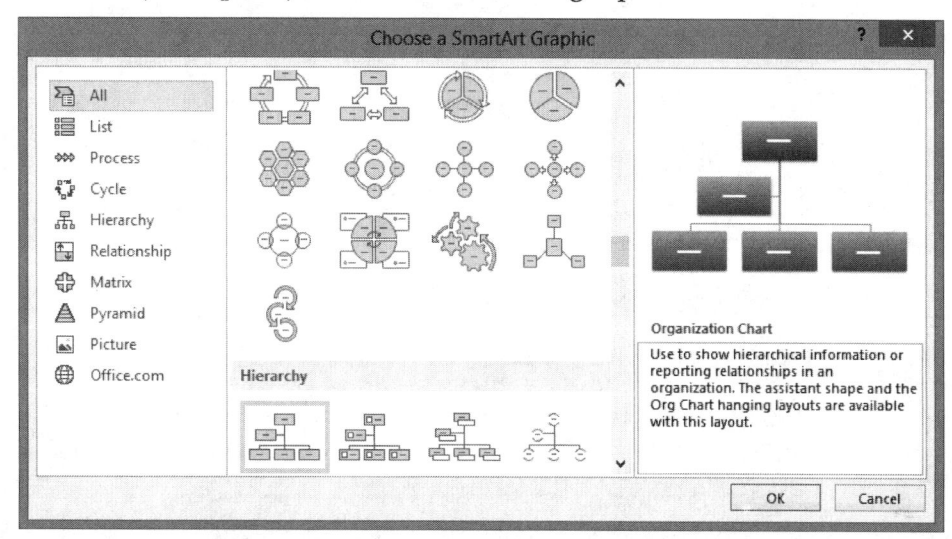

4. Click on **OK**.
   The SmartArt shape is inserted into your document. Alongside the shape is the Text Pane, which can help when entering text. Two new ribbons are displayed with SmartArt Tools (Design and Format). The Design ribbon is active.

How to: Add text

1. Click in a shape and begin typing ~or~
   Click on the **Text** Pane button (Crate Graphic group) begin typing against the appropriate bullet point.
   (Your font size adjusts based on the text entered).

How to: Insert a shape

1. Click on the shape you want to insert before/after, etc. 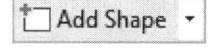
2. Click on the Design ribbon, then click on the Add Shape down-arrow (Create Graphic group).
3. Click on the required option, e.g. Add Shape After.

How to: Adjust the branch layout

1. Click on the required shape. 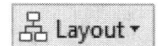
2. Click on the **Layout** button (Create Graphic group).
3. Click on the required option, e.g. Standard.

How to: Delete a shape

1. Click on the shape you want to delete, then press Delete

How to: Change the chart style

1. Double-click on the chart.

2. On the Design ribbon, point to any option in the **SmartArt Styles** gallery to see the design effect previewed on your chart. Click on the **More** button to display the full gallery of styles.

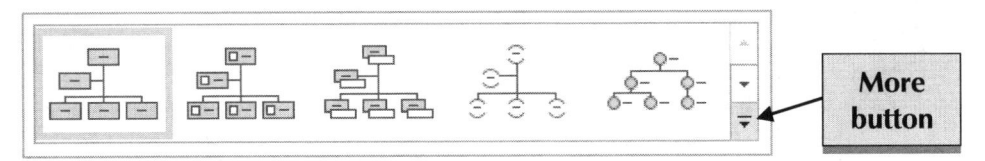

3. Click on the required style to apply.

How to: Change chart colours

1. Double-click on the chart.
2. On the Design ribbon, click on the **Change Color** button, then click on a colour of your choice.

How to: Position a chart

1. Double-click on the chart.
2. Drag the chart by the border (to another paragraph marker) ~or~ Display the Format ribbon, click on the **Position** button.
3. Click on the required position.

Hands-on exercise 33

In this exercise you practice inserting and editing SmartArt.

- Create a blank document.
- Display the Insert ribbon and click on the **SmartArt** button (Illustrations group).
- Under Hierarchy click on Name and Title Organisational Chart.
- The organisational chart is added to your document and 2 new ribbons, SmartArt Tools/Design and Format.
- Click into the top level and type: *Manager*
- Click into the smaller box under it and type: *James Hunt*
- Click into the next level and type: *Assistant Manager*
- Click into the smaller box under it and type: *Kelly Stock*
- Click on the border of the middle box on the bottom line and press the **Demote** button (Create Graphic group).
- Complete the following:

Topic 8 – Inserting charts and SmartArt

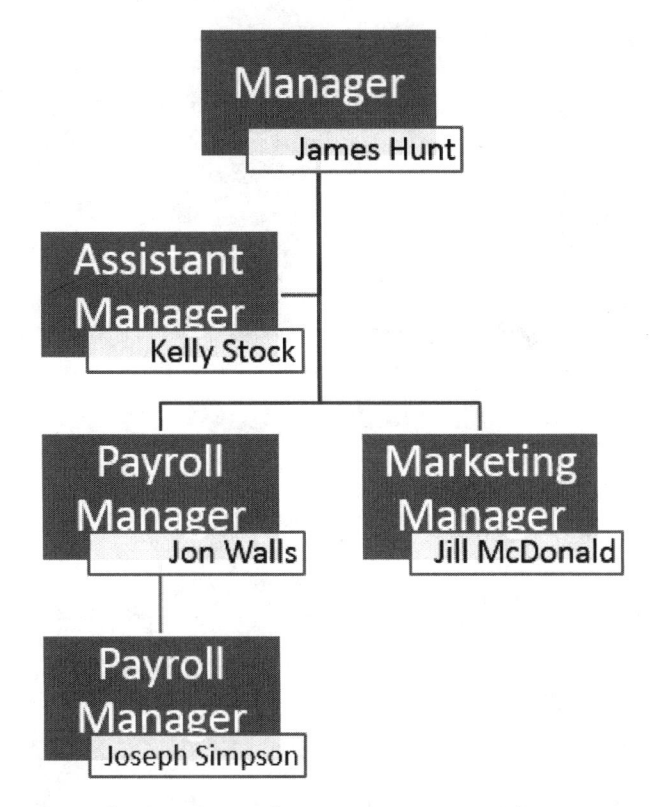

[Organizational chart showing:
- Manager: James Hunt
  - Assistant Manager: Kelly Stock
    - Payroll Manager: Jon Walls
    - Marketing Manager: Jill McDonald
    - Payroll Manager: Joseph Simpson]

- Save your document with an appropriate title.
- Click on the Change Colors button and select Colorful Range – Accent Colors 4 to 5.
- In SmartArt Styles, click on the more button, then under 3D, select Polished.

Next we change the colour of one of the levels.

- Select the box outside the Assistant Manager.
- Display the SmartArt Tools/Format ribbon, then click on the **Shape Fill** button.
- Select a red colour (ensure the white text can still be seen).
- **Save** and **close** your document.

Hints & tips

You can use these SmartArt skills to create different SmartArt graphics. Investigate the Lists group and the Pictures group for instance.

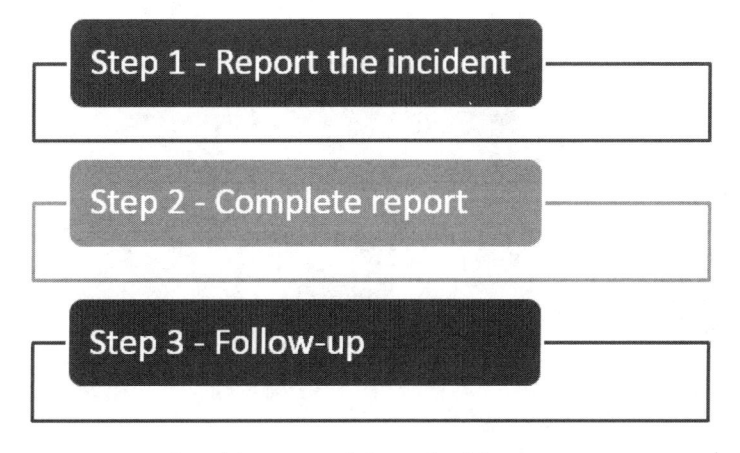

[Graphic showing three steps:
- Step 1 - Report the incident
- Step 2 - Complete report
- Step 3 - Follow-up]

Graphics created from the List group

Graphics created from the Picture group

Consolidation task 12

In this task you create 2 organisational charts to be inserted into the SuperFood annual report.

- Open the document *SuperFood annual report 2*.
- Move to the heading: This Year's Highlights and create a new paragraph at the end of the section.
- Type the following:
- This year we are pleased to announce a new structure to our marketing and accounts departments. Please see the new structure in these departments.
- Create the following 2 organisational charts after the new paragraph.
- Format as appropriate.
- Insert a suitable heading for: Marketing Department, Accounts Department.
- Review your document in Print Preview.
- **Print** a copy of your document.
- **Save** your document and **close**.

Topic 8 – Inserting charts and SmartArt

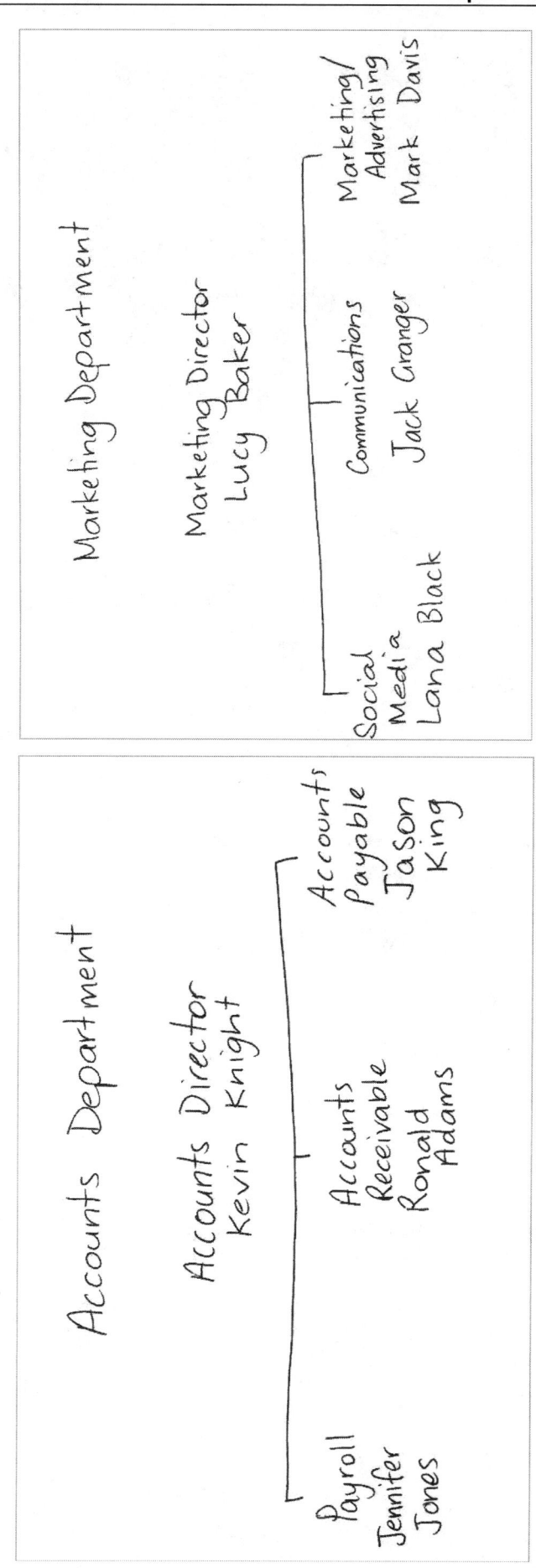

Accounts Department

Accounts Director
Kevin Knight

- Payroll — Jennifer Jones
- Accounts Receivable — Ronald Adams
- Accounts Payable — Jason King

Marketing Department

Marketing Director
Lucy Baker

- Social Media — Lana Black
- Communications — Jack Granger
- Marketing/Advertising — Mark Davis

Topic 9 – Adding comments, tracking changes & comparing content

When collaborating on a document it can be useful to leave **comments** as you go, explaining why you have made changes or suggesting places where additions might be necessary.

To ensure that changes to a document are clearly identified, you can **track** changes, i.e. mark where you have added, deleted or modified text. These changes can then be reviewed (perhaps by your manager) and accepted or rejected.

If tracking was not switched on, and you wanted to know what changes had been made to a document, you can **compare** two versions of a document.

Adding comments to your document

Comments can easily be added, reviewed and deleted.

How to: Add a comment

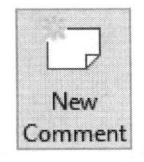

1. Select the text that you want to comment on.
2. Display the Review ribbon, then click on the **New Comment** button (Comments group). A Markup Area opens. Note your initials in the comments balloon (as shown under Word *Options/General*).

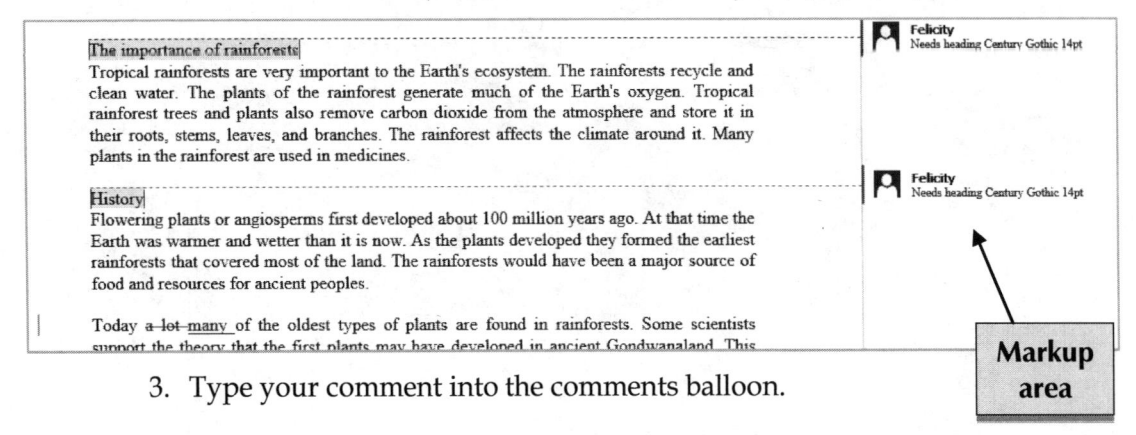

3. Type your comment into the comments balloon.

Topic 9 – Adding comments, tracking changes & comparing content

How to: Review your comments

1. Display the Review ribbon, then click on the **Next Comment/ Previous Comment** buttons (Comments group).

How to: Review your comments using the Reviewing Pane

1. Display the Review ribbon, then click on the **Reviewing Pane** down arrow (Tracking group), then click on **Reviewing Pane Vertical**.
   The reviewing pane will open on the left of the document.

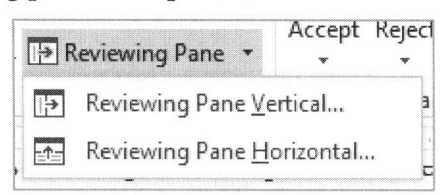

2. The reviewing pane will display a summary of the markups.

3. Double-click on a markup to display it in the document.

How to: Delete a comment(s)

1. Show your comments

2. Right-click on a comment balloon, then click on **Delete Comment** ~or~

3. Display the Review ribbon, click on the **Delete** down-arrow (Comments group), then click on **Delete All Comments in Document**.

How to: Change your view

1. Display the Review ribbon, click on the **Display for Review** down-arrow (Comments group), then click on the required view.

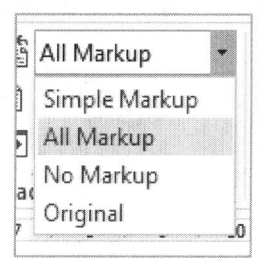

Hands-on exercise 34

In this exercise you practice working with comments.

- **Open** the document *Rainforest report*.
- Display the document with the **Reviewing Pane** showing.
- In the Reviewing pane summary, how many revisions are there?

  _____

- How many of the revisions are insertions?

  _____

- Close the reviewing pane (click on the button again).
- Highlight the second paragraph (One of the earliest written...), then click on the **New Comment** button (Comments group).
  A Markup Area opens. Note your initials in the comments balloon.

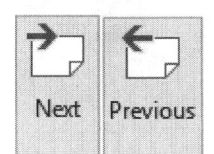

- Type the following comment into the comments balloon:
  Can we add this paragraph to the one before or after or is there more we can add to it?
- Select the words: Broad-leaved trees:
- Click on the **New Comment** button (Comments group).
- Type the following comment into the comments balloon: Can we give a definition of a broad-leaved tree?
- Select the words: Conifers:
- Type the following comment into the comments balloon: Can we give a definition of a conifer?
- Select the bold word after the characteristics heading: Buttresses:
- Type the following comment into the comments balloon: Can we include a picture?
- Go to the top of the document.
- Click on the **Next Comment** button to display each comment.
- Click on the **Display for Review** down-arrow (Tracking group), then click on **Final**. Your document is displayed in its final state.
- Click on the **Display for Review** down-arrow, then click on **Final: Show Markup**. Your document is displayed in its final revision state but with the comments showing.
- Find the comment: "I don't really like this word, can you please find another one from the thesaurus".
- Right-click on the first comments balloon, then click on **Delete Comment**.
- Find the comments: "Can we give a definition of a broad-leaved tree?" And "Can we give a definition of a conifer?"
- Click on the **Delete** button (Comments group) to delete both of these comments.
- **Save** your changes.

Tracking document changes

If your manager asks you to review a document, but they want to see the changes you have made and decide whether to accept or reject them before the final document is distributed, then tracking is the feature to use.

How to: Turn tracking on/off

1. Display the Review ribbon, then click on the **Track Changes** button (Tracking group). The button is highlighted.
2. Make your changes to the text. Altered text is marked and changes are noted in the Markup Area.
3. To switch tracking off, click back on the **Track Changes** button. The highlight is removed from the button.

How to: Accept revisions

1. Ensure you are displaying Markups.
2. Display the Review ribbon, then click on the **Accept and Move to Next** button (Changes group) ~*or*~
   Click on the **Accept** down-arrow, then click on **Accept All Changes in Document**.

How to: Reject revisions

1. Ensure you are displaying Markups.
2. Display the Review ribbon, then click on the **Reject and Move to Next** button (Changes group) ~*or*~
   Click on the **Reject** down-arrow, then click on **Reject All Changes in Document**.

How to: Move between revisions

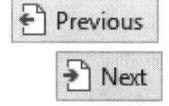

1. Display the Review ribbon, then click on the **Next Change/ Previous Change** buttons (Changes group).

Hands-on exercise 35

In this exercise you practise tracking.

- Using the document *Rainforest report*, click on the **Track Changes** button (Tracking group). The button is highlighted.

- Select the paragraph at the top of the document commencing: One of the earliest written descriptions...

- Delete this paragraph. Note the text is displayed in red with a strikethrough. Note the vertical line in the left margin.

- Apply the heading as noted in the comment: The importance of rainforests.
  The change is noted in the Markup Area. Note the vertical line in the left margin.

- Click on the **Display for Review** down-arrow (Comments group), then click on **Original: Show Markup**. Note how formatting changes are not displayed in this view, just detailed in the Markup area.

- Return to the view **Final: Show Markup**.

- Go to the heading: Emergents.

- Type the following text beneath the existing paragraph:

- Some of these trees are known to grow as high as 60 meters above the rainforest with trunks that measure up to 5 meters around. These huge trunks are usually supported by an extensive root system to protect them from harsh winds.

- The altered text is shown in red and underlined (with a solid underline).

- Keeping this edit in view, click on the **Display for Review** down-arrow (Comments group), then click on **Original**. Note the original text without revision is displayed.

- What changed in the document?

  _____

- Click on the **Display for Review** down-arrow, then click on **Final**.
- What changed in the document?

  _____

- Click on the **Display for Review** down-arrow, then click on **Final: Show Markup**.

Next, you now work through accepting or rejecting the revisions and editing the document.

- Go to the top of the document.
- Click on the **Next Change** button (Changes group).
- Make the change needed throughout the document and click on the **Accept and Move to Next** button (Changes group).
- To insert a picture of a buttress root system, search on the internet and save a picture. Search with the words: Buttress root system and click on images (if using Google as your search engine).
- Right-click on the picture and click on Save picture as…
- What was the URL of the website you saved the picture from:

  _____

- Format your picture appropriately.
- Scroll to the end of your document and type the URL into the Bibliography (in alphabetical order). Buttress root system image:

Finally, you switch off tracking.

- Click on the **Track Changes** button (Tracking group).
  The highlight is removed from the button.
- Display your document as **Final**.
- Scroll through your document and make any other necessary changes.
- **Save** your changes.

Comparing and merging content

If tracking was not switched on, and you needed to know what changes had been made to a document, you can **compare** two versions. Compare allows you to **merge** the differences between two documents into a single new document, reviewing each change. The documents being compared are not altered.

> *As an aside* … *Compare documents is best used when the original and revised documents do not contain tracked changes, as tracked changes are treated as accepted.*

How to: Compare two documents

1. Display the Review ribbon, click on the **Compare** button, then click on **Compare** (Compare group). The Compare Documents dialogue box is presented.

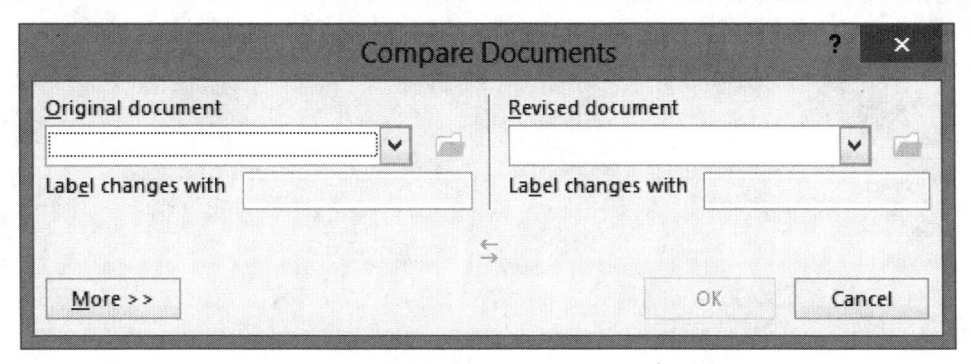

Topic 9 – Adding comments, tracking changes & comparing content

2. Select your **Original document**. (Use the folder icon to Browse.)
3. Select your **Revised document**. (Use the folder icon to Browse.)
4. Click on **OK**.

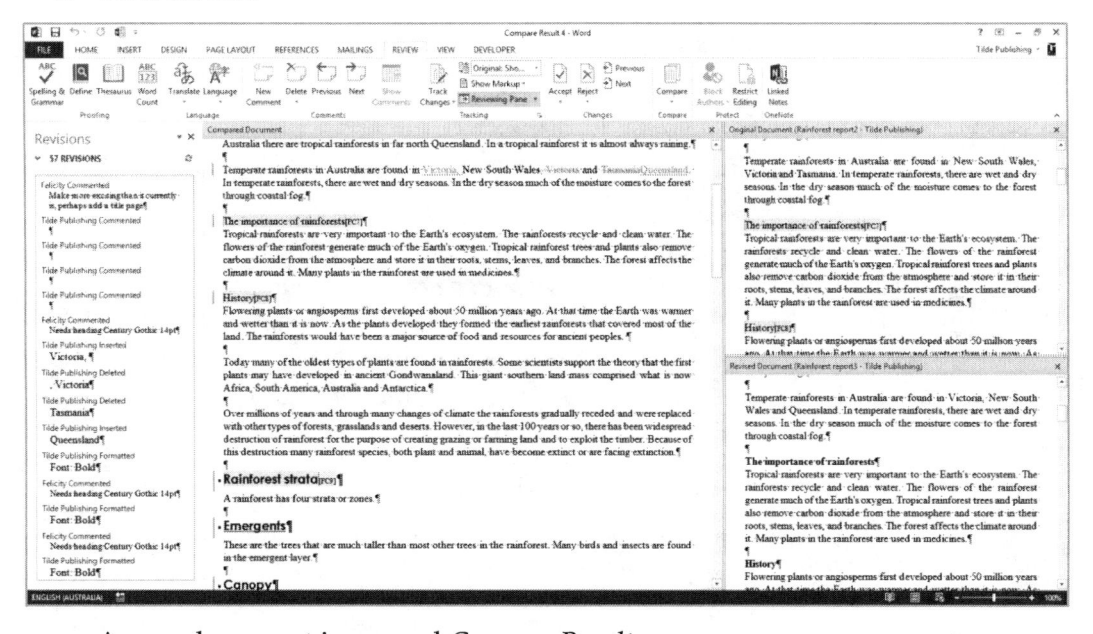

A new document is opened *Compare Results* ...

5. To review the documents with the Review Pane, click on the **Compare** button. Select **Show Source Documents**, **Show Both**.
   The Reviewing Pane is opened on the left of the screen.
   At the top of the Reviewing Pane the differences are summarised (between the original and the revised version).
   On the right of the screen are your two document versions (Original Document and Revised Document).
   The new Compared Document is in the middle.
6. Use your **Accept/Reject/Next** and **Previous** buttons (Changes group) to view and accept or reject changes.
7. **Save** your new compared document.

Hands-on exercise 36

In this exercise you practise comparing two documents.

- Display the document *Rainforest report* and open the document *Rainforest report v2*.
- Scroll through the document *Rainforest report v2*. You will notice it is the document you have just worked on but without any of the changes.

- Display the Review ribbon, click on the **Compare** button (Compare group), then click on **Compare**... The Compare Documents dialogue box is presented.

- Select *Rainforest report v2* as your **Original document**.
  (Use the drop-down box to view recently opened documents or the folder icon to Browse. Click on **Open**.)

- Select *Rainforest report* your **Revised document**.
  (Use the drop-down box to view recently opened documents or the folder icon to Browse. Click on **Open**.)

- If either of your documents still contain tracking changes, the following message will appear.

- Click on Yes.

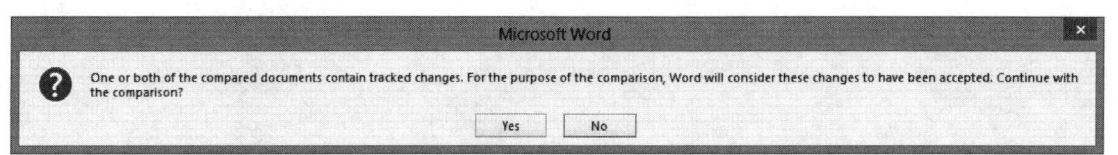

> Microsoft Word
> One or both of the compared documents contain tracked changes. For the purpose of the comparison, Word will consider these changes to have been accepted. Continue with the comparison?
> [Yes] [No]

- A new document is opened *Compare Results* ...
  The Reviewing Pane is opened on the left of the screen.
  At the top of the Reviewing Pane the differences are summarised (between the original and the revised version).
  On the right of the screen are your two document versions (Original Document (top) and Revised Document (bottom).
  The new Compared Document is in the middle.

- How many revisions are there? _____

- How many of the revisions are formatting? _____

- How many of the revisions are deletions? _____

- Click on the **Next Change** button (Changes group).
  You are taken to the first change. Note the information in the Reviewing Pane (**Inserted -** and by whom).

- Click on the **Accept and Move to Next Change** button.

- You are taken to the next change.
  Note the information in the Reviewing Pane (**Deleted**).

- Click on the **Accept and Move to Next Change** button.

- You are taken to the next change.

- Click on the **Accept and Move to Next Change** button.

- Click on **OK** to the message re comments and tracked changes.

- **Save** your new document as *Final version – Rainforest report v3*.

- **Close** all of your document.

- Re-**open** *Final version – Rainforest report v3*.
  Ensure it is displayed in Print Layout view. If tracking changes are shown, mark as Final.

- Review your document.

- **Close** your document.

As an aside ... Compare is used when comparing two documents. Combine is used when comparing two or more documents. If tracking is present these appear as tracked changes in the combined document.

Hints & tips

To add a Track Changes indicator on the Status bar, right-click on the Status bar and click on Track Changes in the list presented.

To prevent you from inadvertently distributing documents that contain tracked changes and comments, Word displays tracked changes and comments by default. (**Final: Show Markup** is the default option in **Display for Review**.)

Terms & concepts review

- Why use **comments**?

  _____

  _____

- What does **tracking** create in a document?

  _____

  _____

  _____

  _____

- What happens when you **compare** two documents?

  _____

  _____

- Where do you find the following buttons and what do they do?

	Ribbon? Group?	What does this button do?
Compare		
Reject		
Next		
Previous		

Topic 10 – Calculations in Word

You can perform calculations in Word. However, Word does not provide full spreadsheet functionality, so there are limitations to what it can do. For this reason, performing calculations in Word is most appropriate where the following conditions apply:

- the amount of numbers requiring calculation is small
- the likelihood of change to these numbers is low
- the layout of the numbers is unlikely to change.

Inserting automatic totals

In Word, you can perform calculations when you have numbers organised in a **table**.

How to: Sum numbers above or to the left

1. Click your insertion point in the appropriate cell (in the table) which has numbers above or to the left. 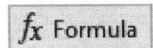
2. Display the Layout ribbon, then click on the **Formula** button (Data group). The Formula dialogue box is presented. 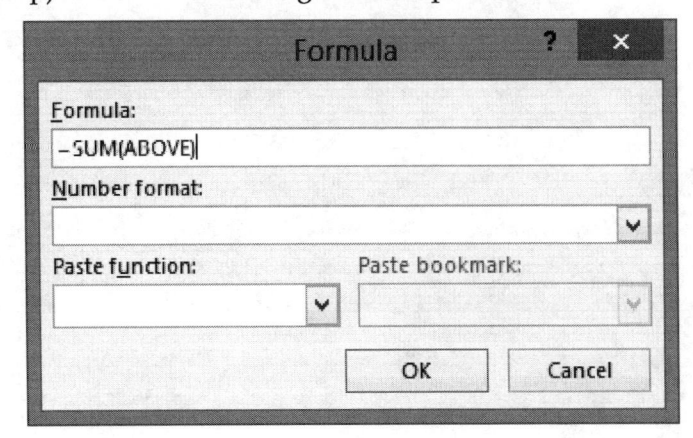
3. Excel anticipates the calculation you want to perform (**Formula**).
4. Click on **OK**.

As an aside ... *The range of an AutoSum calculation, i.e. SUM(ABOVE) or SUM(LEFT), stops when a blank cell is encountered. To avoid your calculations being incorrect, consider inserting a zero (0) instead of leaving a cell blank to ensure you have a continuous range of cells.*

How to: Update calculations

1. Select the calculation(s), i.e. field(s), to be updated.

2. Press [F9] ~or~
   Right-click on the selected cells, then click on **Update Field**.

Hands-on exercise 37

In this exercise you practise inserting automatic calculations into a Word document.

- **Open** the document *Commissions*.
- Locate the first table in this document.
- Position your insertion point in the first blank cell in the TOTAL column (April).
- Display the Layout ribbon, then click on the **Formula** button (Data group). The Formula dialogue box is presented.
- Note the **Formula** is SUM(ABOVE).
- Click on **OK**.
- Repeat the previous step for the first blank cell in the TOTAL row (A. Davis). Note the Formula is SUM(LEFT).
- Management advise an updated figure for J. Bromley's June sales. Change 24,450 to 28,960.
- Select the row sum (132,800), then press [F9]
- What other sum(s) are also affected?

  _____

- Select the other sum(s) to be updated, then press [F9]
- **Save** your changes.

As an aside ... *Each calculation inserted in this topic is simply a Word field. For more information, see below.*

Inserting custom calculations

If the calculations you require are not simply totals, or the rules of AutoSum are not appropriate, Word makes available a number of other common calculations or **functions** for you to use. Alternatively you can build your own formula.

Whether inserting a pre-defined function or performing your own calculation, the formula defined is inserted as the Word field *formula*. This field has the syntax:

$$\{= \text{Formula [Bookmark] [\textbackslash\# Numeric Picture]}\}$$

Where:

- **Formula** is any combination of numbers, operators (e.g. +, -, *, etc), functions, table cell references, or bookmarked cells/values.
- **Numeric Picture** is the number format by which the result should be displayed.

Before you can insert an existing function or create your own, you first need to understand a little more about formulas.

Explaining table cell references

Table **cell references** can be used when you want to create a calculation in a table. These cell references refer to one or more cells in a table. You need to begin thinking of the cells in your table as a grid, similar to that which you would find in an Excel worksheet, with letters representing columns and numbers representing rows. These letter and number combinations are referred to as cell references.

A1	B1	C1
A2	B2	C2
A3	B3	C3

Cell references in a three row, three column Word table.

Cell references include:

- **individual cells**:
  separate the references with commas, e.g. A1, B2, C3
- a **range of cells**:
  separate the first (top left) and last (bottom right) cell references with a colon, e.g. A2:B4

> *As an aside ...* Unlike Excel, if you add or delete rows or columns within your table, cell references within formulas do not automatically update. So, if you do make any structural changes to your table, check each formula to ensure that it is making the calculation you require.

Explaining bookmarks and formulas

If you wish to use a value in your formula that exists elsewhere in a document, that value – or the table containing that value – must be bookmarked to ensure it can be accessed by your formula.

Once created, to reference a bookmark outside of a table, you simply use the bookmark's name. To reference cell(s) within a bookmarked table, use the bookmark's name followed by the cell reference.

How to: Create a bookmark

1. Select the text or table to be bookmarked. 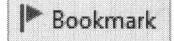
2. Display the Insert ribbon, then click on the **Bookmark** button (Links group). The Bookmark dialogue box is presented.

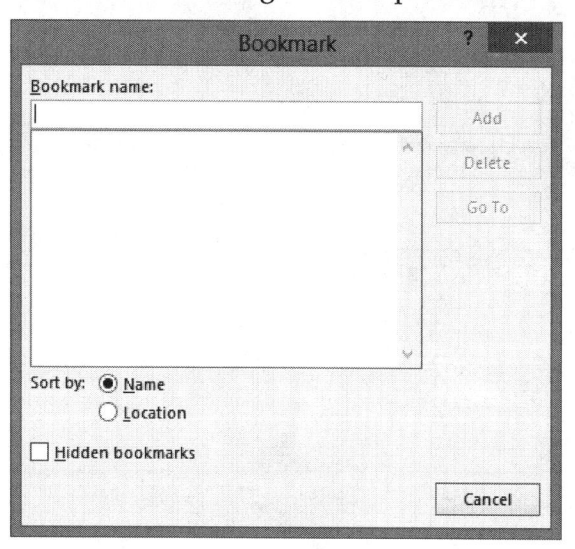

3. Type a **Bookmark name** (no spaces).
4. Click on **Add**.

Interpreting number formats

To ensure your calculation always appears formatted in a particular way, e.g. as a dollar value with two decimal points, you can apply number formatting. Formats are defined using zeros (0) and hashes (#). These are **placeholders** which define how a number in a given position should be displayed.

Word makes available a number of pre-defined number formats for you to apply to your calculation; or, you can create your own.

A number format is built by combining one or more of the placeholders '#' and '0' with text, e.g. #,##0.00

Both placeholders display the number if one exists. However, with the # placeholder, if no number exists then nothing is displayed, whereas with the 0 placeholder, if no number exists then a 0 is displayed.

For example ... With the number format #,##0.00 applied, the number 1126 is displayed as 1,126.00, while .5 is displayed as 0.50.

Building your calculation

With a greater understanding of the components of the formula field, you can now insert your own formulas using whichever combination of components is appropriate.

How to: Insert custom calculations

1. Click your insertion point in the cell to contain the calculation. 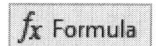
2. Display the Layout ribbon, then click on the **Formula** button (Data group). The Formula dialogue box is presented.

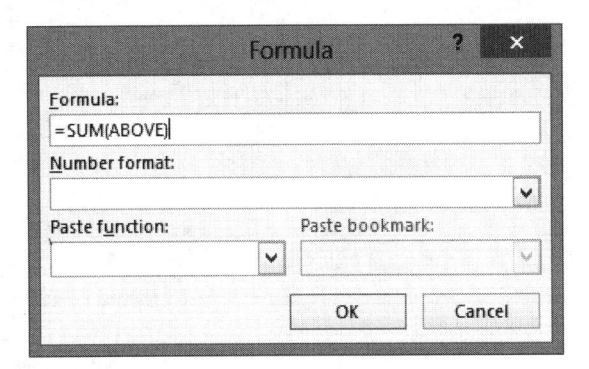

3. Delete the current **Formula**, leaving just the equals (=) sign.

4. Type your formula in the Formula box, incorporating the appropriate numbers, operators, functions, cell references, or bookmarked cells/values.

5. To insert a pre-defined function, click on the required function in the **Paste function** list. Selecting automatically inserts the function into the Formula box.

6. Within the parentheses of the function, type the appropriate cell reference(s). Note: like Excel, functions can also be nested within other functions.

7. To apply a number format to your calculation, click on the required format in the **Number format** list.

8. Click on **OK**.

How to: View your formula

1. Click at the beginning of the field to be viewed.

2. Press [Shift] [F9] ~or~
   Right-click, then click on **Toggle Field Codes**.

3. Repeat the above two steps to re-display the formula's result.

As an aside ... While viewing your formula, you can change the formula directly without needing to access the Formula dialogue box.

Creating your own formula

Now you understand all the components of a formula you can create your own from scratch, e.g. outside a table.

How to: Insert a formula manually

1. Click your insertion point where you require the calculation.

2. Press [Ctrl] [F9]
   Word inserts the field {} parentheses. Note these parentheses cannot be typed manually.

3. Type your calculation according to the syntax rules shown on page 122.

Topic 10 – Calculations in Word

Hands-on exercise 38

In this exercise you practise creating and updating calculations to determine departmental average sales.

- Ensure the document *Commissions* is open on your screen.
- Click in the cell immediately to the right of AVERAGE.
- Display the Layout ribbon, then click on the **Formula** button (Data group). The Formula dialogue box is presented.
- Delete the current Formula, leaving just the equals (=) sign.
- Click on the **AVERAGE** function in the **Paste function** list. Word automatically inserts the function into the Formula box.
- Within the brackets of the function, type: B2:B6
- Click on #,##0.00 in the Number format list.
- Click on **OK**.
- Repeat this process to calculate the May average, i.e. for range C2:C6.
- **Copy** and **paste** this last calculation to the June average cell.
- Right-click, then from the list click on **Toggle Field Codes**.
- Edit the field, changing the range to D2:D6.
- Right-click, then click on **Toggle Field Codes**.
- With the field still active, press [F9] to update the calculation.
- **Save** your changes.

Hands-on exercise 39

In this exercise you practise creating and updating calculations to determine commissions payable for sample figures.

- Ensure the document *Commissions* is open on your screen.
- Scroll down to the second table.
- Click in the blank cell in the **Old Comm.** column in the second table.
- Display the Layout ribbon, then click on the **Formula** button (Data group). The Formula dialogue box is presented.
- Delete the current **Formula**, leaving just the equals (=) sign, then type: B2*D2
- Delete the current **Number format**, then type: $#,##0.00; ($#,##0.00)
- Click on **OK**.
- Click in the blank cell in the **New Comm.** column.
- Press [Ctrl] [F9]
  Word inserts the {} parentheses.
- Within the {}, type: =C2*D2 \#"$#,##0.00;($#,##0.00)"

Copyright © 2014 Tilde Publishing & Distribution

- Select the calculation, then press [F9] to update it.
- Change the **New rate** for **25,001 – 50,000** to 3.2%.
- Select the related calculation in the **New Comm.** column, then press [F9] to update.
- **Save** your changes.

Hands-on exercise 40

In this exercise you practise creating and updating calculations appearing in the text of your document and accessing data within a table.

- Ensure the document *Commissions* is open on your screen.

First, you bookmark the table.

- Select the first table in the document.
- Display the Insert ribbon, then click on the **Bookmark** button (Links group). The Bookmark dialogue box is presented.
- Type the **Bookmark name:** QTR2Sales
- Click on **Add**.

Next, you create a formula that references that table.

- Position your insertion point at the end of the sentence located below the table: This represents average monthly sales of
- Press [Ctrl] [F9]
  Word inserts the {} parentheses.
- Within the {}, create the following formula: =AVERAGE (QRT2Sales B9:D9\ #"$#,##0.00")
- Select the calculation you have just typed, then press [F9] to update it
- **Save** your changes.
- **Close** your document.

Consolidation task 13

In this task you perform some calculations on exam results data.

- **Open** the document *Class of 2013*.
- Sum the columns: Mid-Term, Final, and Term Project.
- Sum the Total Points across the rows.
  (Ensure that these calculations are summing to the left.)
- Sum the Total Points column.
- Add an extra row to the bottom of the table.
- Type in the first cell of the new row: Class averages
- Calculate the averages for the columns: Mid-term, Final, and Term Project.

- Edit the figures for P Collins to read: 59, 86 and 92 for the Mid-Term, Final and Term Project columns respectively.
- Update all the calculations affected by these changes.
- How many calculations were affected?

- **Save** your changes.
- **Close** all open documents.

Topic 11 – Customising and automating tasks

Word offers a variety of features to enable you to customise and automate the tasks you repeatedly perform.

Customising the Quick Access Toolbar

You may find that you have several frequently-used commands that you require quicker access to. Command buttons can easily be added to the Quick Access Toolbar.

How to: Add basic commands to the Quick Access Toolbar

1. Right-click on a command button, then click on **Add to Quick Access Toolbar** ~or~
   Click on the **Customize Quick Access Toolbar** button, then click on the additional commands required from the list presented.

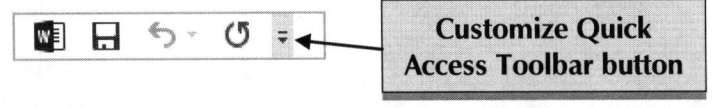

   Customize Quick Access Toolbar button

How to: Add more commands to the Quick Access Toolbar

1. Display **Backstage** view, then click on **Options**.
   The Word Options pane is presented.

2. Click on Quick Access Toolbar in the left panel.

3. In the pane presented, click on the **Choose commands from** down-arrow, then click on a category, e.g. All Commands.

4. Click on a command from the list presented on the left (list presented in alphabetical order).

5. Click on **Add**.

6. Your command button is added to the list on the right.

7. Use the up/down arrows to change the order of items added.

8. Click on **OK**.

9. Note the new button on the Quick Access toolbar.

How to: Remove buttons from the Quick Access Toolbar

1. Right-click on a command button added to the Quick Access Toolbar, then click on **Remove from Quick Access Toolbar**.

Hands-on exercise 41

In this exercise you practise adding/removing buttons from the Quick Access Toolbar.

- Click on the **Customize Quick Access Toolbar** button, and add the following commands to your toolbar: **New, Open, Print Preview**.
- Display **Backstage** view, then click on **Options**.
  The Word Options pane is presented.
- Click on **Quick Access Toolbar** in the left panel.
- In the pane presented, click on the **Choose commands from** down-arrow, then click on **All Commands**.
- Scroll down and click on **Save All** from the list presented on the left.
- Click on **Add**.
- Your command button is added to the list on the right.
- Scroll down and click on **Close/Close All** from the list presented on the left.
- Click on **Add**.
- Your command button is added to the list on the right.
- Scroll down and click on **Print Documents...** from the list presented on the left.
- Click on **Add**.
- Scroll down and click on **New** from the list presented on the left.
- Click on **Add**.
- Click on **OK**.
- Note the new buttons on the Quick Access toolbar.

Customising shortcut keys (direct key combinations)

Many Word commands already have shortcut keys assigned to them, e.g. the command to open a document `Ctrl` `O` (see *Appendix I*). You can assign additional shortcut keys to commands that you use regularly.

Shortcut keys are stored in templates. For your shortcut keys to be available in all documents, you must store them in the Normal template.

How to: Create shortcut keys in the Normal template

1. Display **Backstage** view, then click on **Options**.
   The Word Options pane is presented.

2. Click on **Customize Ribbon** in the left panel.

3. At the bottom of the pane, click on the **Keyboard shortcuts: Customize** button. The Customize Keyboard dialogue box is presented.

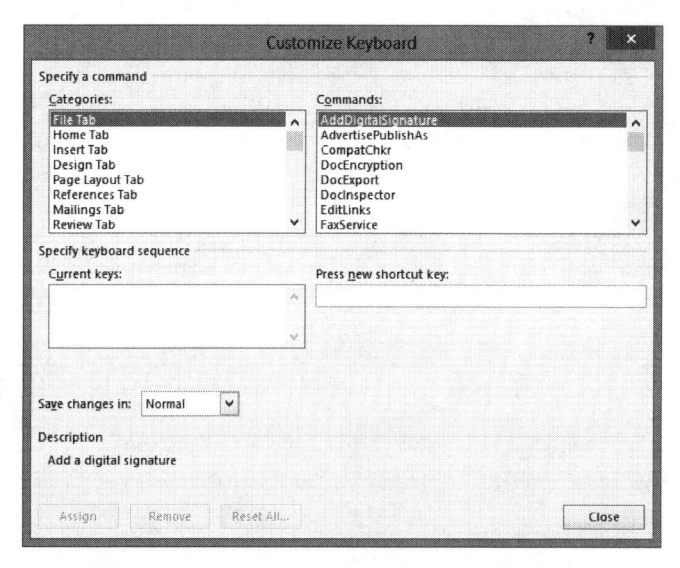

4. Ensure the **Save changes in** option displays **Normal**.
   (By storing your shortcut keys in the Normal template, they will be available to all documents.)

5. Select from the list of **Categories**, then select from the list of **Commands**.
   (If a key combination is already assigned to a command, it will be displayed in the **Current keys** box.)
   Note: The word **Tab** in the list of categories refers to a ribbon – so the Home Tab displays the commands on the Home ribbon.

6. Click in the **Press new shortcut key** box.

7. Press the shortcut key combination you require.
   (If the key combination selected is already assigned, the command will be displayed beneath the **Press new shortcut key** box.)

8. Click on **Assign**.

9. Click on **Close** in the Customize Keyboard dialogue box.

10. Click on **OK** in the Word options pane.

As an aside ... You can remove a shortcut key combination within the Customize Keyboard dialogue box. Click on the command, in the **Current keys** box click on the key combination, then click on **Remove**.

Hands-on exercise 42

In this exercise you practise assigning shortcut keys.

- **Open** the document *Reduce waste*.

First, you review existing shortcut keys.

- Display **Backstage** view, then click on **Options**.
  The Word Options pane is presented.

- Click on **Customize Ribbon** in the left panel.

- At the bottom of the pane, click on the **Keyboard shortcuts: Customize** button.
  The Customize Keyboard dialogue box is presented.

- Ensure the **Save changes in** option displays Normal.

Topic 11 – Customising and automating tasks

- From the list of **Categories**, click on **Home Tab**.
- Click on the following **Commands** and note their shortcut keys (displayed in **Current keys**):

    Bold   _____

    EditCopy   _____

    EditPaste   _____

- From the list of **Categories**, click on **All Commands** (near bottom of list).
- Click on the following **Commands** and note their shortcut keys (displayed in **Current keys**):

    ApplyHeading1   _____

    ApplyHeading2   _____

    ApplyHeading3   _____

- Click on **Close**.
- Click on **Cancel** to close the Word Options pane.
- Experiment with the shortcut keys above in your document.

Next, you create a new shortcut key - one that applies a border.

- Display **Backstage** view, then click on **Options**.
  The Word Options pane is presented.
- Click on **Customize** in the left panel.
- At the bottom of the pane, click on the **Keyboard shortcuts: Customize** button.
  The Customize Keyboard dialogue box is presented.
- Ensure **Save changes in** is displaying Normal.
- From the **Categories** list, click on **Home Tab**.
- From the **Commands** list, click on **BorderOutside**.
- Click in the **Press new shortcut key** box.
- Press [Alt] [Ctrl] [B]
  (Note that this shortcut key is not assigned.)
- Click on **Assign**.
- Click on **Close**.
- Click on **OK**.
- Experiment with your new shortcut key in your document (select a paragraph and apply).
- **Save** your changes.
- **Close** your document.

Hints & tips

*The following is a simpler method when creating shortcut keys for styles. Display the Styles task pane. Click on the down-arrow beside a style name. Click on **Modify**. Click on the **Format** button, then click on **Shortcut Key**.*

Assigning a Quick Part item to a shortcut key

Standard paragraphs of text can be saved in the **Quick Parts** gallery. These paragraphs can then be quickly inserted into documents. Word refers to these as building blocks.

Shortcut keys can be applied to Quick Part items using the same process as above, however in the Customize Keyboard dialogue box Quick Part items are known as **AutoText**.

First, we remind ourselves how to create a Quick Part item (before we assign a keyboard shortcut to it).

How to: Add to the Quick Parts gallery

1. Select the text to be stored.
2. Display the Insert ribbon, click on the **Quick Parts** button, then click on the **Save Selection to Quick Parts Gallery** option (Text group). The Create New Building Block dialogue box is presented.

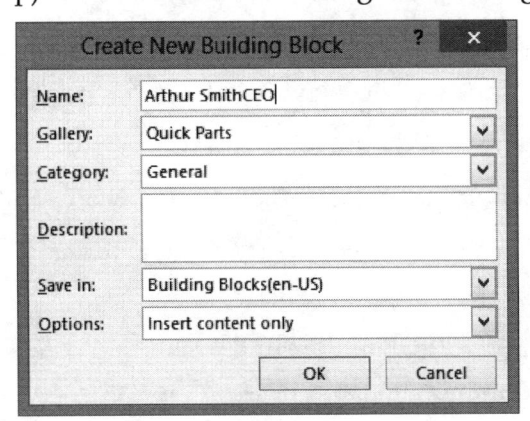

3. Complete the following information:

Name	Be unique and descriptive.
Gallery	There are many. If you store under the default **Quick Parts** gallery the item can quickly be selected later from the Quick Parts list.
Category	**General** is the only one to begin with. More can be created later to manage extensive lists.
Description	Be clear to help locate later on.
Save In	Select **Building Blocks** so the item is available to all documents you create, or the item can be stored in a specific template to restrict availability to only specific types of documents.
Options	Select **Insert content only** to insert item wherever required (most flexible), **Insert content in its own paragraph**, to make item into its own paragraph (paragraph markers before and after), or **Insert content in its own page**, with page breaks before and after, e.g. for a cover page.

4. Click on **OK**.

As an aside …If you want to retain the paragraph formatting of selected text when inserted, ensure that you include the paragraph marker in the initial selection.

How to: Insert a Quick Part item

1. Position your insertion point where the item is required.
2. Display the Insert ribbon, click on the **Quick Parts** button (Text group).
3. Note your item under **General** in the Quick Parts list.

Topic 11 – Customising and automating tasks

4. Click on the item required.

Hands-on exercise 43

In this exercise you first create a Quick Part item for a letter closure. Then, you assign this to a shortcut key.

- **Open** the document *Eagle legal letter*.

First, you create a Quick Part item using a letter closure.

- Select the letter closure. (Yours sincerely, plus name and company.)
- Display the Insert ribbon, click on the **Quick Parts** button, then click on the **Save Selection to Quick Part Gallery** option (Text group).
  The Create New Building Block dialogue box is presented.
- **Name** the Quick Part item: LetterClosure1
- Click on **OK**.
- Delete the existing closure from your letter.
- To insert the Quick Part item, click on the **Quick Parts** button, then click on LetterClosure1.
- Delete the closure again from the letter.

Next, you assign your Quick Part item to a shortcut key.

- Display **Backstage** view, then click on **Options**.
  The Word Options pane is presented.
- Click on **Customize Ribbon** in the left panel.
- At the bottom of the pane, click on the **Keyboard shortcuts**: **Customize** button.
  The Customize Keyboard dialogue box is presented.
- Ensure **Save changes in** is displaying Normal.
- Scroll down the **Categories** list, then click on **Building Blocks**.
- Click on the **Building Blocks**: LetterClosure1
- Click in the **Press new shortcut key** box.
- Press [Alt] [L]
- Click on **Assign**.
- Click on **Close**.
- Click on **OK**.
- Use your new shortcut key to insert your letter closure.
- **Save** your changes.

*As an aside ... To reset all key combinations back to their original settings, in the Customize Keyboard dialogue box (see above), click on **Reset All**.*

Hints & tips

Avoid assigning actions to ALT H, N, P, S, M, R or W as these are used for the new Word access keys (See Appendix I), and no warning is given in the dialogue box that they are assigned.

Assigning Quick Parts to the Quick Access toolbar

Alternatively, you can assign Quick Parts to the Quick Access Toolbar.

Hands-on exercise 44

In this exercise you practise assigning Quick Parts to the Quick Access Toolbar.

- Display **Backstage** view, then click on **Options**.
  The Word Options pane is presented.
- Click on **Quick Access Toolbar** in the left panel.
- In the pane presented, click on the **Choose commands from** down-arrow, then click on the category **All Commands**.
- Click on the command **Quick Parts** from the list presented on the left.
- Click on **Add**.
- Your command button is added to the list on the right.
- Click on **OK**.
- Note the new button on the Quick Access toolbar.
- **Close** your document.

Recording a macro

If you repeatedly perform a task that has many steps, you can automate that task using a **macro**. A macro is simply a series of actions that are grouped together under a single command.

For example ... Macros can be used to combine a series of steps to speed up routine editing or formatting.

The easiest way to create a macro is to record your actions using Word's macro **recorder**. Once the recorder is switched on, it records all your keystrokes and mouse actions until you switch it off again.

Macros are usually stored in templates. By default, Word stores macros in the Normal template so that they are available for use with every Word document. Macros can be assigned to run from shortcut keys or the Quick Access Toolbar.

How to: Record a macro in the Normal template

1. Display the Developer ribbon, then click on the **Record Macro** button (Code group). The Record Macro dialogue box is presented.

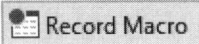

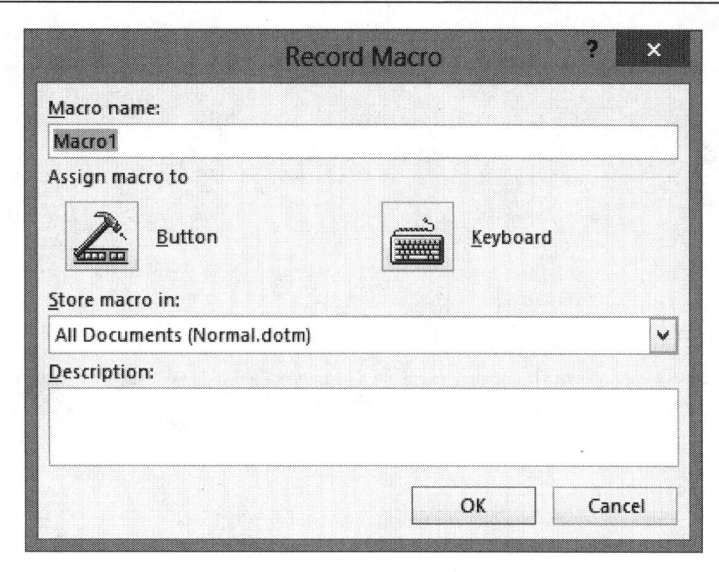

Topic 11 – Customising and automating tasks

2. Type a **Macro name**.
   Macro names must begin with a letter and cannot contain spaces.

3. Under **Store macro in**, ensure **All Documents (Normal.dotm)** is selected.

4. Type a **Description** (optional) to help you identify your macro later. The current date and author are added automatically.

5. Click on **OK** to begin recording.
   The Recording pointer is displayed and the **Stop recording** indicator in the Status bar.

6. Perform the actions you want to record.

7. When you have finished your actions, click on the **Stop Recording** button (Code group) ~or~
   Click on the **Stop recording** indicator in the Status bar.

Hands-on exercise 45

In this exercise you practise creating a macro by recording the steps to print the current page of a document. (This will make a dialogue box option more accessible.)

- **Open** the document SuperFood annual report.

- Display the Developer ribbon, then click on the **Record Macro** button (Code group). The Record Macro dialogue box is presented.

- Type the **Macro name**: PrintCurrentPage

- Under **Store macro in**, ensure **All Documents (Normal.dotm)** is selected.

- Click on **OK** to begin recording.
  The Recording pointer is displayed and the **Stop recording** indicator in the Status bar.

- **Display Backstage** view, click on **Print**, then click on **Current Page**. Click on **Print**.

- Click on the **Stop Recording** button (Code group) ~or~
  Click on the **Stop recording** indicator in the Status bar.

Running a macro

Macros can be assigned to run from shortcut keys and the Quick Access Toolbar. However, you should first test your macro by running it manually from the Macros dialogue box.

How to: Run a macro manually

1. Display the Developer ribbon, then click on the **Macros** button (Code group). The Macros dialogue box is presented.

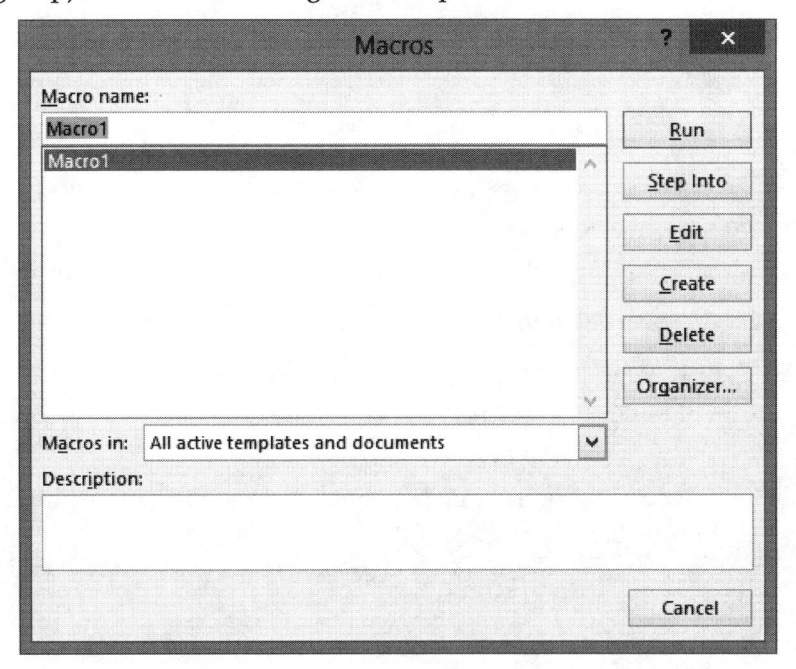

2. Click on the **Macros in** down-arrow, then click on the required template, e.g. **Normal.dotm (global template)**.

3. Click on the required macro in the **Macro name** list.

4. Click on **Run**.

Hints & tips

To delete a macro, display the Macros dialogue box (above), click on the macro, then click on **Delete**.

If your macro contains an error, it is easier with small macros to simply re-record the entire macro.

Hands-on exercise 46

In this exercise you practise running your macro manually.

- Ensure the document *SuperFood annual report* is displayed (page 1).
- Display the Developer ribbon, then click on the **Macros** button (Code group). The Macros dialogue box is presented.
- Click on the **Macros in** down-arrow, then click on **Normal.dotm (global template)**.
- Click on the *PrintCurrentPage* macro in the **Macro name** list.
- Click on **Run**. Your macro prints the current page of your document.

Topic 11 – Customising and automating tasks

Assigning a macro to a shortcut key

Macros can be assigned to shortcut keys using the previous process.

Hands-on exercise 47

In this exercise you assign your PrintCurrentPage macro to a shortcut key.

- Display **Backstage** view, then click on **Options**.
  The Word Options pane is presented.

- Click on **Customize Ribbon** in the left panel.

- At the bottom of the pane, click on the **Keyboard shortcuts: Customize** button. The Customize Keyboard dialogue box is presented.

- Ensure **Save changes in** is displaying **Normal**.

- From the list of **Categories**, scroll down and click on **Macros**.

- From the list of **Macros**, click on the macro **PrintCurrentPage**.

- Click in the **Press new shortcut key** box.

- Press `Alt` `Ctrl` `P`
  (This key combination is currently assigned - it will now be overwritten and re-assigned to your macro.)

- Click on **Assign**.

- Click on **Close**.

- Click on **OK**.

Now, you test your shortcut key combination.

- Go to the end of the document.

- Press `Alt` `Ctrl` `P`
  The final page of the document is printed.

- **Save** your changes.

- **Close** your document.

Hands-on exercise 48

In this exercise you create a macro which displays a new document based on the supplied template *Company letter*. This template should have been previously copied into your Templates folder (see **Preface, Before You Start**).

- Display the Developer ribbon, then click on the **Record Macro** button (Code group). The Record Macro dialogue box is presented.

- Type the **Macro name**: CallLetter

- Under **Store macro in**, ensure **All Documents (Normal.dotm)** is selected.

- Click on **OK** to begin recording.
  The Recording pointer is displayed and the **Stop Recording** indicator in the Status bar.

- Display **Backstage** view, click on **New**, click on **My templates**, click on *Company letter*, then click on **OK**.
  A new document is displayed based on the *Company letter* template.
- Click on the **Stop Recording** indicator on the Status bar.
- You have now finished recording your macro.
- **Close** your document, without saving.

Now, you test your macro (manually).

- Display the Developer ribbon, then click on the **Macros** button (Code group). The Macros dialogue box is presented.
- Click on the **Macros in** down-arrow, then click on **Normal.dotm (global template)**.
- Click on the *CallLetter* macro in the **Macro name** list.
- Click on **Run**. Your macro creates a new document based on the *Company letter* template.
- **Close** your document, without saving.
- Assign your macro to the shortcut key `Alt` `Ctrl` `L` (overwriting any other assignment)
- Test your keystroke combination.
- **Close** your document, without saving.

Assigning a macro to the Quick Access Toolbar

Alternatively, macros can be assigned to the Quick Access Toolbar.

Hands-on exercise 49

In this exercise you practise assigning your CallLetter macro to the Quick Access Toolbar.

- Display **Backstage** view, then click on **Options**.
  The Word Options pane is presented.
- Click on **Quick Access Toolbar** in the left panel.
- In the pane presented, click on the **Choose commands from** down-arrow, then click on the category **Macros**.
- Click on your CallLetter macro from the list presented.
- Click on **Add**.
- Your command button is added to the list on the right.
- Click on **OK**.
- Note the new button on the Quick Access toolbar.
- Practice using your new button.
- **Close** all open documents.

Modifying a command button image

You will have noticed that the button allocated to the Quick Access Toolbar in the exercise above is not very attractive or meaningful (and would be repeated for all macros added). You can however modify button images.

How to: Edit a button image

1. In the Customize pane (Word Options), when you have added a button to the list on the right, ensure the item is still selected, then click on the **Modify** button (or return to the pane at any time and follow these steps). The Modify Button dialogue box is presented.

2. Click on a new image.
3. Edit the **Display name** as required.
4. Click on **OK**.
5. Note your new button image on the Quick Access Toolbar.

Hands-on exercise 50

In this exercise you will practise creating custom buttons for your toolbars.

- Display **Backstage** view, then click on **Options**.
  The Word Options pane is presented.

- Click on **Quick Access Toolbar** in the left panel.

- Click on the CallLetter item in the RIGHT pane, then click on the **Modify** button. The Modify Button dialogue box is presented.

- Click on a new image, e.g. .

- Edit the **Display name** as: Company letter.

- Click on **OK**.
  Note your new button image on the Quick Access Toolbar.

Tilde *skills* Design & Develop Complex Text Documents

```
┌─────────────────────────────────────────────────────────────┐
│                    Consolidation task 14                    │
└─────────────────────────────────────────────────────────────┘
```

In this task you practise creating another macro. Your supplied exercises include a template called *Weekly report* which is used in this exercise. This template should have been copied into your Templates folder (see **Preface, Before You Start**).

- Create a macro called CallReport which presents a document based on the supplied *Weekly report* template.
- Test your macro.
- Assign your macro to the Quick Access Toolbar.
- Test your new button.
- **Close** all open documents.

```
┌─────────────────────────────────────────────────────────────┐
│                    Consolidation task 15                    │
└─────────────────────────────────────────────────────────────┘
```

In this task you create a macro to help you to format documents. The macro will contain the following steps:

- create a macro that finds the two spaces between sentences and replaces with a single space;
- add a **space after** paragraph measurement of 6 pts; and
- format all the text in the document with the font **Arial** and the font size **11 pts**.

The first steps you record in your macro use the Find feature to find two spaces (one after the other), then replace them with one space. Note: If you make any mistakes in recording the macro simply stop and start again, and when prompted overwrite the previous macro.

- **Open** the document *Photography course*.
- Begin recording a new macro called: **StripParas**
  Ensure it is stored in the Normal template.
- Display the Home ribbon, then click on **Find**.
  The Find and Replace dialogue is presented.
- Click on the Replace tab
- In **Find what** press: [Spacebar] [Spacebar]
- Click in **Replace with** then press: [Spacebar]
- Click on **Replace All**.
- Click on **OK**, then click on **Close**.

Next, while still recording, you select the entire document and change the paragraph spacing.

- Press [Ctrl] [A] to select your entire document.
- Display the Page Layout ribbon, then increase the **Space After Paragraph** measurement to **6 pt**.

Next, while still recording, you apply the required font and font size.

Topic 11 – Customising and automating tasks

- Ensure your document is still selected.
- Display the Home ribbon and format the select text as **Arial, 11 pt**.
- Return to the top of the document - `Ctrl` `Home`
  (This step is simply to remove the highlighting and reposition your insertion point.)
- You have now completed recording your macro.
  Click on the **Stop Recording** icon on the Status bar.
- Assign your macro to a customised Quick Access Toolbar button.
- Save and close your document.
- **Open** the document *Great Ocean Road* and use your macro to format it.
- **Save** and **close** your document.

Creating a customised template

As you have noticed in previous exercises, your Quick Part items, shortcut key assignments and macros are stored in templates. So far you have only stored your customised items into the Normal template so that they are available for use with any documents you create.

You can, however, store customised items into a specific template, if they will only be required when creating documents of a certain type.

For example ... A Quick Part item to insert a legal disclaimer that is only required when you use the Contracts template should be stored in the Contracts template (not the Normal template).

Hands-on exercise 51

In this exercise you open a legal template, create a number of Quick Part items and save them to the legal template (only). Note: Your supplied exercises include a template called *Tenancy agreement* which is used in this exercise. This template should have been copied into your Templates folder (see **Preface, Before You Start**).

- **Open** the *Tenancy agreement* template.
- Leave the template open on your screen.

First, you create your Quick Part items and store them in the tenancy agreement template.

- Go to the end of the document.
- Select the final bulleted paragraph.
- Create a new Quick Part item called: Carpets. Ensure in the Create New Building Blocks dialogue box under **Save in**, that you select **Tenancy agreement**. Click on **OK**.
- Delete the sentence from the template.
- Select the previous paragraph about animals and reptiles. Save as a Quick Part item called: Animals. Again under **Save in**, ensure that you select **Tenancy agreement**. Click on **OK**.
- Delete the sentence from the template.

Next, you create shortcut keys and store them in the tenancy template.

- Display **Backstage** view, then click on **Options**.
  The Word Options pane is presented.
- Click on **Customize Ribbon** in the left panel.
- At the bottom of the pane, click on the **Keyboard shortcuts: Customize** button.
  The Customize Keyboard dialogue box is presented.
- Ensure **Save changes in** is displaying **Tenancy agreement**.
- Scroll down the **Categories** list, then click on **Building Blocks**.
- Click on the **AutoText**: Carpets
- Click in the **Press new shortcut key** box.
- Press `Alt` `C`
- Click on **Assign**.
- Assign another shortcut key combination to the Animals Quick Part (try `Alt` `A`).
- Click on **Close**.
- Click on **OK**.
- **Save** your template, and **close**.

Next, create a new **blank** document, i.e. so it's based on the Normal template.

- Click on the Quick Parts button on your Quick Access Toolbar.
  Note that the Carpets and Animals Quick Part items are not available.
- **Close** this document without saving.

Next, you create a document based on the Tenancy agreement template –

- Display **Backstage** view, click on **New**, click on **My Templates**, then on the **Tenancy agreement** template.
- Click on **OK**.
- Click on the **Quick Parts** button on your Quick Access Toolbar.

Note that the Carpets and Animals Quick Part items **ARE** available.

- Go to the end of the document.
- Use your new shortcut keys to add your new items.
- **Close** your document without saving.

Terms & concepts review

- What does a macro do?

_____

_____

_____

- When would you store macros in the Normal template?

- When would you store macros in a customised template?

Topic 12 – Creating a master document

As a document gets larger you can continue to work in a large file or break it down into smaller ones using Word's **Master Document** feature.

A master document is a document that contains links to one or more separate documents called **subdocuments**. The individual subdocuments can be worked on separately, but when you open the master document all the separate documents are brought together as one. In the one file you can view, edit and print the entire contents as though it were one file.

Inserting subdocuments

The master document feature is accessed through Outline view.

How to: Insert a subdocument

1. Create a **new** blank document, or open any existing document that will be your master.
2. Display Outline view.
3. Click on the **Show Document** button (Outlining ribbon, Master Document group). When this button is active the Master Document group is expanded.
4. Click on the **Insert** button (Outlining ribbon, Master Document group). The Insert Subdocument dialogue box is presented.
5. Select your subdocument, then click on **Open**.
6. Repeat for each subdocument you need to insert.
7. **Save** your master document.

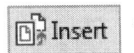

How to: Collapse and expand subdocuments

1. Click on **Collapse Subdocuments** (Outlining ribbon, Master Document group), to see the links to the external documents.
2. Click on **Expand Subdocuments** (Outlining ribbon, Master Document group) to return to the full contents.

Topic 12 – Creating a master document

Hands-on exercise 52

In this exercise you practise creating a master document.

- Create a **new** blank document.
- Display Outline view.
- Click on the **Show Document** button (Outlining ribbon, Master Document group). When this button is active the Master Document group is expanded.
- Click on the **Insert** button.
  The Insert Subdocument dialogue box is presented.
- Select the subdocument *Book review 1*, then click on **Open**.
- Repeat for the documents *Book review 2* and *Book review 3*.
- **Save** you master document as *Book reviews - March*.
- Go to the top of the document.
- Click on **Collapse Subdocuments** (Outlining ribbon, Master Document group), to see the links to the external documents.
- Click on **Expand Subdocuments** to return to the full contents.
- Note the heading in the first subdocument.
- **Close** your master document.
- **Open** the document *Book review 1*.
- Apply the Heading 1 style to the title.
- **Save** and **close** the document.
- Re-open your master document, *Book reviews – March*.
- **Expand** your subdocuments.
- Note the change in the individual file is also made in the master.
- Scroll down the document and apply the Heading 1 style to the heading at the start of the second subdocument (Shackleton's Way...).
- **Save** and **close** the master document.
- **Open** the document *Book review 2*.
  Note that the change from the master is also reflected in the subdocument.
- **Close** your subdocument.
- Re-open your master document, *Book reviews – March*.
- To open a subdocument from within the master, double-click on the subdocument icon alongside the first link.
- Note in the Title bar you are in *Book review 1*.
- **Close** *Book review 1*.
- Back in the master document note the locked icon alongside each subdocument. This indicates that each subdocument is locked while someone is working in the master.

- Go to the top of the document. With your insertion point flashing at the very top of the master document, click on the **Lock Document** button to lock the master document, so that any further changes you make to the master document are not propagated to the subdocuments.

- **Save** and **close** your document.

Workplace scenarios

These Workplace Scenarios have been developed as a set of tasks within a fictitious company that provides tuition services. To complete the scenarios you will need to refer to the following files which are stored with your exercise documents. Print out each file to refer to (you may have already printed some). Ask your instructor if you need assistance to locate these files:

- *OH&S guide* (PDF)
- *Org style guide - letter standard* (Word document)
- *Org style guide - memo standard* (Word document)
- *Org style guide - fax standard* (Word document)
- *Tuition Services DocProc* (Word document).

First, you need to create a folder on the **C:** drive called **Tuition Services – Your Initials**, e.g. **Tuition Services - FC***. You will store all your documents here. Within this folder create a sub-folder called **General Documents**, i.e. **C:\Tuition Services – FC\General Documents**.

Read through the whole question before starting the exercise so you understand what the question is asking and devise an outcome. Think of it like a work situation - your supervisor would ask you or email you a task and you need to comprehend it before you begin.

* The initials are simply to distinguish the folder if several people are sharing one computer. Omit if unnecessary.

Workplace scenario 1

You have been asked to create a certificate for students successfully completing courses.

- First, using the *OH&S guide*, check your workstation setup.
- Next, in a document, create the following layout for a certificate, inserting **Fill-in** fields as requested.
- **Save** your document as a **template** using a suitable file name, then **close**.

Tilde Education

Certificate of Competency

(Insert a fill-in field to prompt for the student's name)

has successfully completed a course in:

(Insert a fill-in field to prompt for name of course)

on:

(Insert a fill-in field to prompt for the date(s))

_____   _____
Education Co-ordinator   Instructor

Note: The detail at the bottom of the certificate can be created using a three column table as follows:

Draw this:

Then remove the lines as follows:

- From the saved template create a new document, then enter fictitious details.
- **Save** this document into your **General Documents** folder, referring to the naming conventions specified in the document procedures guide *Tuition Services DocProc*.

Workplace scenario 2

You have been asked to create mailing labels to accompany letters being produced by your Marketing department. The Marketing department stores their data in Excel.

- Produce mailing labels using the Excel worksheet *Mailing list*. Ensure the college name is shown after the customer names.
- Merge to a new document.
- **Close** your output document without saving.
- **Save** your main document (label layout) into your **General Documents** folder, referring to the naming conventions specified in the document procedures guide *Tuition Services DocProc*.
- **Close** all open documents.

Workplace scenario 3

You have been asked to create an account statement to notify customers of any outstanding monies due. Customer data is already held in a Word document.

- Create the following in a document:

Statement of Account

Attention:		Date:	
College:		Amount Due:	$
Street:			
Suburb:			
State:			
Post Code:			

- **Save** your document into your **General Documents** folder, referring to the naming conventions specified in the document procedures guide *Tuition Services DocProc*.

- Commence a mail merge for letters.
  Use the (Word) file *Accounts data* as the data source.

- Insert merge fields at suitable locations.

- Include a date field.

- Merge to a new document, selecting only those customers who have purchased more than 50 books.

- **Save** your output document into your **General Documents** folder using the name: Accounts statements – over 50.

- **Close** your output document.

- Produce labels to accompany your statements (not the entire data source).

- **Save** your output document into your **General Documents** folder using the name: Accounts statement labels – over 50.

- **Close** your output document.

- **Save** your main document (label layout) into your **General Documents** folder, referring to the naming conventions specified in the document procedures guide *Tuition Services DocProc*.

- **Close** all open documents.

Workplace scenario 4

You have been asked to send out a variety of form letters to tutors. Data required for the merge is already held in a Word document.

- **Open** the document *Enrolment data*.
  This is your data source. Review the data, then close the file.

- Referring to your *Org style guide - letter standard*, create the following letter to tutors, advising them that course enrolment starts on 4th January.

> Dear (tutors name to be inserted)
>
> Please be advised that course enrolments for (dept. name to be inserted) commence on 4th January

- **Save** your document into your **General Documents** folder, referring to the naming conventions specified in the document procedures guide *Tuition Services DocProc*.

- Commence a mail merge for letters. Use the existing Word document *Enrolment data* as the data source.

- Insert a merge field for the tutor's name and tutor's department.

- Merge to a new document, selecting only those tutors who work in the Computing department.

- **Save** your output document into your **General Documents** folder using the name: Computing dept letters.

- **Close** your output document.

- Merge to a new document, selecting only those tutors who work in the Computing department in the evening.

- **Save** your output document into your **General Documents** folder using the name: Computing dept evening letters.

- **Close** your output document.

- **Save** and **close** your main document.

Workplace scenario 5

You have been asked to create letters to inform customers of a change to company telephone numbers. Data required for the merge is already held in a Word document.

- Referring to your *Org style guide - letter standard*, create a letter to inform customers that your company telephone numbers have changed.

- Select the Word file *Enquiry data* as the data source.

- Insert a Word field which will achieve the following:
  - If the customer lives in Queensland, a local phone number is quoted in the text for customers to call.
    (Make up a phone number.)
  - If the customer does not live in Queensland, a national phone number is quoted instead.
    (Make up a phone number.)

- **Save** your main document into your **General Documents** folder, referring to the naming conventions specified in the document procedures guide *Tuition Services DocProc*.

- Merge to a new document. Scroll through your output.

- **Close** your output document without saving.

- **Close** all open documents.

Workplace scenario 6

You have been asked to send out letters to students advising them of course commencement.
Data required for the merge is already held in a Word document.

- Referring to your *Org style guide - letter standard*, create a letter to all students advising them of course enrolment dates.

- Select the Word file *Enrolment data* as the data source.

- If the student is enrolled in the Computing department, then course commencement should be specified as the 4th January. For all others it should specify the 5th January.

> Dear { MERGEFIELD Student_First_Name }
>
> Our records indicate that you are enrolled in the { MERGEFIELD Tutors_Dept } Department. Please note that enrolment will commence on the { IF { MERGEFIELD Tutors_Dept } = "Computing" "4th January" "5th January" }.

- In the same letter, if the student is from overseas, add a paragraph asking them to bring in a copy of their tertiary qualifications. All others to bring a copy of their HSC.

- **Save** your main document into your **General Documents** folder, referring to the naming conventions specified in the document procedures guide *Tuition Services DocProc*.

- Merge to a new document. Scroll through your output.

- **Close** your output document without saving.

- **Close** all open documents.

Workplace scenario 7

You have been asked to prepare a standard letter for candidates who have been selected for a job interview. You have a database of the candidates' names and other details, but you do not want to add interview times to this database as these times are one-offs and do not need to be permanently recorded.

Therefore, you decide to prepare a merge letter and use a fill-in field to prompt for the interview time as each record is being merged.

- Create a data source to hold the name and address information of four people. Ensure you hold the information in a table.

- **Save** your data source into your **General Documents** folder, referring to the naming conventions specified in the document procedures guide *Tuition Services DocProc*.

- Referring to your *Org style guide - letter standard*, create a letter inviting your candidates for interview one week from today. Leave out any variable data including the time of the interview.

- **Save** your main document into your **General Documents** folder, referring to the naming conventions specified in the document procedures guide *Tuition Services DocProc*.

- Insert the required merge fields into your letter.
  Insert a Fill-in field for the time of the interview.
  Leave the default fill-in text blank.

- Edit your Fill-in field to prompt with the name of the candidate.
- **Save** your main document.
- Merge to a new document.
  Enter the prompt information as required.
- Scroll through the letters created.
- **Close** your output document without saving.
- **Close** all open documents.

Workplace scenario 8

You have been asked to send a letter to students advising them of their tutor's name.

Referring to your *Org style guide - letter standard*, create the following form letter using the data source *Enrolment data*.

> Dear (insert students name)
>
> Please be advised that your tutor is (insert tutor's name) (Insert He or She depending on tutor's gender) will be available to answer all of your enrolment queries.

> Dear { MERGEFIELD Student_First_Name }
>
> Please be advised that your tutor's name is { MERGEFIELD Tutors_First_Name } { MERGEFIELD Tutors_Last_Name }. { FILLIN "Type He/She here for { MERGEFIELD Tutors_First_Name } { MERGEFIELD Tutors_Last_Name }:" \d "He" } will be available to answer all of your enrolment queries.

- **Save** your main document into your **General Documents** folder, referring to the naming conventions specified in the document procedures guide *Tuition Services DocProc*.
- Create labels to accompany the letters using student name and tutor's department only.
- **Save** your label document into your **General Documents** folder, referring to the naming conventions specified in the document procedures guide *Tuition Services DocProc*.
- Merge the letter to all students.
- **Close** your output document without saving.
- **Close** all open documents.

Workplace scenario 9

You have been asked to create an automated fax template to ensure a consistent layout for fax communications.

Referring to your *Org style guide - fax standard*, create a fax layout in a new template.

- Include Fill-in fields to prompt for relevant information.
- **Save** your template using a suitable name.

- Test your automated template.
  You do not need to save any documents you create from your template.

Workplace scenario 10

You regularly insert the contents of a file maintained by the Accounts department into a report for management. You decide that this routine task could be automated using a macro.

- Create a **new** blank document.

- Create a macro called **InsertResults** that inserts the file: *Sales results*.
  Ensure the macro is stored in the Normal template.
  (When recording macros that look for a file, use the **Look in** drop-down list to select the full path of the file you are looking for.)

- Assign the macro to the keystroke combination: `Alt` `R`
  Ensure you save your keystroke combination in the Normal template.

- Test your macro by inserting the Sales Results file at the bottom of the document: *SuperFood annual report*.

- **Save** your changes and **close** all open documents.

Workplace scenario 11

You have been asked to create a template which will assist in the creation of general company correspondence.

- Referring to your *Org style guide - letter standard*, create a letter template. Include a date field at the top of the letter.

- Create a Quick Part item for a letter closure and a standard paragraph thanking someone for telephoning. The Quick Part items should be stored in the letter template only.

- Assign your Quick Part items to shortcut keys – stored in the letter template.

- **Save** your template using a suitable name, then **close**.

- Ensure you can create a document from your letter template. **Close** your document without saving.

- Record a macro that presents a document based on your letter template. (Consider when recording your macro that it should be available to all templates, and not just confined to the letter template.)

- Add your macro button to the Quick Access toolbar.

Workplace scenario 12

You have been asked to collect information about your company's perceived performance via a customer survey form.

Include at least the following fields on the form.

Information to be included…	Nature of information	Order / Position
Form Title		
Name		
Company		
Company size		
Please rate your level of satisfaction in our:		
response to your enquiries		
tuition services		
Tutor knowledge		
Are there any areas you feel the company could improve its performance?		
Closing		

- Identify any further fields that could add value to the form.
- Order the list appropriately.
- Sketch a basic design layout on paper prior to creating the form in Word.
- Create your form in a Word template, with appropriate **content controls**.
- **Protect** your form.
- **Save** your template using a suitable name.
- **Close** your template.

Skills challenges & Assessment tasks

The following *challenges* and *tasks* are undertaken by a student on his or her own at the completion of the course.

Read through the whole question before starting the exercise so you understand what the question is asking and devise an outcome. Think of it like a work situation - your supervisor would ask you or email you a task and you need to comprehend it before you begin.

Creating a working area

In the following exercises you create and amend a number of files. To ensure these are efficiently organised, you need to have a suitable location in which to store the files.

In your student download files you will find a folder called: *Challenges and Assessment task files*. Throughout these challenges and assessment tasks you will be asked to open various folders and files.

Ensure you refer back to your *OH&S guide* in your student folder to remind yourself of your seating position, rest breaks and exercises.

Skills challenge 1

Environmental Challenges Australia (ECA) operates several earth sanctuaries in Australia where native flora and fauna are established and regenerated.

You have joined Environmental Challenges Australia's Finance department. Your title is Finance Manager – Subscriptions and Shares and your job is to manage ECA's members and shareholders.

Your first task is to download the company style and procedures guide from the company intranet. This document has been password protected for changes, but read-only access is available.

> *As an aside* ... Many organisations have their own requirements for the presentation of documents, e.g. size and style of text used and document layout. Standards are usually presented in a company Style Guide or Procedures Manual.

- In your student downloaded files you will find a folder Challenges and Assessment task files/1 About this Organisation.
- In the folder Standard files, locate the file: Complex style and procedures guide.doc.
- Open the document as read-only, print and review the company's style and procedures guide. (You will refer to this document throughout the course for organisation requirements relating to document style and image.)
- Close your document.

Skills challenge 2

Your next task is to send out the yearly Membership renewal letters. You receive the following email from the Finance Director.

> Please send out Membership renewal letters to all our members, using our letter template. I have set our yearly Membership cost at $75 for overseas members and $50 for Australian members. The membership data is stored on the intranet in the Managing Members & Events folder under Membership.
>
> Thanks.
>
> Doug.

- You will be using a letter template. You begin by finding out where *your* templates are stored. Review your template storage locations and note down the location for User templates.

- Locate the document: *ECA letter template.dot* (*1 About this Organisation, Standard files*). Place this template into your **User templates** folder. Retain the original file name.

First, you create a renewal letter to members.

- **Create** a new document using the ECA letter template, then add the following text, leaving room at the top of the letter for date and address information.

> Dear
>
> We have had a great year here at Environmental Challenges Australia! Read all about it in our Newsletter included with this letter.
>
> Your membership expires at the end of this month. The cost of renewing your membership is $
>
> Membership covers free entry to our earth sanctuaries and a reduced rate on our tours and at our retail outlets. We hope you will come and visit our new attractions, participate in our guided adventure walks, our education programs or enjoy our unique accommodation and restaurant facilities.
>
> Please complete the attached Membership Renewal form and send it with your membership fee to:
>
> Environmental Challenges Australia Ltd
> Challenges House
> Wildlife Lane
> Manly NSW 2095
> Australia
>
> If you have any queries, please call me on 02 9976 0843.
>
> Yours sincerely
>
>
> (key in your name)
>
> Finance Manager – Subscriptions and Shares

Save your letter into your *Membership* folder using a suitable filename.

Skills challenges & Assessment tasks

- Perform a spelling and grammar check on your document.
- **Preview**, print and proof read your document for accuracy.

Next, you create a merge document.

- Use your letter as the merge document.
- Identify the data file as the Excel file that you downloaded from the company intranet: *ECA membership.xls* (2 *Managing Members and Events / Membership*).
- Select the table: **Members**
- Insert an address block at the top of the letter.
  If necessary, match the address fields to your data.
- Insert today's date, using a field.
- Delete the text "Dear" and add a suitable greeting line.
  For invalid names use: Dear Member.
- After the $ in the second paragraph, insert the Word field If..Then..Else for the $75 membership fee to change to $50 when the country is Australia.
- **Save** your changes.
- **Preview** your merge output using records from your data source.
- **Merge** the letter to a new document. After viewing your merge output, close it without saving.

Next, you create labels to accompany your letters.

- Create a new document to hold your label layout and commence a mail merge for labels.
- Refer to the Complex Style and Procedures guide for the label size.
- Use the file *ECA membership.xls* as your data source.
  Select the table: **Members**
- Insert an address block using suitable fields for your label.
  Replicate it for all labels.
- Once you have created your label layout, save it into your *Membership* folder using a suitable filename.
- **Merge** the labels to a new document. After viewing your merged output, close it without saving.

Finally, you decide to create a directory or Mailing list of all the members you sent the renewal letter to.

- Create a new document to hold your list, then commence a mail merge for a directory.
- Use the file *ECA membership.xls* as your data source.
  Select the table: **Members**
- **Sort** the data by Last Name.
- Insert suitable name and address fields for your list.
  If necessary match the fields to your data.
- **Save** your directory into your *Membership* folder using a suitable filename.

- **Merge** the directory to a new document.
- **Print** your directory list.
- After printing your list, close it without saving it.
- **Close** all open documents.
- At the completion of this task you should have stored in your *Membership* folder:
  - a membership renewal letter with merged fields,
  - membership labels with merged fields,
  - a membership directory list with merged fields, and
  - the *ECA membership.xls* file.

Skills challenge 3

A Membership Renewal form is required with the Membership renewal letter. Your supervisor gives you a hand-drawn rough guide on what they want on the form. You create a form to be returned with the member's payment.

- In a new blank A4 document, create a form using the fields below. You may use tables and create a layout similar to the form below or design your own form, using the same fields.
  See the Complex Style and Procedures guide for correct logo, fonts and sizes. Use the *Logo.wmf* (*1 About this Organisation / Standard* files).
- When you have completed your form, **save** it into your *Membership* folder using a suitable filename.

(Hand-drawn form sketch showing:)

Logo
Environmental Challenges Australia
Membership Application/Renewal

Membership details
Name: ....
Address: ....
Suburb: .... State: ....
Please tick one of the following:
New Member: ☐   Existing Member: ☐
Member Number: ....

Payment details
I am paying by
☐ Cheque (made out to ECA) for $..........
☐ Credit card: ☐ Visa ☐ Mastercard
Card Number: .... Expiry Date: --/--
Card Holder's Name: ....
Signature: ....

Skills challenge 4

You have submitted your Membership renewal form to the Finance Director for approval. He leaves you the following voice mail.

> "Hi, the Membership renewal form looks great; however I also want to give members the opportunity to subscribe on-line. Could you duplicate this form as an online form? You will also need to make mention of this in the Membership renewal letter. Also, can you please add a footer to the form with our details. Thanks."

First, you create an on-line form.

- **Open** your Membership renewal form.
- Remove the payment by cheque option as online payments must be made using a credit card.
- **Save** your form as a template, using a suitable filename.
- Insert form fields at the appropriate locations.
  Think about where you can add drop-down fields, default text, or help text to assist the member complete the form.
- When your form is complete, protect the template.
- **Save** your changes and close your template.

Next, you test your on-line form.

- **Open** a document based on your renewal form template.
- Complete the form, testing each of your fields.
- **Close** your form, without saving.
- If necessary, open the form template and make any modifications to your form. **Save** your changes.

Finally, you update your Membership renewal letter.

- **Open** your Membership renewal letter. Edit the fourth paragraph of the letter to become:

> You may either log on to www.challenges.com.au and renew on-line or complete the attached Membership Renewal form and send it with your membership fee to:

- **Close** your letter, saving your changes.

Skills challenge 5

To save mailing costs, ECA are including their quarterly newsletter with the Membership renewal letter. You have agreed to create the newsletter as long as they provide the data and pictures. You receive the following email.

> Thanks for helping out with the Spring issue of Sanctuary Snippets. The newsletter file **Spring issue text** and the photos are on the intranet. The Newsletter should be two pages. Please add a Table of Contents on the front page. I am happy for you to change the size of photos or move articles around to get a good fit.
>
> Please send me a copy of the final result before it is distributed. Thanks.
>
> Roger.

- In a new document, create the following banner headline for your newsletter.
  Use the Complex Style and Procedures guide to identify the font style.
  Use the *Logo.wmf* (*1 About this Organisation / Standard files*).

Sanctuary Snippets
Environmental Challenges Australia Newsletter — Spring Issue

- Underneath the banner, insert a section break and change to a three column layout.

- **Insert** the document *Spring issue text.doc* (*2 Managing Members and Events / Historical Publications / Old newsletters*) directly into the three column section.

- Change the font and size of the body text and add some paragraph spacing to make the text easier to read.

- Select the heading: Warrawong News
  To make the heading stand out, put it in a single cell table. Remove the table border and add shading to the cell.
  Format the heading's font and size to a suitable style.

- Create a Heading1 style based on the heading Warrawong News and apply this style to the headings: Little River News, Hello from Hanson and Competition.

- **Save** your newsletter into your *Membership* folder using a suitable filename.

- **Insert** the pictures *Jodie.bmp, Sunset.bmp,* and the *Long nosed Potoroo* (*2 Managing Members and Events / ECA photos*). (Jodie is the winner of the competition and the Sunset is for the night walks.) Size and position the pictures to look attractive with text flowing around them.

- Add captions to each picture. Refer to the Complex Styles and Procedures Guide for general rules on captions.

- Add the following footer with a top border, the page number and total number of pages.

For more info about our Earth Sanctuaries, visit our website on www.challenges.com.au

- On the first page of the newsletter, using WordArt, add the text 'Newsletter' with a grey colour.
- **Save** your changes.
- **Close** your newsletter.

Skills challenge 6

The last part of the membership renewal is the receipting process. Each month you collect the receipted file from the company intranet. You create a letter that includes a receipt for all Australian members. (International members will require a different receipt.) Then merge it to your receipted file to create individual receipts.

- Create a new document using the ECA letter template to be used as the receipt letter to members. Add the following text, leaving room at the top of the letter for date and address information.

Dear

Thank you for becoming a member of Environmental Challenges Australia. We hope you will enjoy a year of visits and value at our award winning earth sanctuaries.

Your membership entitles you to free entry to our earth sanctuaries and a reduced rate on our tours and at our retail outlets. Just look for the "Member Deals".

Yours faithfully,

(key in your name)

- At the bottom of the letter, add the following receipt.

Environmental Challenges Australia

Membership Number:

Name:

Address:

Suburb: State:

Receipt Number: Date of Issue:

- Separate the letter and the receipt with a broken line and insert the scissors symbol from the Wingdings font.

  ✂ --

- **Save** your letter into your *Membership* folder using a suitable filename.
- Perform a spelling and grammar check on your document.
- **Preview**, print and proof read your document for accuracy.
- Correct any minor errors and save your changes.

Next, you create a merge document.

- Identify the data file as the Excel file that you downloaded from the company intranet: *ECA receipted members.xls* (*2 Managing Members and Events / Membership*).
  Select **Sheet1**.
- Select only records where the Country is Australia and sort the records by Last Name.
- Insert an address block at the top of the letter.
  Match your data's fields to the address fields.
- Insert today's date, using a field.
- Delete the text "Dear" and add a suitable greeting.
  For invalid names display: Dear Member
- Insert suitable merge fields to all the receipt fields, including the Membership number.
- **Save** your changes.
- **Preview** an output document using records from your data source.
- **Merge** the letter to a new document. After viewing your merge output, close without saving.

Next, you create labels to accompany your letters.

- Create a new document to hold your label layout and commence a mail merge for labels.
- Select the label size as specified in the Complex Style and Procedures guide
- Use the file *ECA receipted members.xls* as your data source.
  Select **Sheet1**.
- Select only records where the Country is Australia and sort the records by Last Name.
- Ensure that suitable fields are included in an address block and replicate for all labels.
- Once you have created your label layout, save it into your *Membership* folder using a suitable filename.
- **Merge** the labels to a new document. After viewing your merged output, close it without saving.

Skills challenge 7

As part of your role as Finance Manager – Subscriptions and Shares, you also compile the Environmental Challenges Australia's Annual Report, which is issued to shareholders.

- **Create** a new document. On the first page create a title page for the report, including ECA's, name and address and the report title.
- **Insert** the pictures *Logo.wmf* (*1 About this Organisation / Standard files*) and *Quoll.bmp* (*2 Managing Members and Events / ECA photos*) and position them appropriately.
- Note: A possible appearance of the title page is shown at the end of this skills challenge.

Next, you insert some text files and create your report styles.

- On the second page, type the heading: Table of Contents
- On the third page, insert the word document *Our vision.doc* (*1 About this Organisation / General information*).
- Select the heading: Our vision and create a Heading1 style with a top border. Refer to the Complex Style and Procedures guide for more information on the heading font, size and paragraph spacing. An example of the heading is below:

Our Vision

- Change the Normal style to include a paragraph spacing of 6pt before, then apply the new Normal style to the body text.
  Refer to the Complex Style and Procedures guide for more information on the font and size for body text.
- On the next new page, type the heading: From the Managing Director
- Apply the Heading 1 style to the new heading.
- **Insert** the word document *MD address.doc* (*1 About this Organisation/ General information*) then apply the Normal style to the body text.
- On the next new page, type the Heading 1: Review of Operations
- Under the new heading, type the Heading 2: Overview
- **Format** the Heading 2 style to your choice, refer to the Complex Style and Procedures guide for information on the heading font, size and paragraph spacing.
- On the next page type the Heading 2: Financial Statements
- Under the heading Financial Statements type the Heading 3: Profit and Loss Statement.
- **Format** the Heading 3 style to your choice. Refer to the Complex Style and Procedures Guide for information on the standard heading font, size and paragraph spacing.

Next, you copy financial information into the report.

- Under the Heading 3: Profit and Loss Statement, copy and paste from the *ECA financial statements.xls*
  Sheet: **Profit/Loss** the range of cells **A3:C16**

- Key in the Heading 3: Finance Statement.
- **Copy** and paste from the *ECA financial statements.xls*
  Sheet: **Finance** the range of cells **A3:C21**
- Key in the Heading 3: Cash Flow Statement.
- **Copy** and paste from the *ECA financial statements.xls*
  Sheet: **Cash flow** the range of cells **A3:C22**
- **Save** your annual report into your *Shareholders* folder using a suitable filename.

Next, you improve the look of your report, increasing the white space, adding a header and footer and pictures.

- Ensure your page orientation is portrait and set your top, bottom, left and right margins all to 4 cm.
- Design your report so that the first page has no header or footer. Begin your footer on page 2 of the report (Our Vision) starting the page numbering at 1. Make the footer display on the right side of odd pages and on the left side of even pages. The footer text is:

  Environmental Challenges Australia 1

- Begin your header on page 2 of the report (Our Vision). Make the header display on the right side of odd pages and on the left side of even pages. The header text is:

  Annual Report

- With the page numbering continuing through the document, insert a section break at the topic: Review of Operations and change the header to:

  Annual Report - Financial

- In the topic "Our Vision" add the photo of *John.bmp* (2 *Managing Members and Events/ ECA photos*). Add a caption to the picture. Refer to the Complex Style and Procedures Guide for more information on caption standards.
- Size and position the picture to look attractive on the page with the text flowing around it.
- In the topic "From the Managing Director" add the photo of *Janet.bmp* (2 *Managing Members and Events / ECA photos*). Add a caption to the picture. If necessary crop the picture and/or position it so that the Managing Director information fits on two pages.
- **Save** your changes.
- Finally, you add numbering to your headings and create an Index and Table of Contents for your report.
- With your cursor on a heading, apply the outline numbering displayed here (1, 1.1, 1.1.1).
- Select at least two key words on each page of the report and mark them as index entries.
- Add a final page to your report. Add the Heading 1: Index then generate the index.
- On the second page of your report, generate a table of contents.

- **Save** your changes.
- **Close** your report.

Skills challenge 8

You receive the following email from the Finance Director.

> Hi, I've put together the text for the Review of Operations chapter of the Annual Report. Could you please add a Profit and Loss chart and a Revenue chart which are linked back to the *ECA financial statements.xls* file. Thanks.
> - Doug

- **Open** your annual report document.
  Under the heading: Review of Operations, Overview insert the document: *Review of operations.doc* (2 Managing Members and Events/ Operational Information)
- Delete the additional heading and format the text to the Normal style of the report.
- Mark at least two index entries in the new text.
- **Save** your changes.

Next, you insert the following footnotes for clarification.

- Under the heading Overview, insert footnote 1 at the end of the first paragraph of the new text and insert footnote 2 at the end of the third paragraph. The footnotes are:

[1] See the Financial Statements in the Annual Report for more detail.
[2] Full details of fauna under the Company's care are available from Environmental Challenges Australia's head office.

- **Save** your changes.

Finally, you insert two linked charts.

- **Copy** the Profit and Loss chart from the *ECA financial statements.xls* on the Sheet: **Profit/Loss**.
  Paste the chart.
- **Copy** the Revenue chart from the *ECA financial statements.xls* on the Sheet: **Profit/Loss**.
  Paste the chart.
- Size and position the charts to look attractive on the page with the text flowing around them.
- **Save** your changes.
- **Preview** your report and check its layout.
- **Close** your report.

Skills challenge 9

- This year, to attract more shareholders to the Annual General Meeting (AGM), you are including in the Annual Report information on a free tour that will be offered to all shareholders before the AGM.
- **Open** the Annual Report document. Locate a suitable position for the new page.
- Create a new page, and add the Heading 1: Shareholder Benefits
- Key in the following text:

> Being a shareholder in Environmental Challenges Australia offers a number of benefits. Every shareholder is entitled to a **20% discount** on most goods and services at our Earth sanctuaries, excluding food.
>
> Throughout the year we offer special Shareholder Events. These events allow members to view ECA projects and add their input. You also receive a quarterly newsletter to keep in touch with what is happening at the sanctuaries and new developments.
>
> This year we are offering a **free** Night tour of our Warrawong sanctuary before the Annual General Meeting. Come and see our wonderful native animals in the '"wild". The tour starts from the Warrawong Reception at sunset and lasts for one hour. Tea and coffee will then be served in our Conference Centre prior to the commencement of the Annual General Meeting.

- Mark at least two index entries in the new text.
- **Save** your changes.
- Perform a spelling and grammar check on your new text.

Next, you add a map of the tour.

- Use Drawing tools to draw the following map.

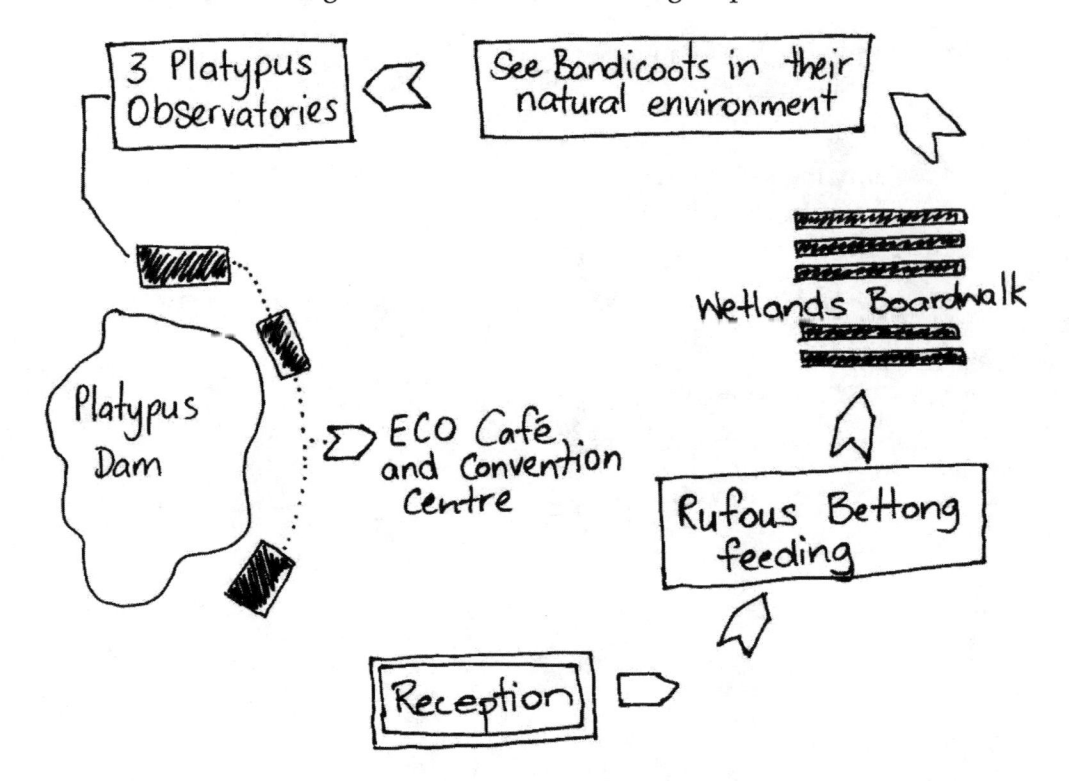

- **Save** your changes.
- Next, update your Table of Contents and your Index to include the Review of Operations and Shareholder information.
- **Save** your changes.

Finally, review your report.

- **Preview**, print and proof read your document for accuracy.
- Check your report thoroughly. Make any adjustments to make the report look professional and its design enhances the readability of the document.
- **Save** your report.
- **Close** your report.

Skills challenge 10

You use the ECA letter template all the time. It needs improving. You add a footer to the letter in line with company standards. To speed up your keying, you create an AutoText entry for Environmental Challenges Australia and an AutoText entry for your closing.

- **Open** the document template *ECA letter template.dot*
- Note: You previously identified where your templates are stored and downloaded the template to this location.
- Display the document's **footer** and insert the following footer with a top border. Check the Complex Style and Procedures Guide for the font and size of the footer.

---
www.challenges.com.au
ACN: 078 809 659

- Create an **AutoText** entry of ECA for Environmental Challenges Australia and store it in the ECA letter template.
- As other people use this template, create an **AutoText** entry for closing your letters and store it in the ECA letter template.

```
Yours sincerely


your name
Finance Manager – Subscriptions and Shares
```

- **Save** your changes and **close** your template.
- Finally, check the changes to your template.
- Create a new document using the ECA letter template.
  Check the new footer displays. Test your two new AutoText entries – one for ECA and one for your closing.
- **Close** your document without saving.

Skills challenge 11

- You receive the following voice mail from the Promotions manager.

> "As part of promoting the earth sanctuaries, could you send out a generic letter to all our shareholders advising them of their discount?
>
> Thanks."

Create a new document using the ECA letter template.

- Insert today's date.
- Remove the recipient address information at the top of the letter.
- Add the letter text below.
  Use your ECA AutoText entry to enter the full company name and your closing AutoText entry for the end of the letter.

Dear Shareholder

Your shareholders discount

As a shareholder in Environmental Challenges Australia, you are entitled to a 20% discount on most goods and services, where no other discount applies. This discount is limited to Shareholders only and applies to the Shareholder and their immediate family.

Your savings can really add up! For example if you decided to stay with us at Warrawong for the weekend:

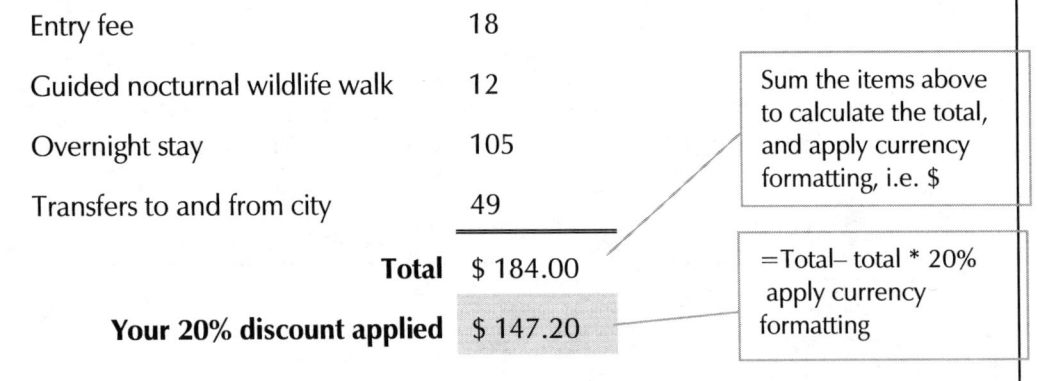

Entry fee	18
Guided nocturnal wildlife walk	12
Overnight stay	105
Transfers to and from city	49
Total	$ 184.00
Your 20% discount applied	$ 147.20

(Sum the items above to calculate the total, and apply currency formatting, i.e. $)

*(=Total– total * 20% apply currency formatting)*

We hope you will visit one of Environmental Challenges Australia's award winning sanctuaries soon.

Yours sincerely

(your name)
Finance Manager – Subscriptions and Shares

- **Save** your letter into your *Shareholders* folder using a suitable filename.
- **Close** your document.

Skills challenge 12

Replying to correspondence takes up much of your time. You decide to create a letter template, based on the ECA letter template, with fields that prompt for the letter information. You also create three separate text documents to answer the three most commonly asked questions: How do I become a member; How can I volunteer; and, When are the open days?

First, you create a new template based on the ECA letter template.

- Create a new document based on the *ECA letter template.dot*.
- Leave the date as you will fix this later.
- At each address line, use the FILLIN field to replace the text with a prompt.
- Also put a FILLIN field to prompt after "Dear" and a FILLIN field to prompt for the subject line.
- Leaving some space to insert some letter text, add the letter closing using your key combination.
- **Save** your document as a **template** called *Finance letter template*. (Note that everything in the ECA letter template, including the AutoText and Key Assignments will be in your Finance letter template.)
- Leave your template open, so that your Key assignments and AutoText commands are available.

Next, create some text documents that can be inserted when required.

- **Create** a new blank document (based on the Normal template) and key in the following text.

Becoming a member of Environmental Challenges Australia helps ensure that the land within the sanctuaries is preserved as it has been for thousands of years. Our conservation successes continually draw people from around the world.

Your membership entitles you to a free quarterly newsletter, keeping you up to date on the latest developments and new attractions at our award winning sanctuaries.

It also gives you free entry to our earth sanctuaries and a reduced rate on our tours and at our retail outlets. We hope you will come and visit our sanctuaries, participate in our guided adventure walks, our education programs or enjoy our unique accommodation and restaurant facilities.

The cost of a Membership is $50.00. Please complete the attached Membership form and send it with your membership fee to Environmental Challenges Australia.

- **Save** your document as *Become member.doc* in your *Standard files* folder.
- Perform a spelling and grammar check on your document and proof read your document for accuracy.
- **Save** any changes then **close** your document.
- **Create** a new blank document (based on the Normal template) and key in the following text.

> Our growing group of volunteers has made a huge difference to our sanctuaries. All volunteers are required to be members of Environmental Challenges Australia (ECA). Members are covered by insurance for volunteering opportunities for work carried out in ECA sanctuaries.
>
> Each month volunteers work at Warrawong on maintenance, weeding and planting. At Little River, volunteers assisted in upgrading an area for Quoll breeding facilities. At Waratah Park many new volunteers have been busy getting the new sanctuary ready for opening.
>
> Come and join the fun and help our environment too! Ring Julie on 02 1122 5555 to volunteer.

- **Save** your document as *Volunteering.doc* in your *Standard files* folder.
- Perform a spelling and grammar check on your document and proof read your document for accuracy.
- **Save** any changes then **close** your document.
- **Create** a new blank document (based on the Normal template) and key in the following text.

> A great way to find out more about Environmental Challenges Australia is to come to one of our open days. For one day each year our sanctuaries are open to the public, free of charge. There are also special events which have free entry as well. This year, at the opening day of our new Waratah Park earth sanctuary, entry will be free.
>
> Here at Environmental Challenges Australia we believe that all Victorians should have the opportunity to see its native wildlife in the wild. Therefore at the reintroduction of Eastern Quolls to Little River Earth Sanctuary, entry will be free. Join the Wildlife Adventure Walks to see these beautiful yet unknown marsupials just as the early explorers did, wild and free.
>
> **The opening days for this year are**:
> Little River   6 April
> Waratah Park 12 May – Opening Day
> Warrawong 19 September
> Little River   15 October – Quoll release
> Hanson Bay 24 October

- **Save** your document as *Open days.doc* in your *Standard files* folder.
- Perform a spelling and grammar check on your document and proof read your document for accuracy.
- **Save** any changes then **close** your document.
- **Close** your template.
- Finally, you test your template using data you received on a note from the Finance Director.

> Could you please let Mrs Thomas, 14 Spring Street, Springville SA know how to become a volunteer.
>
> Cheers, Doug

- Create a new document based on the template *Finance letter template.dot*.
- Complete the FILLIN prompts.
- Insert the file *Volunteering.doc*.
- At the top of your document, insert the correct date.
- **Save** your letter as *Thomas Springville.doc* in the *Membership* folder.
- **Preview** your document.
- **Close** your document.

Skills challenge 13

Since your enquiry from Mrs Thomas, you realise that you need to speed up generating your letter, so that it can be done whilst the member is on the phone. You decide to create macros to:

- insert today's date in the correct format;
- insert the required text file;
- print the letter; and
- print the membership form (created on page 158).

- **Open** the document template *Finance letter template.dot*.
- When you record your macros ensure that they are stored in the Finance letter template. Assign a meaningful name for the macro – it will become the tool tip for your button, e.g. OpenDay.
- **Record** a macro that will select the 'Date' text at the top of the letter and insert today's date in the required format *without* the option to Update automatically. Refer to the Complex Style and Procedures Guide for the correct date format for letters.
- **Record** a macro to insert the file *Become member.doc*
- **Record** a macro to insert the file *Open days.doc*
- **Record** a macro to insert the file *Volunteering.doc*
- **Record** a macro to open, print, then close your Membership form, stored in the **Members** folder.

Next, you test your template. You receive the following voice mail:

> "Hi, my name is Kerry Whyte and I would like to become a member of Environmental Challenges Australia. Could you send me an application form? I live at 44 Hilly Road, Hilldale 4040.
>
> Thank you."

- Create a new document based on the Finance letter template.
- Respond to the FILLIN prompts.

- Insert the date.
- Insert the membership information via BecomeMember macro.
- **Save** your letter as *Whyte Hilldale.doc* in the *Membership* folder.
- Use your MembershipForm macro to print the form.
- **Print** your letter.
- **Close** your letter.

Assessment tasks

This chapter contains realistic Assessment tasks. They are designed to provide a final check of your ability to design and develop complex text documents through a number of real world scenarios.

Output from Assessment tasks should be submitted to your teacher or assessor for review. Consult with your teacher or assessor as to how and when they require completed work to be submitted, i.e. emailed as attachments or in a printed format.

Assessment task 1

The Personnel Manager says that a document has been posted on the company intranet re health and safety standards which she wants you to review.

- Locate and open the document: Company health and safety policy.doc (1 About this Organisation/ Standard files).
- Print and review the document. Ensure that your workspace and work organisation meet company standards, and that you remind yourself of energy and resource conservation techniques.

You have received the following email from the General Manager.

> The Board of Directors has decided to release an additional 100,000,000 shares in order to raise capital to fund the purchase of several parcels of land. These locations will, after some restoration of the habitat, be established as wildlife sanctuaries. The share price will be set within 5 per cent of the share price at June 25. As at today, the share price was $0.79.
>
> I need you to generate the documents associated with releasing this share offer to the public. Initially I need a letter outlining the new share offer to existing members. Use the letter (Initial share offer.doc (*3 Shareholders*) used for the initial share float as a starting point – it's on the company intranet, in the Keeping Members Informed folder under Share float. Please update the letter to reflect the new release as well as appropriately incorporating the information I have supplied in the previous paragraph.
>
> The letter then needs to be sent to our existing members – details of which are in the spreadsheet ECA membership.xls (Members Aus sheet). Use this information to generate personalised letters as well as labels according to the company standard.
>
> Please show me a draft of one of the letters before they are all printed.
>
> Thanks

- Check with your teacher or assessor for the timeline on this task.

- Create a new letter following the consistent corporate image based on the information supplied by the General Manager.
- Ensure the letter is accurate and error free.
- Save the letter using a suitable name in an appropriate folder.
- Update the letter to include the merge information. Use Help if required.
- Print off one of the letters. One possible output appears at the end of this task.
- Create a document containing labels to accompany the letters.
- Ensure the labels are accurate and error free.
- Save the labels document using a suitable name.
- Submit your completed documents to your teacher or assessor for assessment.

Assessment task 2

In response to receiving a draft of your letter to shareholders, the General Manager has left you the following voicemail.

> "Thanks for the draft of the shareholder letter. We have received some advice from our Legal Department. Until some paperwork is processed in South Australia and Victoria, we cannot send the letters to these members. As a result, just generate letters and labels for all members except those residing in these two states. For quality control, the letters and labels should both be ordered by last name.
>
> Thanks again"

- Check with your teacher or assessor for the timeline on this task.
- Modify the letter and label documents created in the previous assessment task as indicated in the voicemail above.
- Save your changes to both documents.
- Generate the letters and labels as required.
- Review the output checking its accuracy.
- For the purposes of assessment, save both output documents using suitable names.
- Submit your completed documents to your teacher or assessor for assessment.

Assessment task 3

Following instructions, you have made contact with the Legal Department regarding the prospectus to be included with the share offer mail out.

During your discussions regarding the prospectus work to be performed, you noted that a draft prospectus *Prospectus text.doc* is currently on the company intranet – *3 Shareholders/Share float* folder. It currently contains text but requires full formatting.

- Check with your teacher or assessor for the timeline on this task.
- Improve the appearance of the document ensuring the design and layout is consistent, and applying the report layout standards across the report.

- To achieve this improvement, ensure you consider: applying heading styles; adding a table of contents; adding headers and footers; adding graphics (with captions where appropriate); using columns; and adding an index.

- Note: A picture of Greg Conners can be found on the intranet – (2 *Managing Members and Events/ ECA photos*).

- Incorporate data from a number of external sources into the prospectus:
  - In the Managing Director's message, insert a chart from the spreadsheet *ECA financial statements.xls* (ProfitLoss sheet).
  - Insert the contents of the document *Shareholder information.doc* (3 *Shareholders*)
  - Under the Our Performance heading, include a link to all data in *ECA financial statements.xls* on the Assets sheet.
  - Under the Directors' shareholding heading, copy or embed the data from *Directors share holding.xls*. (1 *About this Organisation/ Staff files*)

- Save the revised document using a suitable filename.

- Print and proof read the prospectus for accuracy, adherence to organisational standards and readability.

- Make any adjustments as required.

- Save your changes.

- Submit your completed document to your teacher or assessor for assessment.

Assessment task 4

The Marketing Manager has requested you create a form for individuals responding to the share offer to complete in Word. During your discussion, you make the following notes:

> Existing form only available in Adobe PDF format on the intranet – Share application form.pdf, (3 *Shareholders*), Standard forms heading – so will need to create a new form from scratch.
>
> Update form using online facilities where available, e.g. drop downs for state, amount of shares and payment methods. Include default text where useful.
>
> Include a check box at the bottom of the form for if they don't want to receive further mail outs. Also ensure the postcode is captured – it was missing from the printed version.

- Check with your teacher or assessor for the timeline on this task.

- Redevelop the form for completion online in Word, ensuring it contains prompts for all the necessary information. Also ensure the resulting document meets the task requirements and corporate guidelines. Use Help if required.

- Note: A possible solution appears below.

- Save the form using a suitable filename.

- Test your new form.

- Print and proof read the form. Ensure it is accurate and error free.
- Write a procedure on how to use this form and save it in your folder: *1 About this Organisation, Standard files.*
- Print and follow your procedure and present to your assessor for assessment.
- Present the functionality of your newly created form to your teacher or assessor for assessment.

Assessment task 5

You have also been asked to prepare a Shareholding certificate that will be issued to all new shareholders.

- Check with your teacher or assessor for the timeline on this task.
- Develop a template for this statement. Consider using fill-in fields and a table formula (to calculate the current share value). A possible initial layout and design appears over the page.
- If able, automate the template so the current value can be automatically updated (regardless of your cursor position) by a button on the Quick Access Toolbar or a keystroke combination. Consider bookmarking the cell to help with the formula update.
- Add an attractive seal to the bottom right of the statement, indicating the company is an 'ECO Certified Company'. Consider using a variety of drawing tools or WordArt to enhance the certificate.
- Write a procedure on how to use this form and save it in your folder: *1 About this Organisation, Standard files.*
- Print and follow your procedure and present to your assessor for assessment.
- Present the functionality of your newly created template to your teacher or assessor for assessment.

Challenges with

Manage Business Document Design & Development

Skills Challenges & Assessment tasks

The following *challenges* and *tasks* are undertaken by a student on his or her own at the completion of the course.

Creating a working area

In the following exercises you create a number of files. To ensure these are efficiently organised, you need to have a suitable location in which to store the files.

There are also supplied files that can be found in a folder under the student exercises downloaded from our website <www.tilde.com.au> called Manage Business Document Design & Development (within your student files for Design and Develop Complex Text Documents). Throughout these challenges and assessment tasks you will be asked to open, edit and create various folders and files.

Skills challenge 1

The documents generated by individuals within your organisation typically follow standards. However these standards have only ever been communicated verbally or noted down within departments.

In this challenge you review a number of generated documents (following the accepted standards) as well as review existing standards used by one department. All documents have been published on the intranet. You use this information to prepare a standards document satisfying the organisation's requirements.

- Locate the following folders and documents from the downloaded student exercises folder: *Manage Business Document Design & Development*.
- Open the following documents from the *4 Internal Docs Archive* folder.
    - *04-08-12 Correspondence JJP.doc*
    - *04-12-15 Memo re J Simms annual leave JS.doc*
    - *03-12-20 Fax re draft report FW.doc*
- Locate the folder: *5 Corporate Comms Group/Standard files* and open *Comms dept style guide.pdf* (partially developed) and *Printing policy.doc*.
- Locate the folder: *6 Info Systems Group/ Data Storage*. Open the document: *User data storage standards.doc*.
- Review the contents of each document.
- Based on these documents, prepare a document detailing the company's existing documentation standards. Headings/categories in the document should at least cover:
    - Company logo and associated text
    - Standard fonts for text and headings
    - Page margins and text alignment
    - Accepted document formats
    - Document naming and storage conventions
    - Standard documents – location, description and samples
    - Printing.
- Save your document using a suitable filename and location.

You need to ensure that current and future technology capabilities within your organisation have been taken into consideration in your documentation standards.

- Locate the folder: *6 Info Systems Group /Capabilities*. Open the document *Technology standards.doc*.
- Review the document.
- Update your documentation standards appropriately.
- Save your changes.
- Close the document.

Skills challenge 2

The Communications Manager has left you the following voicemail:

> "Some information has been posted on the intranet which will be the basis for a hand-out I am developing. Can you edit it for me (*2 Managing Members and Events/ Educational Material folder, Australian wildlife.doc*). Format attractively (within your newly published company guidelines). The document will be published in colour, so use it where you feel it can be beneficial.
>
> Thanks"

- Locate the appropriate folder, then open the document.
- Apply heading styles to attractively format the document while ensuring a consistent appearance. Modify the styles as appropriate to ensure they reflect the standards you have published in your style and procedures guide.
- Update the normal style to reflect the standard font and size. Ensure you improve the readability (e.g. by adding white space between paragraphs).
- Improve the appearance of, then apply styles to standardise each occurrence of:
   - pictures and their captions;
   - scientific name (excluding any other related text);
   - lists of locations; and
   - their status.

  Note: Styles other than paragraph styles may better suit in some of these cases. The captioning style should also always follow the picture style.
- Save your changes.
- Print then close your document.

Skills challenge 3

Despite your initial intranet research, you have begun to notice a variety of formats and designs of faxes being sent by company staff appearing on fax machines across the company's offices. There should be just the one standard fax document in use.

In an effort to bring everyone back to using the one template, you first recognise that you need to identify why they have been varying from the standard. As a result, you decide to interview a number of key contacts throughout the company. A summary of your notes from these discussions is shown below.

Skills Challenges & Assessment tasks

> **Meeting 1**
>
> Employees in this department use Word (and computers) only occasionally. As a result they sometimes struggle to use the template as it was intended. The template needs to be made easier to use as well as have a basic instruction sheet that can be kept by the computer for easy reference when users need to generate a fax.

> **Meeting 2**
>
> Department staff don't believe the current standard reflects the company image adequately, so they have tended to try and customise the template's appearance individually. More of the image used on the marketing material should be used.

> **Meeting 3**
>
> The department has a number of staff who work in remote areas relying mainly on the resources on their laptop. They tend only to have a need to connect to the company server for email etc. every few days. Initial distribution of standard company documents didn't consider these users, so at times they have generated their own templates on the run.

- Review your notes above. Identify at least four actions you could take to address the problems with the use – or lack of use – of the company fax template.

    _____
    _____
    _____
    _____
    _____
    _____

    Open the current marketing brochure *Challenges marketing.pdf* (*5 Corporate Comms Group/ External publications*). Review it against the layout and design of the fax you reviewed in the Skills challenge 1.

- Develop a new fax template from scratch, incorporating the marketing brochure design into the new layout.

    Note: Only layout needs to be added at this stage, as automation (including fill-in fields) and instructional notes will be developed in a later Skills challenge.

- Save the template with an appropriate title and location.

- Create a new document using your fax template, completing basic information to test it.

- Print the test fax.

- Close the document without saving.

Skills challenge 4

While the contents and design of the new standard company fax are being finalised, you decide to also examine the distribution procedures for standard templates. You identify that a document does not exist or cannot be located on the network and decide to prepare one.

- Prepare a document detailing the processes involved in distributing new standard templates and withdrawing/deleting any old versions.

    You may want to consider using the following headings:
    - Template storage location(s) for general use
    - Master template storage location
    - Communicating changes across the organisation

- Save your document using a suitable filename and location.
- Print then close your document.

Skills challenge 5

Following receipt of your updated Australian wildlife document, the Communications Manager sent you the following email:

> The new formatting looks great! I realise that I will be adding details of a number of animals to this document. Can you do something to make entering the details of each new animal more straightforward?
>
> I will also be creating similar documents for different animal groupings in the future, so what can you do to make this easier for me?
>
> Having easy access to just the styles I need to use in this document would be great too?
>
> Just to make sure I don't do anything incorrectly, as I develop this and other similar documents over the coming days, can you give me some instructions on how I should use the document.
>
> Thanks

- Upon reviewing the Communication Manager's requests, what items or documents do you identify need to be prepared or created to best satisfy the requirements?

    _____
    _____
    _____
    _____
    _____
    _____
    _____

- Develop these solutions, ensuring any documents created are saved with suitable filenames.

- Write a procedure for the Communications Manager to easily update documents with styles. Where appropriate, use Screenshots or diagrams to help others visually. Save with an appropriate title and location.

Skills challenge 6

The Communications Manager has left you a voicemail relating to the documents you have under development from the previous skills challenge.

> "I have just received an email from head office stating that standard documents should only have one space following a full stop. I think I often use two. If you are able to, can you please add a macro to the wildlife document/template you have under development to search for two spaces, then replace this with only one space. If you are not able to do this, can you please search help or online for some possible solutions to the problem as editing all the documents could be time consuming.
>
> Having undergone this final check, the document also needs to be printed to a file – the format required by the external printers. Can you add this process to the end of the macro?
>
> It would be great if you could add this functionality to the quick access toolbar so I don't forget that it's there – you had better also update the instructions you are developing for me.
>
> Thanks"

- Record a macro to be stored in the template you created in the previous skills challenge to satisfy the Communication Manager's request. Research help or online if you have trouble.

- Add the additional functionality requested, updating the accompanying instructions at the same time.

- Email your solutions as attachments to your teacher or assessor with a covering note requesting the Communications Manager test the template and all of its functionality to ensure that it fully meets their requirements.

- In light of the information provided in the voicemail, what should be added to or updated in the style and procedures guide?

  _____
  _____
  _____

- Record these changes to the style and procedures guide document.

Skills challenge 7

Continuing the redevelopment of your fax template begun in Skills challenge 3, you decide to automate the way information is entered into the addressing details for the fax.

- To the template created in Skills challenge 3, insert fill-in fields to help with completion of the address lines.
- Insert appropriate fields for Date and Pages to display these values automatically.
- Save your changes, then close the template.
- Create a new document from your fax template and test it.
- Close the document without saving.
- Prepare a training sheet explaining how basic users should use the template.
- Save the document using a suitable filename.
- Using your training sheet and template, test the materials and template on another individual with basic Word knowledge.
- Gather any relevant feedback, incorporating the changes into both the materials and the template where appropriate.

Skills challenge 8

As sites are identified, ECA plans to organise individuals to help clear rubbish and introduced species from each location. Subsequently, local native plants will be re-established as part of the Bush Buddies program. To help gather volunteers, booths will be set up at local shopping centres and schools.

You have been asked to develop a paper form for each volunteer to complete to help ensure that each day is effectively planned.

In a briefing session with one of the key organisers, you made the following notes:

> We require contact details for each volunteer, e.g. address/ phone/email in case they need to be contacted if the day is changed.
>
> Make request for volunteers to identify specialist skills that we can make better use of, including: arborists, labourers, landscapers, nursery staff, and those with access to related equipment and supplies, e.g. tip truck, bobcat.
>
> Booths may be seeking volunteers for more than one location or day. An area needs to be included for individuals to nominate the location and day they are volunteering to work as well as their expected hours of availability.

- Using these notes, identify content for the form.
- Order the content appropriately.
- On the following page, sketch out a design, ensuring the appropriate company document standards are adhered to.
- Develop the design in Word.
- Save the design as a template using a suitable filename.

- Preview, print and proof read your form for accuracy.
- Complete the printed form using your own personal details to check its ease of use.
- In order to further test your design, provide printed copies of the form to at least four other individuals, asking them to complete the form using their own details.
- Review the completed documents, identifying any areas you believe require amendments.
- Ask the individuals for any comments they may have regarding the form's ease of use.
- Make any appropriate adjustments to fine tune your form's design.
- Save your changes and close the document.
- On a scrap piece of paper, sketch your design.

Skills challenge 9

As part of the Bush Buddies program, you want to review the paper form developed in the previous skills challenge with a view to saving both on paper and on the time required to enter the data. If a few PCs could be incorporated into the information booth for volunteers to enter their details directly, these savings could be achieved.

As a result, you decide to redevelop the form for online entry in Word.

- Given the different way in which you plan to use the form, review your design from the previous Skills challenge.
- Redevelop the design in Word, this time accommodating features for efficient completion within Word.
- Save the design as a template using a suitable filename.
- Preview, print and proof read your form for accuracy.
- Complete the form in Word using your own personal details to check its ease of use.
- In order to further test your design, ask at least two other individuals to complete the form with their details in Word.
- Review the completed documents, identifying any areas you believe require amendments.
- Ask the individuals for any comments they may have regarding the form's ease of use.
- Make any appropriate adjustments to fine tune your form's design.
- Save your changes.
- Close the document.

You now want to consider other ways in which Word allows you to complete a form electronically in order to better evaluate how advances in technology may improve efficiencies in future.

- Investigate using Help or the internet on other format(s) in which a form can be developed in Word.
- Briefly describe the format and process, particularly key differences that set the process apart from creating a form for completion in Word.

Skills challenge 10

You have been asked to assist in compiling Environmental Challenges Australia's Annual Report. During a meeting to discuss the contents of the report, you made the following notes:

Source documents on the intranet (student exercises folder):

- Our vision.doc and MD address.doc (*1 About this Organisation / General information*).
- ECA financial statements.xls (*3 Shareholders / Share float*).
- John.bmp and Janet.bmp (*2 Managing Members and Events / ECA photos*).
- Review of operations.doc (*3 Shareholders / Operational information*)
- Other fauna images from Clip Art

Report structure:

- Cover page
- Table of contents
- Our vision – insert Our vision.doc and photo of John
- From the Managing Director – insert MD address.doc and photo of Janet
- Review of operations → Insert downloaded doc contents

    subheads: Overview, Financial statements

    further subheads

    Profit and loss
    Financial statement
    Cash flow statement

    Include from downloaded spreadsheet

    Sheet: Profit/Loss – range A3:C16
    Also include linked P&L and Revenue charts below data

    Sheet: Finance – range A3:C21

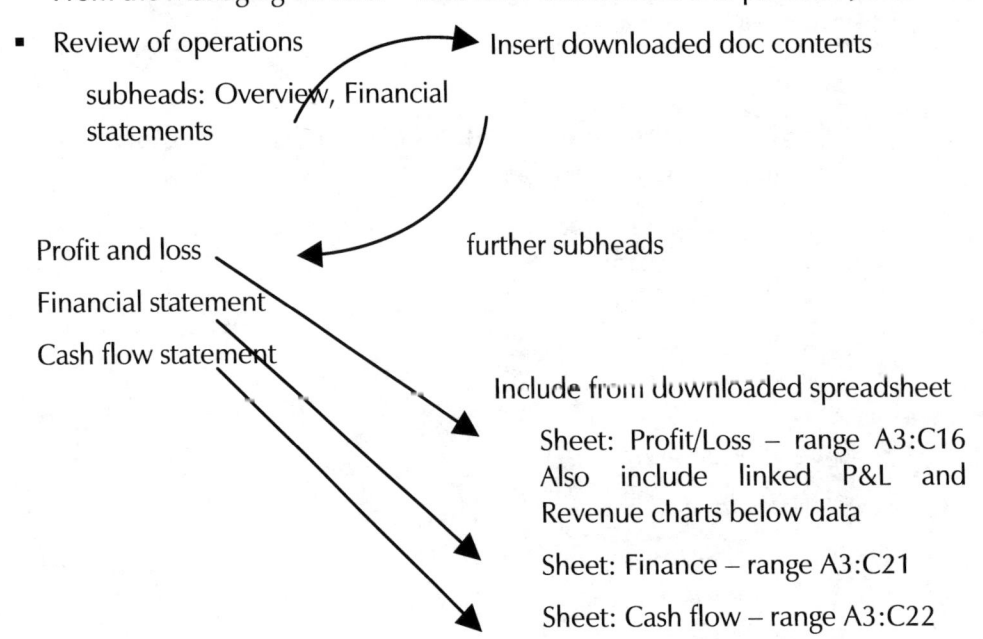

    Sheet: Cash flow – range A3:C22

> - Standard header/footer to start after the table of contents (starting at page 1). Header to read Annual Report (appearing on outside edge of each page). Footer to read Environmental Challenges Australia Ltd on inside edge, with page # of # on outside edge.
> - Index – include relevant keywords throughout report

- Open the required files as recorded in your notes.
- Create a new document for the report, constructing the contents according to your notes. Format it in accordance with the company style and procedures guide you have been developing throughout this course.
- Save your report using a suitable filename and location.
- Preview, proof read and print your report.
- Close your report.

Skills challenge 11

To supplement the standard documents available for use within Word, you have been asked to prepare some sample business cards and With Compliments slips using a desktop publishing application to reflect the company image.

- Using the existing designs as a basis for your design, create a sample business card and With Compliments slip to submit to the Managing Director, reflecting your interpretation of the company image.
- Preview, then print samples of each.
- Save each publication using a suitable filename.
- Close the publications.
- Update your style and procedures guide to indicate the forms that should be used supporting the growing needs of the business.

Skills challenge 12

In Skills challenge 8 you designed a printed form for Bush Buddy volunteers to complete. You also captured the details of a number of individuals during testing.

While further technology will eventually be introduced to capture the data online as volunteers enter it, in the interim the key organiser has asked you to re-enter this data so that it can be used to generate notification letters for the volunteers just to confirm their involvement.

Following your initial discussions, the key organiser has left you the following voicemail.

> "Please create a file to hold the volunteer data. Include in it the four sample sets of data you had from your initial testing of the form. Make sure two different locations are used for the test. I then want to test the process with a basic letter advising each individual of an upcoming regeneration project as well as the skills and/or equipment we have recognised they will be providing on that day.
>
> I will only be generating letters for one location at a time, as at the moment we have only one project per month. I haven't used mail merge in a long time, so once you have tested the process I need you to give me some training in how to generate the letters, including how I can restrict the letters generated to the one event.
>
> Give me a call when you are ready and we can arrange a time to meet.
>
> Thanks"

- Using the forms and data gathered in Skills challenge 8, prepare the required data source.
- Draft a letter incorporating the appropriate information, using various criteria to limit the letters generated to one event location, the time specified, and only including specialist skills and equipment when they have been specified in the data source.

    Note: A sample letter showing where field codes have been used is shown at the end of this challenge.

- Prepare a summary document outlining to the organiser the steps they should perform to complete a merge, given they will change locations each time.
- Save your documents using suitable filenames.
- Provide training and a written procedure to illustrate the process to your teacher or assessor, supporting the demonstration with your explanatory notes. Allow your teacher or assessor to repeat the process without your prompting.

Assessment tasks

Assessment task 1

For an organisation to consistently produce and store standardised, consistent documents and templates, documentation standards need to be put in place that all users must follow. These documentation standards are typically detailed in a document. Throughout this course we have referred to the document as a style and procedures guide.

If you joined a new company and were asked to review existing documentation standards with a view to creating a company style and procedures guide, you would first want to have a document outline. This outline would list the areas you would want covered by the style and procedures guide – to ensure that all aspects of style, standards and company image were adequately addressed. This would be particularly useful if the company lacked any procedures.

In this task, you will prepare such a draft document.

- Check with your teacher or assessor for the timeline on this task.
- Prepare a document listing the areas that should be detailed as a basis for a new style and procedures guide.

- Where appropriate, further detail should be included prompting for specific information, e.g. main heading font, normal text font, standard document types generated, printing standards as well as when internal printing versus external printing facilities should be used.
- You may want to refer to the documents opened as part of Skills challenge 1 for more input.
- Identify topics in the document where developing technology may need to be incorporated, e.g. print quality. This will be appropriate only at the time the contents of the document are finalised.
- Save your document using a suitable filename.
- Submit your completed document to your teacher or assessor for assessment.

Assessment task 2

You have received the following email from the Communications Manager.

> Please design a template to be used to generate each manager's Weekly Management Report. Ensure the presentation compliments other report templates and follows the corporate style guidelines.
>
> Apart from standard document labelling and graphics, the template needs to include the heading categories: Delivered last week; Work in progress; and Scheduled for delivery this week. Information should be entered in bullets under each heading.
>
> Thanks

- Check with your teacher or assessor for the timeline on this task.
- Create a template to satisfy the requirements of this email. Ensure the resulting document follows good document design and layout principles as well as enhances readability and appearance. You should follow the style and procedures guide standards you established during the Skills challenges.
- Save the template using a suitable filename.
- Supply your template to another individual for testing.
- Collect feedback on the document's useability and presentation of information, and incorporates these comments appropriately.
- Present the functionality of your newly created template to your teacher or assessor.

Assessment task 3

The Communications Manager has been drafting an agenda to be used across the company as a standard document for completion online within Word.

Meeting Agenda

Date:	26/02/11	**Time:**	8:00 am–9:30 am	**Location:**	Meeting Rm 1	

Called by: Joshua Fredericks – XYZ Project Manager

Participants: XYZ Project Team

Purpose: Weekly Project Manager's (PMs) meeting

Order of Business

1. Opening of meeting.
2. Apologies.
3. Approval of previous minutes.
4. Agenda Items: Speaker   Duration
   - Unsupported items   SAK   20 mins
   - Standard project plan   HGP   15 mins
   - Departmental status report   RIR   15 mins
5. Any other business.
6. Closing of meeting.

Agenda Distribution

Managing Director (where appropriate)

Department Manager (where appropriate)

Meeting participants

Other interested individuals.

During a meeting with this manager, you note that for meetings there are only four meeting rooms, or alternatively the arranging managers can each use their own offices.

For ease of use, the Communications Manager would also like the process of saving then sending the agenda as an attachment automated as much as possible for the users of the document.

The Communications Manager has also asked for you to prepare a training procedure detailing how to maintain the template, including the release of new versions, allowing him to control the master version of the document in the future.

- Check with your teacher or assessor for the timeline on this task.

- Create a document that contains all the necessary information and automation. Ensure the resulting document suits the needs of the intended audience, is easy to read, and incorporates relevant functionality to allow for efficient production and distribution.
- Save the document using a suitable filename.
- Supply your test document to another individual for testing.
- Collect feedback on the document's useability, incorporating any comments appropriately.
- Prepare the training document to satisfy the Communications Manager's requirements.

    Note: He describes his word processing ability level as a good intermediate user, but lacks knowledge of the more advanced functionality.

- Submit your completed documents to your teacher or assessor for assessment.

Assessment task 4

The Communication's Manager has left you the following voicemail.

> "I released the agenda document you prepared for me onto the network for general use. It has been in use for several weeks now – however I haven't received any feedback from users. Please observe use of the document across a number of individuals as well as documents they have produced to verify its appropriateness and consider any improvements that could be made.
>
> Thanks"

- Check with your teacher or assessor for the timeline on this task.

To satisfy the requirements of this task, you will need to simulate the workplace environment by using at least two individuals to act as workplace users. These individuals should have a reasonable level of competence with a word processor – as well as a degree of familiarity that could be expected with this type of document in a workplace.

- Supply the agenda document to at least two individuals.
- Without your assistance or direct observation, have each individual generate at least two documents using the agenda document.

    Note: You may want to supply sample data (not necessarily following the exact format of the document) to ensure the data entered is realistic.

- While observing, have each individual generate another agenda. Again you may choose to supply sample data. Note any relevant useability issues.
- Review each of the documents produced by your workplace users for any apparent useability problems.
- Discuss with each of your workplace users the document's ease of use and any changes or improvements they might find useful. Note any relevant information as part of the review.
- Prepare a document for the Communications Manager detailing your findings (i.e. user observations and their comments) as well as your

overall recommendations for any proposed amendments to the agenda document seen as useful or appropriate. Ensure you attach copies of the sample forms generated by your workplace users.

- Submit your completed document to your teacher or assessor for assessment.

Assessment task 5

The Managing Director has just announced that the organisation has received international recognition for its environmental work from the world environmental fund. As a result, the organisation is in a position to include a special logo on each of its standard documents.

During a meeting with the Managing Director to discuss the implications on the company's standard documents, you note the following:

> Document regarding guidelines for use of environmental logo – as well as logo on the company intranet – About this Organisation folder under Standard files. ECO logo guidelines.doc and ECO logo.tif.
>
> Update style guide accordingly.
>
> Update weekly management report template firstly for review. Others will be upgraded progressively over the week once MD has approved changes.
>
> Explain procedure for releasing modified templates to Managing Director in an email.
>
> Draft an email to be sent across the organisation regarding the impact of this change to new documents, how existing templates will be replaced, as well as the planned upgrade of templates over the following week. MD will review prior to release.

- Check with your teacher or assessor for the timeline on this task.
- Perform the tasks as recorded in your notes.

    Note: The style guide referred to is the style and procedures guide you created during the Skills challenges. The Weekly Management Report template was created in Assessment task 2.

- Submit your completed documents to your teacher or assessor for assessment.

Assessment task 6

The Managing Director sent you the following email.

> The Directors' Report has been prepared by a temp who was unfamiliar with the company standards. Please reformat it to comply with the ECA standards.
>
> The document could also benefit from a table of contents and an index referencing key terms used. I also want the page numbers of the document to start at 1 on the first page of content following the table of contents – usual footer information to be included.
>
> Under the Financial Statements heading, include the two charts from the Finance sheet of the spreadsheet ECA financial statements.
>
> After the Directors heading and text, add a suitable heading and include the data on the Directors shareholding spreadsheet. You had better make this data linked – in case any changes occur prior to my sign-off.
>
> The files you need can be found on the company intranet. The drafted Directors' Report is in the About this Organisation folder, under Standard files. The Directors shareholding spreadsheet is also in this folder under Staff files. The ECA financial statements spreadsheet is in 3 Shareholders under Share float.
>
> Once you send me a copy of the document to sign-off, the document needs to be provided to the company solicitor for their review in PDF for Word 97- 2003 format.
>
> Thanks

- Check with your teacher or assessor for the timeline on this task.
- Perform the tasks as requested in the email.
- Save the revised report using a suitable name to distinguish it from the original.
- Submit your completed documents to your teacher or assessor for assessment.

Assessment task 7

Susan Harris, the Personnel Manager, has requested your assistance in generating letters to notify particular staff of pay increases they have been granted. She has sent you the following email to advise you of her requirements.

> Thanks for agreeing to generate the pay increase letters. Details of the staff receiving pay increases are on the company intranet in a pay increases document in the *1 About this Organisation* folder, under Staff files. The file is password protected – the password is 1357a.
>
> Create an appropriate letter using their name, department and location as their address. Although this document only includes the amount of their increase, in the body of the letter I would like to show their current wage, their percentage increase and subsequently their new wage amount.
>
> The existing wages for the individuals listed are 87250, 64050, 91000, 23500, 35750, 42500, 51500, 56750, 34750. Update the increase document with these details.
>
> Please close the letter using my details.
>
> At this stage, staff increases in the Communications and Wardens departments are the only ones currently approved. So, once completed, please provide me with printed copies of each of these letters so I can sign them prior to their distribution (sorted alphabetically by surname would be great).

- Check with your teacher or assessor for the timeline on this task.
- Perform the task as detailed in the voicemail.
- Save the revised data source using a suitable filename.
- Submit your completed documents to your teacher or assessor for assessment.

Congratulations on completing the Challenges and Assessment tasks.

Appendix I

Shortcut keys: Direct key combinations

Fundamentals

New document	Ctrl + N	Open document	Ctrl + O
Close document	Ctrl + W	Print	Ctrl + P
Save document	Ctrl + S	Save as	F12
Undo	Ctrl + Z	Redo	Ctrl + Y
Cut	Ctrl + X	Copy	Ctrl + C
Paste	Ctrl + V	Find	Ctrl + F
Replace	Ctrl + H	Go to	Ctrl + G
Return to last edit	Shift + F5	Repeat	F4
Spell & grammar check	F7	Thesaurus	Shift + F7

Character formats

Bold	Ctrl + B	Italics	Ctrl + I
Underline	Ctrl + U	Remove character formats	Ctrl + Spacebar

Paragraph formats

Centre	Ctrl + E	Align left	Ctrl + L
Align right	Ctrl + R	Justify	Ctrl + J
Single line spacing	Ctrl + 1	Double line spacing	Ctrl + 2
1½ line spacing	Ctrl + 5	Remove paragraph formats	Ctrl + Q

Page/line/word division

Manual (hard) page break	Ctrl + Enter	New line (not a new paragraph)	Shift + Enter
Non-breaking space	Ctrl + Shift + Spacebar		

Extra movement keys - text

Beginning of line	`Home`	End of line	`End`
Top of document	`Ctrl` `Home`	End of document	`Ctrl` `End`
Top of previous page	`Ctrl` `Page Up`	Top of next page	`Ctrl` `Page Down`
Select browse object	`Alt` `Ctrl` `Home`		

Extra movement keys - tables

Previous cell	`Shift` `Tab`	First cell in row	`Alt` `Home`
Last cell in row	`Alt` `End`	First cell in column	`Alt` `Page Up`
Last cell in column	`Alt` `Page Down`		
Tab in a table cell	`Ctrl` `Tab`		

Styles

Normal	`Ctrl` `Shift` `N`	Heading 1	`Alt` `Ctrl` `1`
Heading 2	`Alt` `Ctrl` `2`	Heading 3	`Alt` `Ctrl` `3`
Open Apply Styles box	`Ctrl` `Shift` `S`		

Field codes

Insert field brackets	`Ctrl` `F9`	Update fields (Manually)	`F9`
Display fields (All)	`Alt` `F9`	Display fields (Selected)	`Shift` `F9`
Move to next field (useful for editing)	`F11`	Move to previous field	`Shift` `F11`
Lock a field	`Ctrl` `F11`	Unlock a field	`Ctrl` `Shift` `F11`
Insert a DATE field	`Alt` `Shift` `D`	Insert a PAGE field	`Alt` `Shift` `P`
Insert a TIME field	`Alt` `Shift` `T`		

Selecting

Press the `Shift` key with movement keys to select as you move, e.g. `Shift` `End` to select to the end of the line.

To mark a large block of text, click to mark the start of the block. Scroll with the scroll bar, then press `Shift` and click to mark the end of the block.

Shortcut keys: Word 2013 access keys

In Word 2013, you can use an alternative set of key strokes to access ribbons and commands.

How to: Activate access keys

1. Press [Alt]. Letter badges appear against each tab.

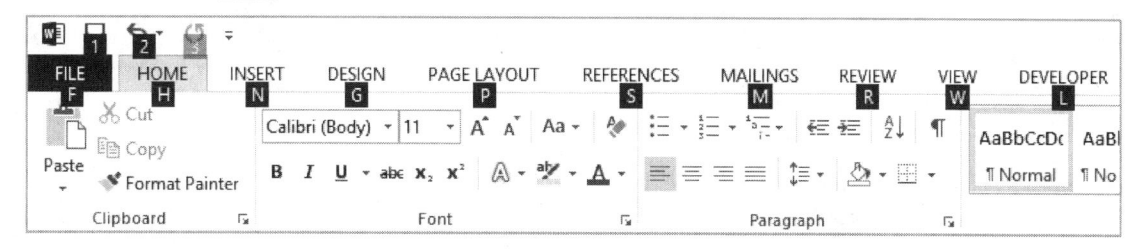

1. Press the required letter to activate a ribbon, e.g. [N] to activate the Insert ribbon. The selected ribbon is presented with more badges.

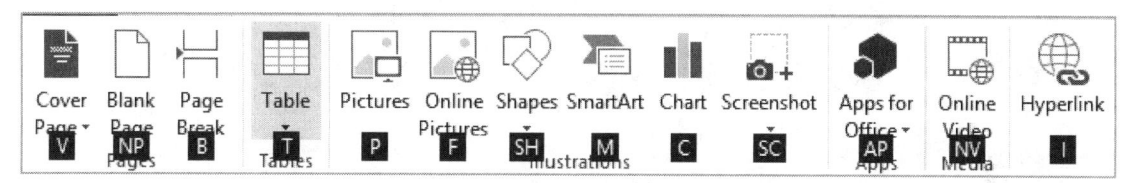

2. Press the required letter for a command, e.g. [B] for Page Break. The command is executed and the badges disappear.

3. Once you have memorised these commands, you can simply type them in sequence, e.g. [Alt] [N], [B].

As an aside ...Press [Esc] *to hide the badges if you display them accidentally.*

Appendix II

Saving to PDF

Word 2013 provides the ability to save a document to a PDF (Portable Document Format).

> *As an aside ... PDF is a popular format for sharing documents particularly on the internet. To read a PDF you need a reader program, the most popular being Acrobat which is available free from the Adobe website.*

How to: Save to PDF

1. Display the required document, then click on **Save As**, then select your storage location.

2. Type a file name if necessary, then in the Save as type, click on **PDF**. The PDF is presented.

Using Help

No matter how good your knowledge of Word, there will be times when you need to look for further information. When you request help if you are connected to the internet you are connected to online help. If you are not connected to the internet (offline), help files stored on your computer are searched. Online help provides access to extended facilities including tutorials and the latest downloads.

How to: Use Help

1. Click on the **Word Help** button.
   The Word Help window is presented.

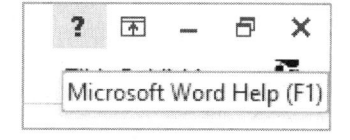

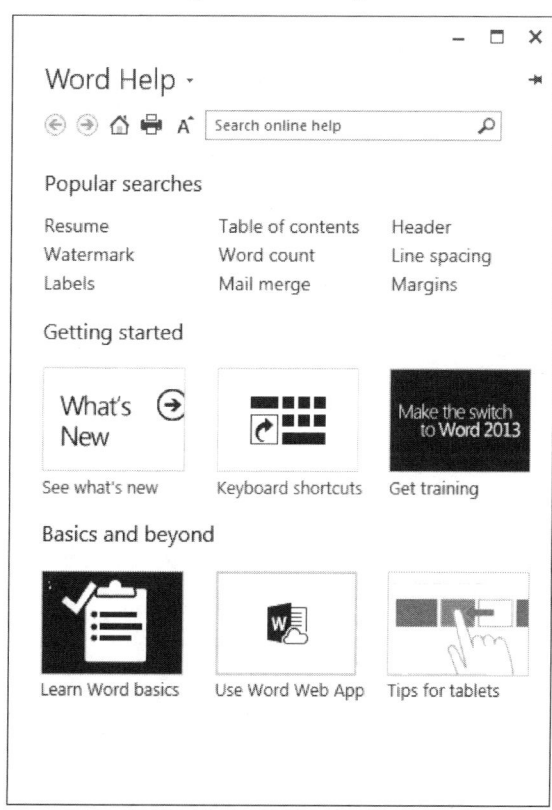

2. Click on one of the links in the Help window, e.g. **Line spacing** ~*or*~
   Type a search word or phrase in the **Search list**, then press Enter

3. If topics are found they are presented in the Help window (as links).
4. Follow the link on the most relevant topic.
5. The following buttons are particularly useful.

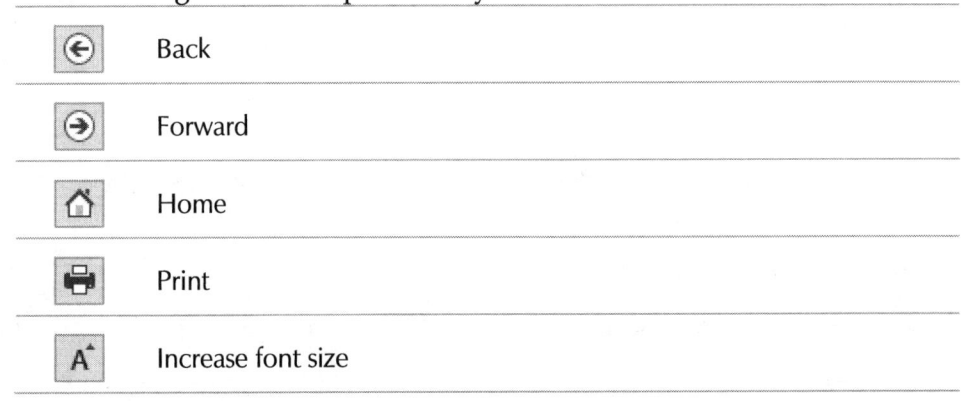

←	Back
→	Forward
⌂	Home
🖶	Print
A⁺	Increase font size

6. Click on **Close** to exit the Help window.

Index

A
AutoShapes, 38

B
Bookmarks, 122
Borders
    Page, 94

C
Calculations, 120
    custom, 122
Character styles, 67
Charts, 101
    Inserting, 101, 107
Command button
    images, 139
Comments, 112
Comparing content, 112, 116
Content controls, 30

D
Developer ribbon, 29
Document
    Views, 1
Drawing a circle, 38
Drawing a square, 38
Drawing a straight line, 38

E
Endnotes, 91

F
Fill-in fields, 22
Footnotes, 91
    Deleting footnotes, 92
    Inserting footnotes, 91
Forms, 20
    content controls, 29
    designing, 27
    layout, 28
    modifying, 33
    planning content, 27

G
Graphics. *See* Drawing objects or pictures

H
Header & footer, 80
Header & footers
    quick parts, 82
    sections, 83
    style reference, 82
Header and footer
    Format page number, 84

I
Index, 87
Insert a picture file, 96

L
Leader characters, 9
Linking
    Excel workbook, 98
List styles, 67
Long documents, 65

M
Macro, 134
Mail merge, 44
    custom labels, 51
    data source, 45
    fill-in field, 56
    if field, 60
    letters, 44
    some criteria, 53
Mail Merge
    labels, 50
Margins, 5
Master document, 144
Multilevel list, 74

N
Numbering headings, 74

O
Organisation charts, 106
Outlining, 69

P
Page
    Breaks, 2
Paper size, 6
Paper source, 6
Paragraph styles, 67
Picture file, 96
Pictures
    Inserting a file, 96
Print
    field codes, 23
Protection, 30

Q
Quick Access Toolbar
    customising, 128
Quick styles, 67

S
Section breaks
    Continuous, 4

  Deleting, 5
  Next page, 4
Shapes, 37
  add text, 38
  callout, 38
  copying, 37
  effects, 38
  fill colour, 38
  inserting, 37
  moving, 37
  outline colour, 38
  resizing, 37
  rotating, 37
  selecting, 39
  style, 38
Shortcut keys
  customising, 129
SmartArt, 106
Styles, 69
  Character styles, 67
  List styles, 67
  Paragraph styles, 67
  Quick Styles Gallery, 94
  Table styles, 67
subdocument, 144

T

Table of contents, 77
Table styles, 67
Tables
  alignment, 13
  borders, 11
  converting text to tables, 14
  creating & modifying, 10
  deleting, 17
  distributing evenly, 17
  height & width, 12
  merging, 14
  moving within, 11
  selecting, 11
  shading, 11
  sorting, 16
  splitting, 14
  styles, 11
Tabs, 7
  Leader characters, 9
Template
  editing, 21
Templates
  Creating templates, 20
  Editing templates, 21
Text box, 40
Text boxes, 40
Tracking changes, 112, 114

V

Views
  document, 1
  Normal, 2
  Outline, 2
  Web Layout, 2

W

Watermarks, 94
WordArt, 37, 40